Memory's Wake

The Official Illustrated Companion Guide

by Selina Fenech

First Published June 2015

Hardcover Edition Published by Fairies and Fantasy PTY LTD

ISBN: 978-0-9943554-1-6

www.memoryswake.com

Memory's Wake

The Official Illustrated Companion Guide

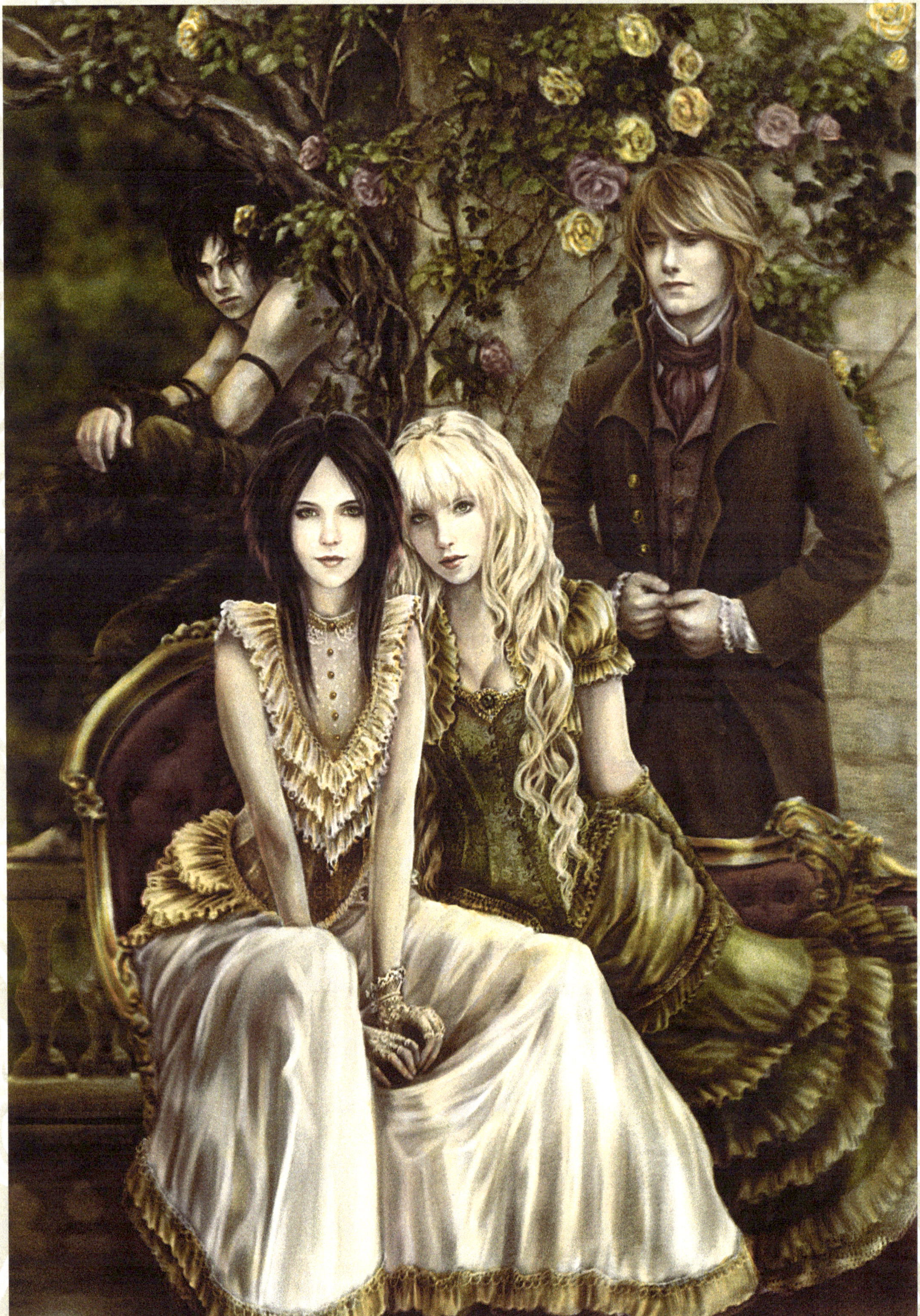

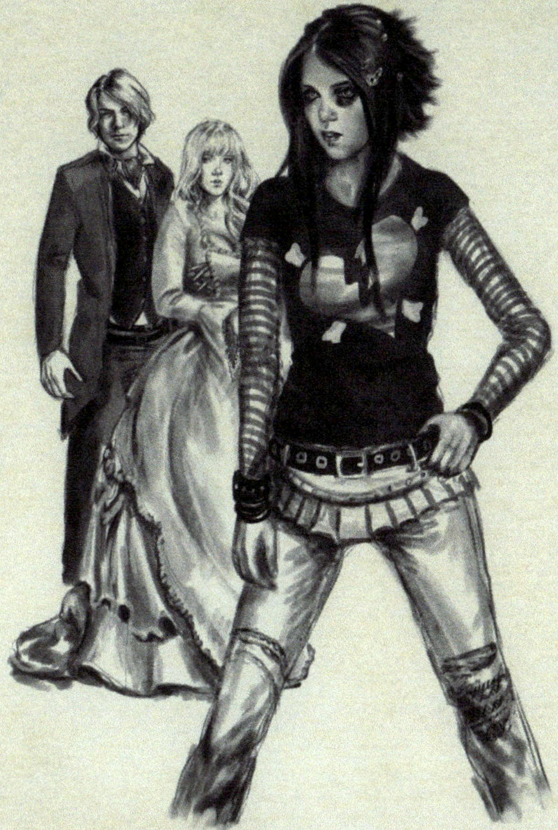

Contents

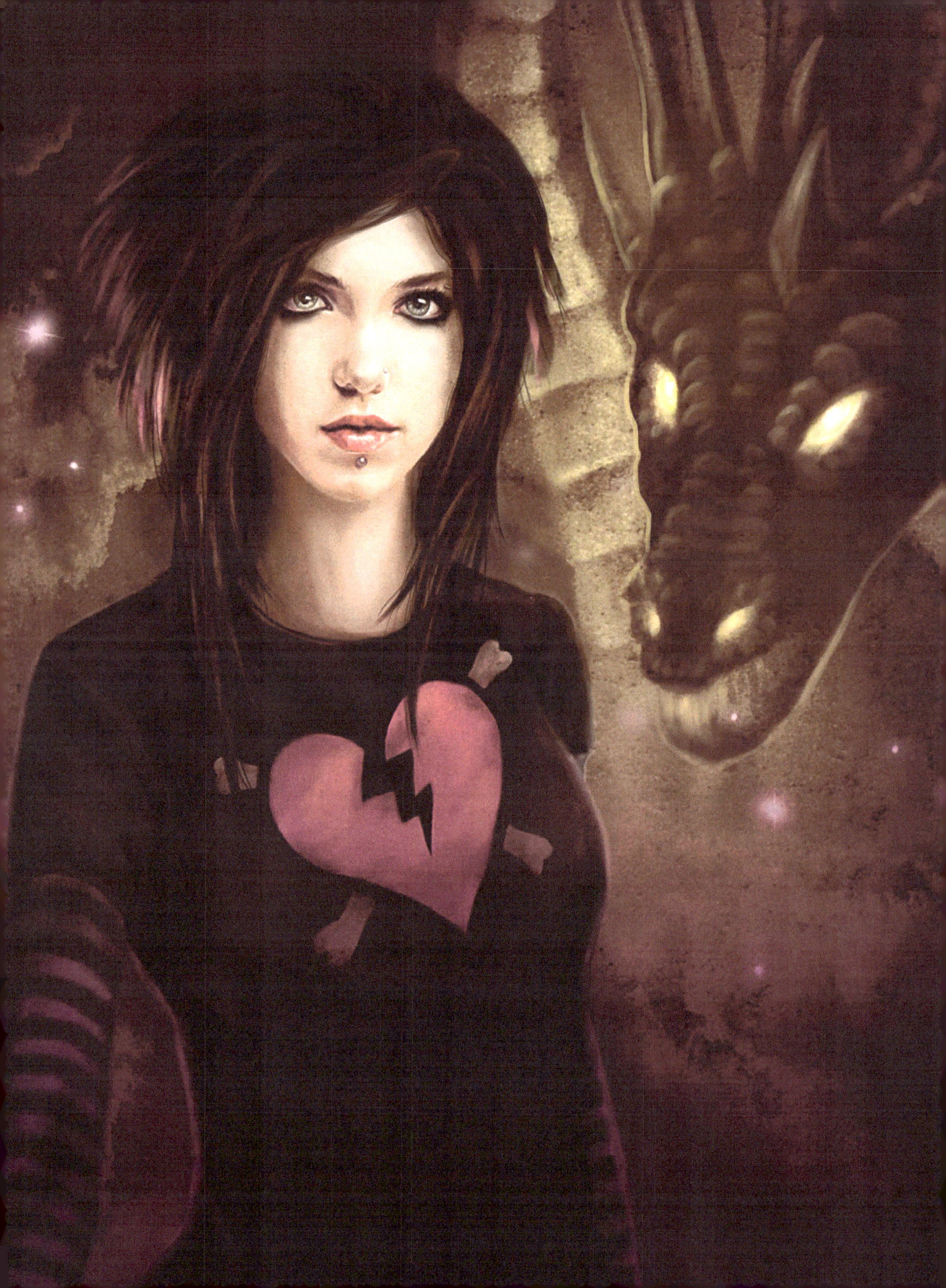

Introduction

They tell me my name is Memory.
They tell me that I did amazing things.
They tell me all about this land I'm in and the changes that are happening here.

It all begins with one tough modern girl, lost and hunted in a fantasy world. By the end, the lands of Avall and its inhabitants have been irrevocably changed.

Memory's Wake is an adventure that encompasses Arthurian mythology, fairies, Victorian era style, danger, magic, politics, twists, romance, and a dragon. As readers, we travel through the fantasy alongside Memory, as she learns all there is to know about the worlds and about herself.

At its heart, the tale is one of family, friendship, belonging, breaking tradition, growth, and betterment.

Revisit the characters and explore the lands of Avall and Tearnan Ogh in this collection of illustrations and information from the Memory's Wake trilogy.

SPOILER WARNING!

This guidebook covers the entirety of the Memory's Wake trilogy and as such contains spoilers! It also contains additional insight into the story from the author that doesn't appear in the books, giving you secret knowledge into the realm of Avall and its inhabitants.

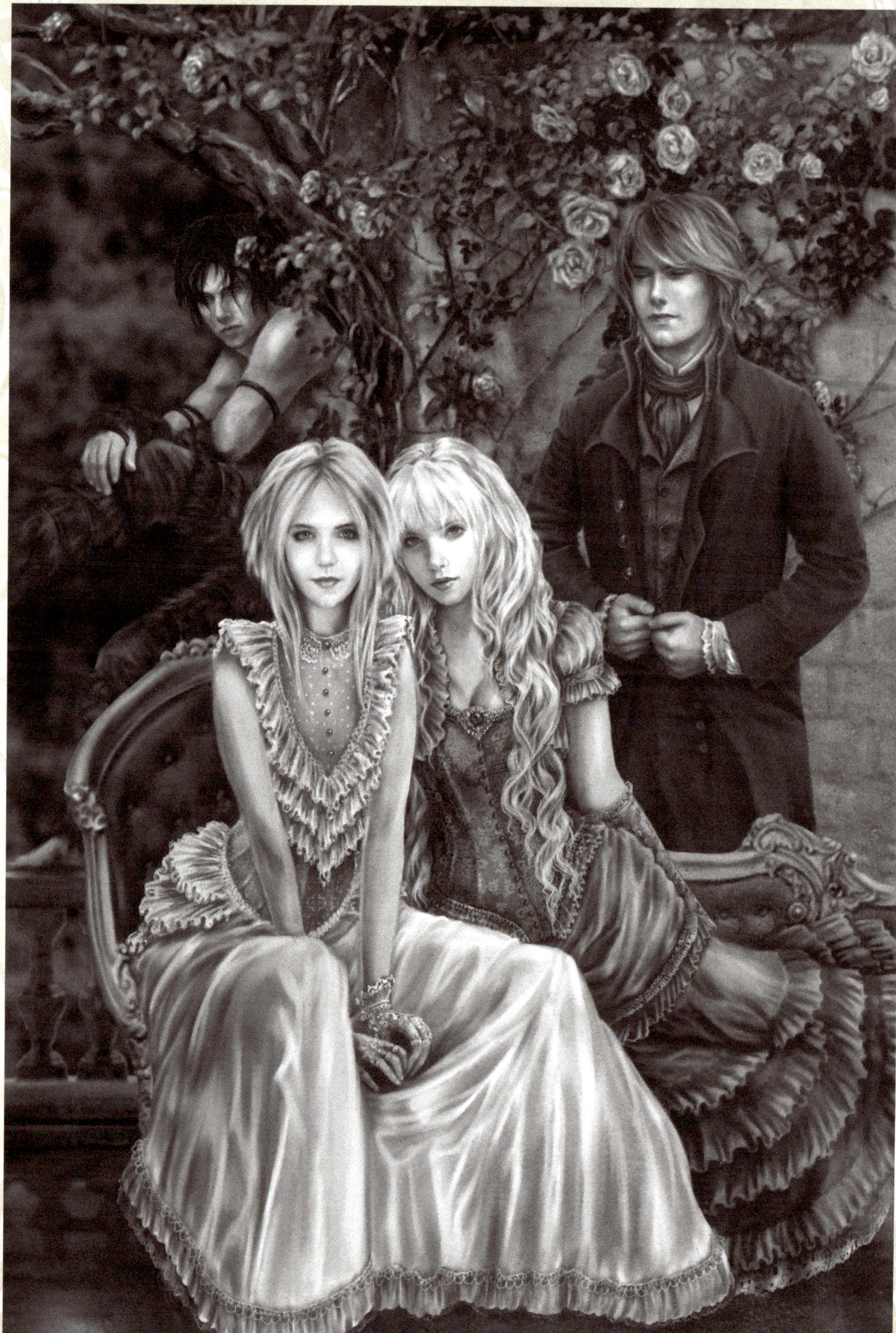

Characters

"I'm the person I am now because of the hurt and the happiness I've lived through. I've lost parts of me before. I never want to lose anything again."

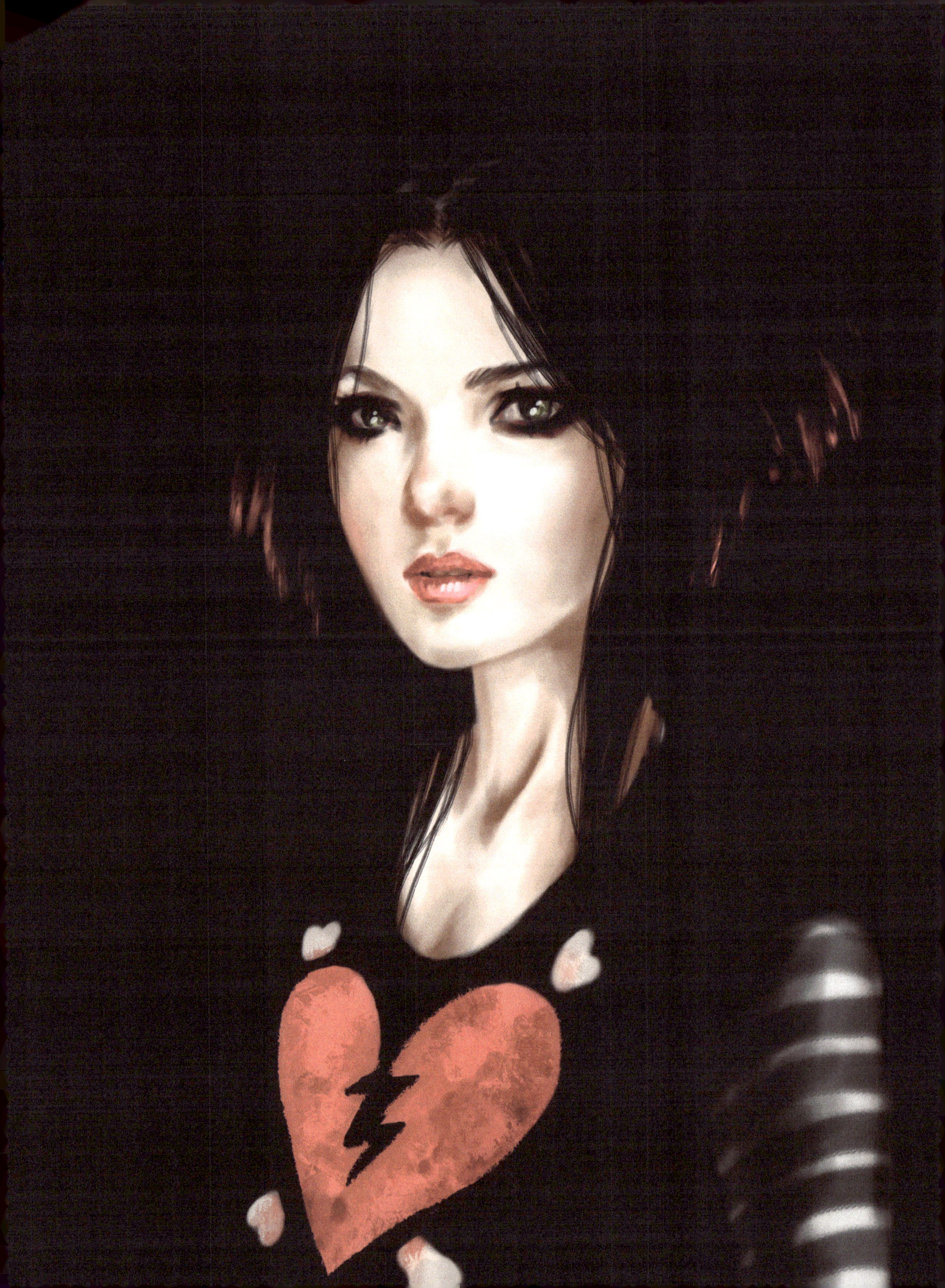

Memory

"I think we all know who is most important here."
Memory's eyes narrowed shiftily.
"Me right? Is it me? Yep. Definitely me."

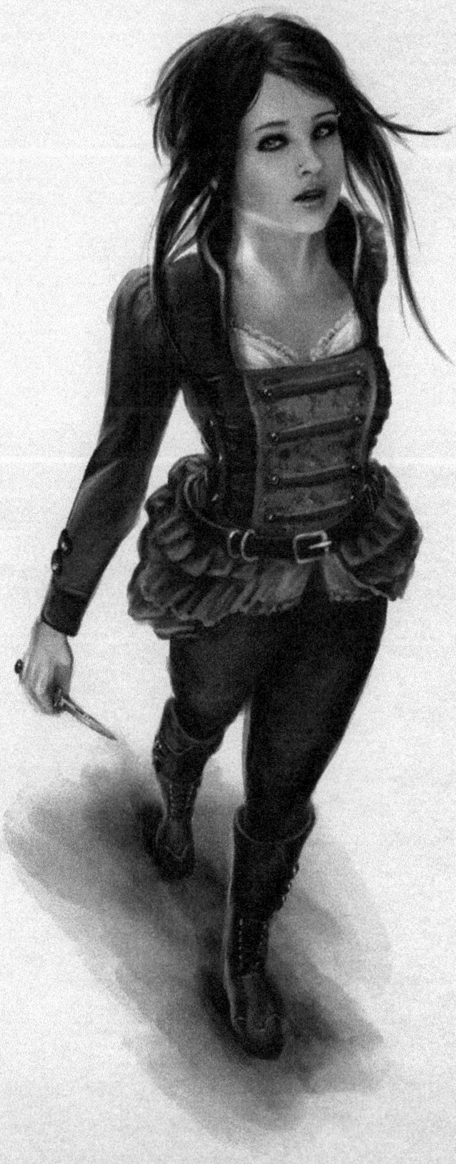

Name: Memory Maellan

Aliases: Mem, Hope Sinclair

Age: 16-17

Height: 5"

Distinguishing Marks: Scar in center of chest

Body Type: Extremely slim and petite

Eyes: Jade green

Hair: Black and pink or blonde or purple and black - changes on a whim

Most prized possession: Iron knife

Flaws: Distrustful, emotionally explosive

Strengths: Quick witted, compassionate

Skills: Magic without behests, quick learner

Family: Eloryn (identical twin sister), Loredanna (mother, deceased), father unknown.

The first born of queen Loredanna Maellan's identical twins, Memory's life was a trial from the moment of her birth. Taken to be used as part of Thayl and Providence's ritual, her chest was carved with magical runes to bind her to Thayl, and then she was sent through a veil door to the rest of the modern human world.

Discovered in Sinclair St and barely alive, she was given the name Hope Sinclair. Due to her long recovery, she wasn't able to be adopted out as a newborn, and was entered into the child welfare system, mostly living in group homes.

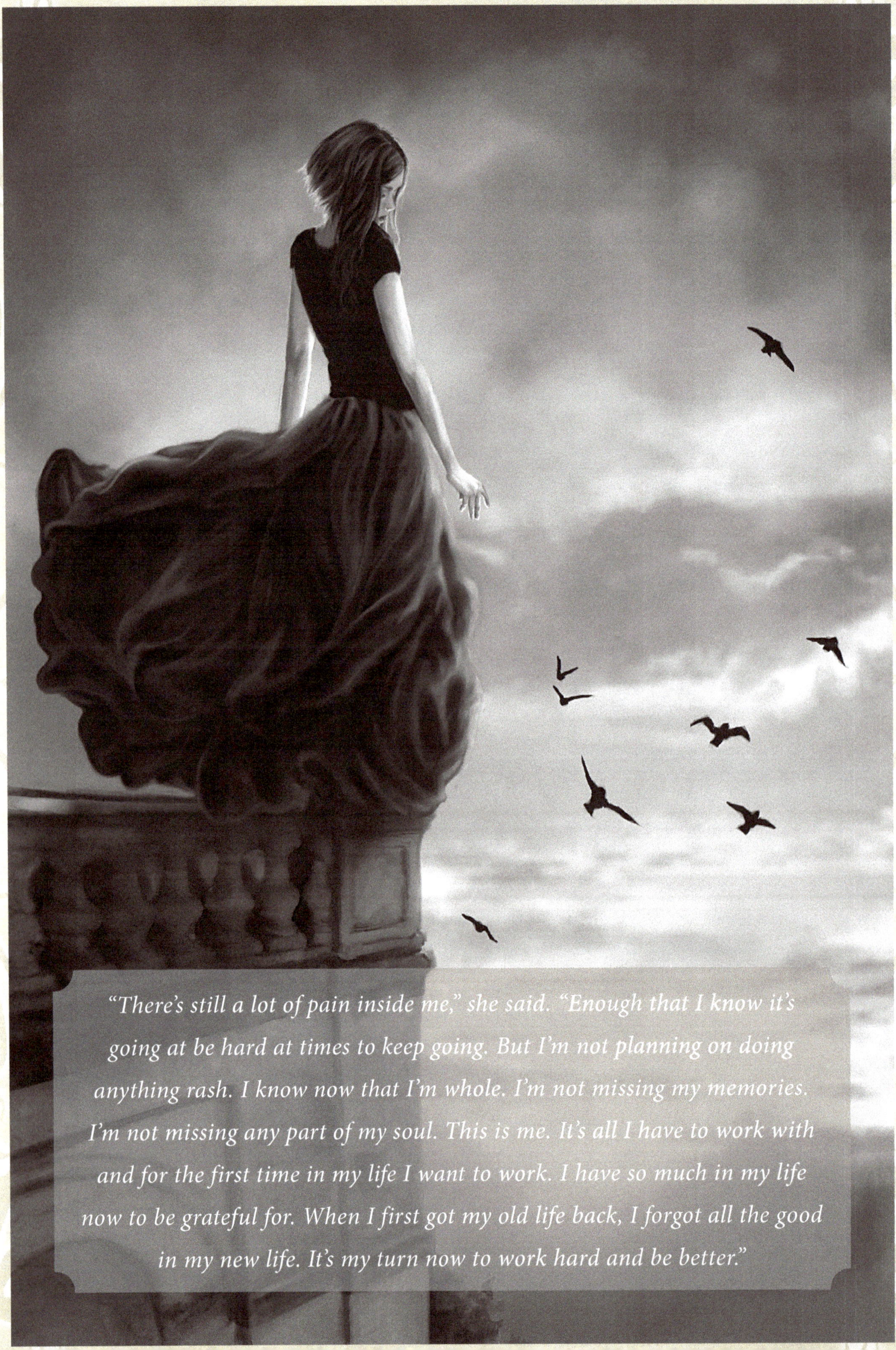

"There's still a lot of pain inside me," she said. "Enough that I know it's going at be hard at times to keep going. But I'm not planning on doing anything rash. I know now that I'm whole. I'm not missing my memories. I'm not missing any part of my soul. This is me. It's all I have to work with and for the first time in my life I want to work. I have so much in my life now to be grateful for. When I first got my old life back, I forgot all the good in my new life. It's my turn now to work hard and be better."

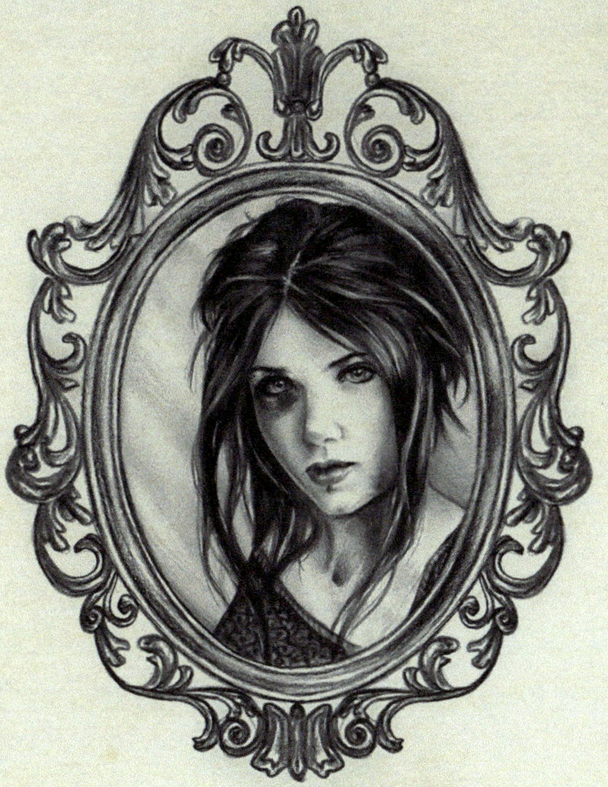

An old, large and twisted scar marked the middle of her chest. NASTY, she thought, wondering how she got it.

As Hope, she grew rough and cynical, regularly getting into fights. With the Spark of Connection inside, and in frequent contact with iron, magic was continually drawn into her for sixteen years. She grew up in constant pain from the heat of that magic, but never knew any different.

There were a few attempts at adoption and foster care, but her troubled nature and strange instances and accidents caused by the magic growing inside her kept sending her back into the system.

Hope's only friend growing up was Will, who started following her around after she "saved his life", defending him from bullies. Much younger than her, and with a kind innocence, Will brought out Hope's natural compassion, and most likely saved her life when he was all she had in her darker moments.

Hope had been sexually abused by a janitor on the group home staff regularly from a young age. At sixteen, she shoplifted a flick-knife and used it to try and warn off her abuser. Her action instead angered the man and he beat her until she defended herself instinctively with magic, killing him.

She fled the group home with nothing but her knife, and only moments later was confronted again by Thayl, come to collect the magic that had been growing inside her.

Thayl attempted to draw all the magic from Hope, and her memories flowed out with it. The ritual was likely to have killed her, had Will not intervened. He had followed hope and attacked Thayl to defend her, and all three fell back through the open veil door. Hope lost grip on Will and was trapped in the veil.

When her twin sister travelled through the veil in a faulty veil door, like called to like and Hope was drawn out beside Eloryn, with no memories or knowledge of who she was. She then became Memory.

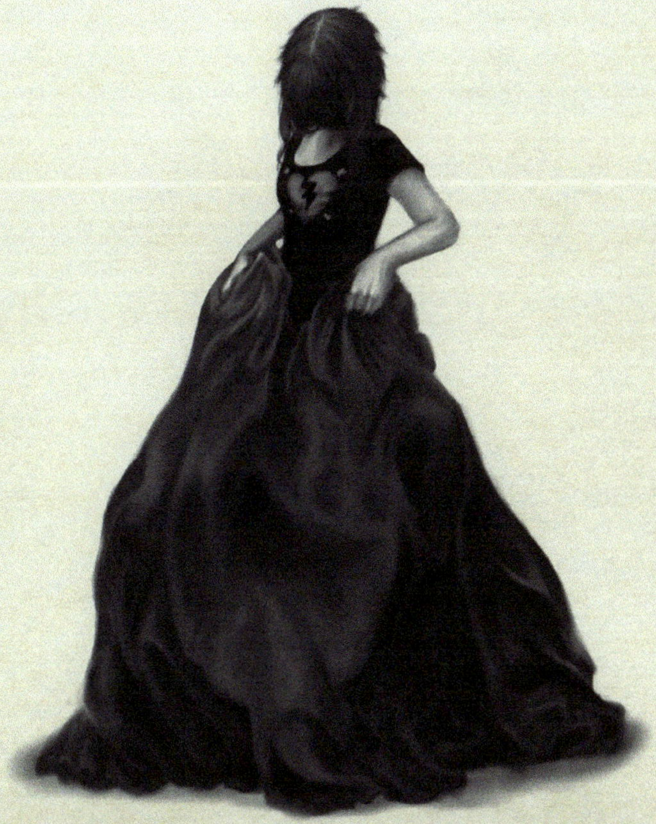

Memory began her new life in Avall confused, emotional, and selfish. She only cared about one thing- finding her family and home. It was the thing she'd wanted her whole life as an orphan, and although she couldn't remember that, she was still driven by those subconscious desires as much as her new need to recover her memories.

In her journey toward that goal, she learned about herself, made new friends, and discovered the truth about her family and that her twin sister was Eloryn.

Together, the twins learned more about the nature of magic and iron's influence on it than anyone in Avall's history. They used that knowledge to defeat Thayl and reclaim their crown, and Memory would also use that knowledge to bring life-magic back into Avall and save the lives of the fae.

Once she became Memory, her life became even more complicated. She went from running for her life in forests and caves, to living in a castle and becoming queen in a matter of months.

She found her family, and also gained new friends, and new enemies. One of her greatest enemies proved to be herself. Memory struggled to accept the love of others, or that she - as

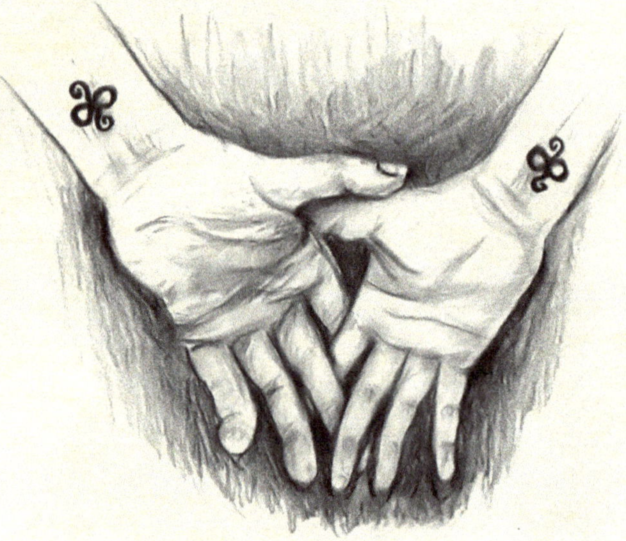

Their wrists matched. Rough inked tattoos of the symbol for eternity with a swirl through the centre.
"Did them ourselves."
"Weren't you like, eight or something?"
"You were my best friend." Will's face heated. "And, kind of a bully."

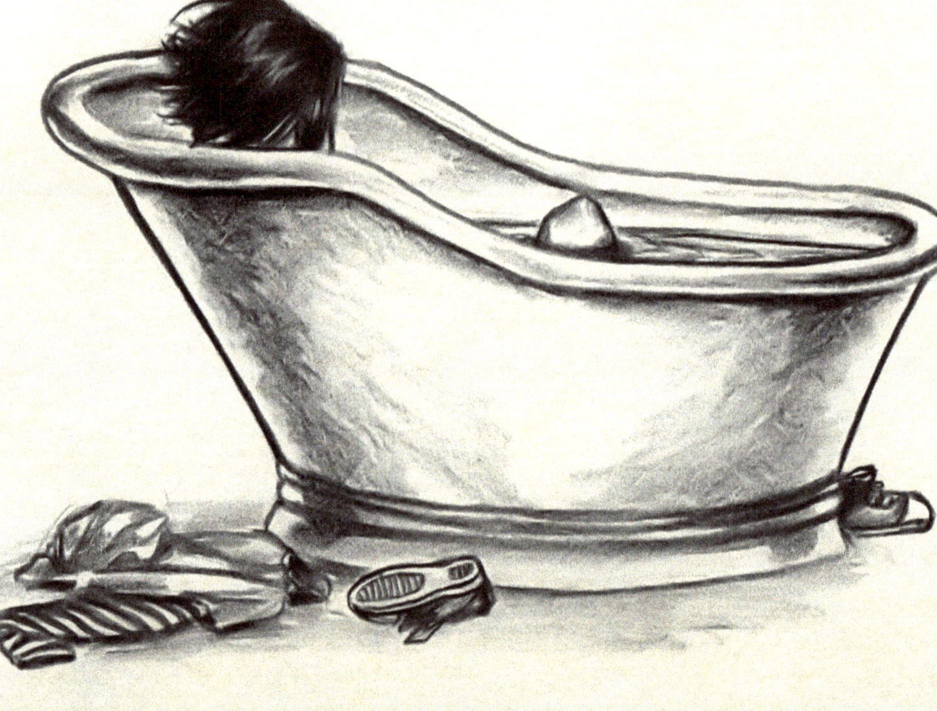

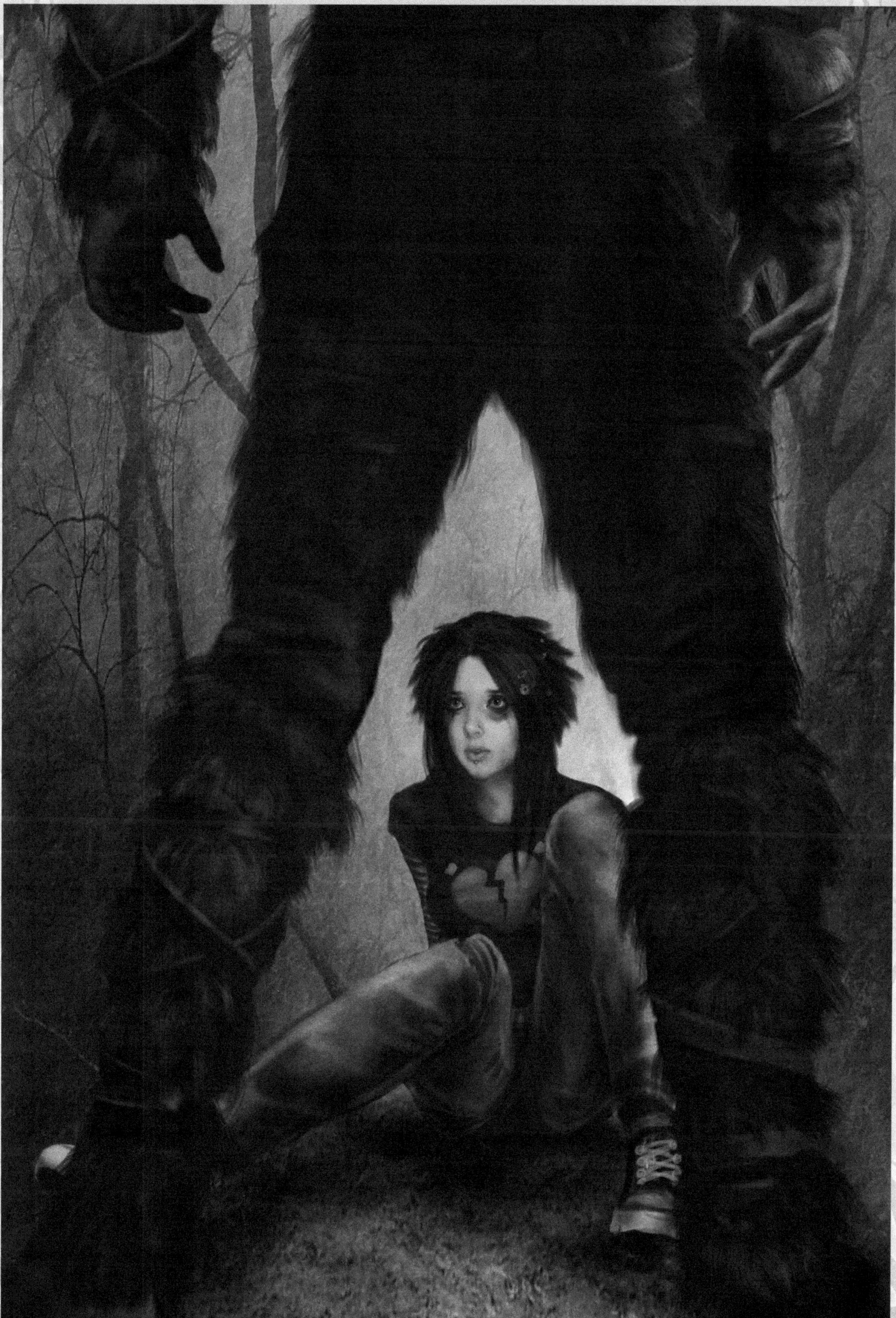

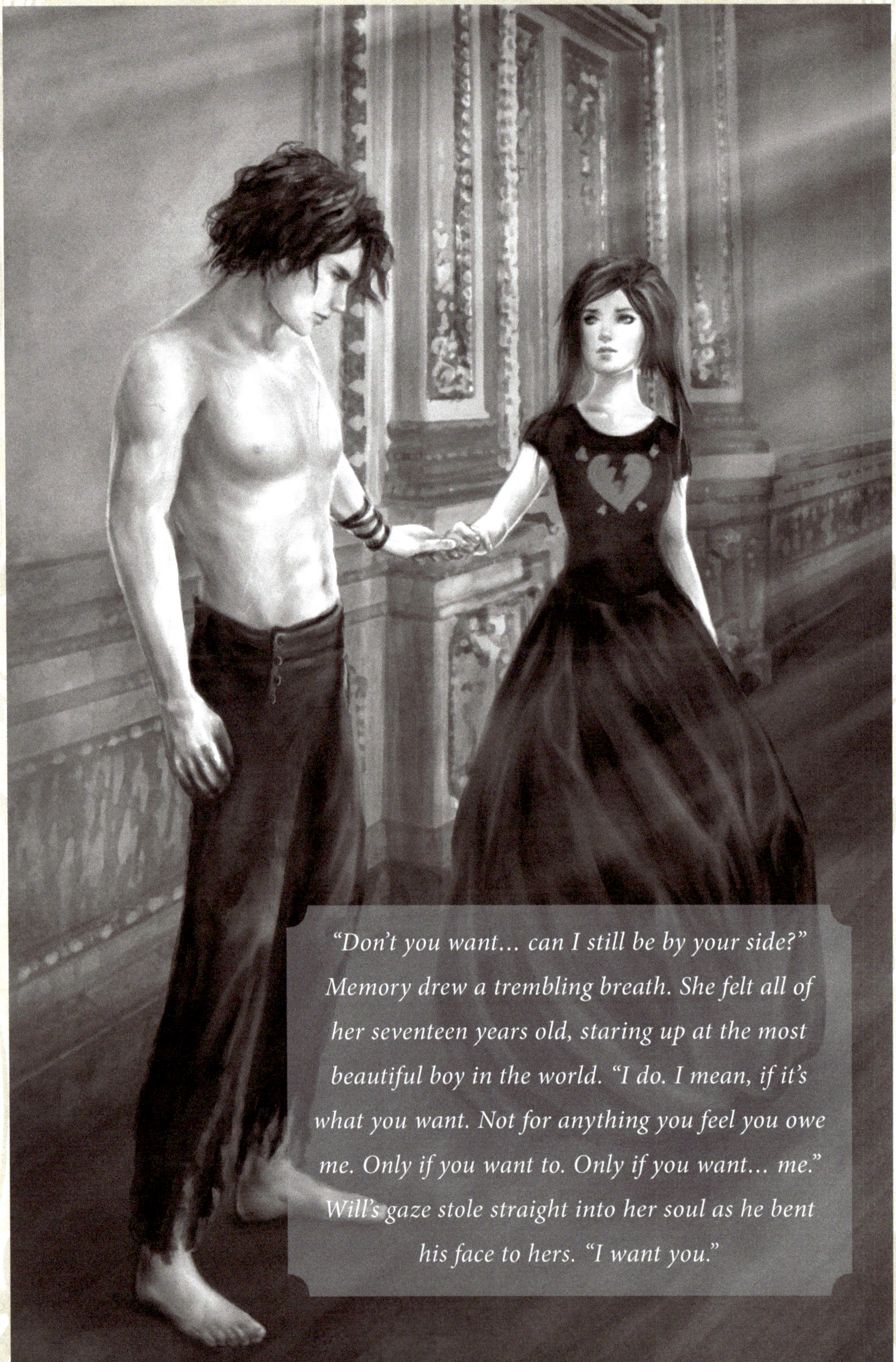
"Don't you want… can I still be by your side?" Memory drew a trembling breath. She felt all of her seventeen years old, staring up at the most beautiful boy in the world. "I do. I mean, if it's what you want. Not for anything you feel you owe me. Only if you want to. Only if you want… me." Will's gaze stole straight into her soul as he bent his face to hers. "I want you."

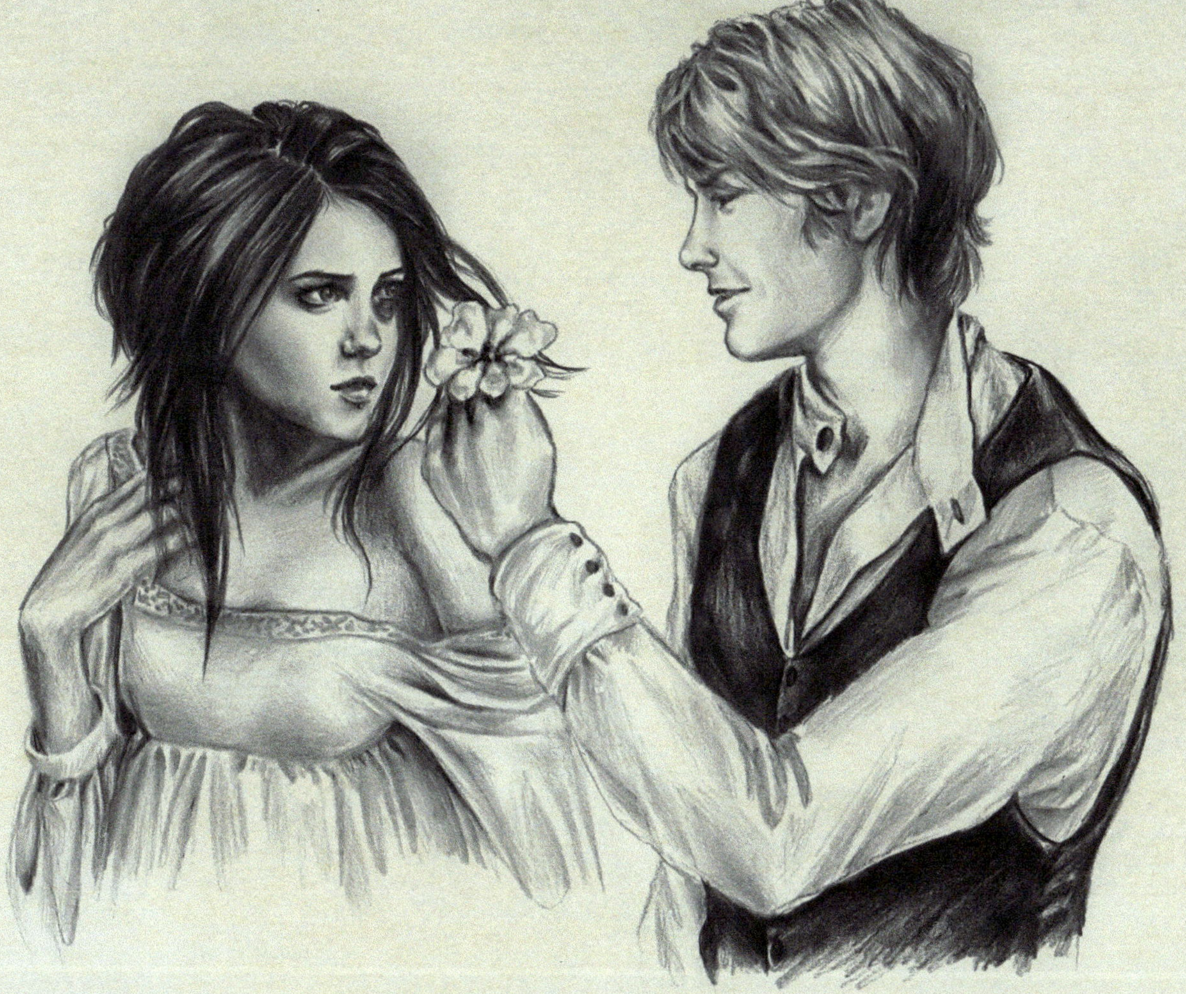

broken and wrong as she believed herself to be - *could* be loved.

When she believed her soul was broken, and that she'd lost everyone she cared about, she came close to ending her own life. But she was saved, and from that moment onwards grew exponentially stronger, buoyed by the love of those around her. Those that could see just how valuable and incredible she really was.

Although sometimes at odds with her sister, her bond with Eloryn is natural and deep. Memory quickly became friends with Roen, and they enjoyed flirting with each other and sharing a sly sense of humor. Even Thayl came to respect Memory, and she to care for him.

From her simple and selfish beginnings to the

"Wow, learned something new about myself. Turns out I'm a cynic. Surprise."

Memory meant so much to him. She was a summer storm, with passion and intensity that awed him and at the same time she was the flower caught within that storm. He would do anything for her.

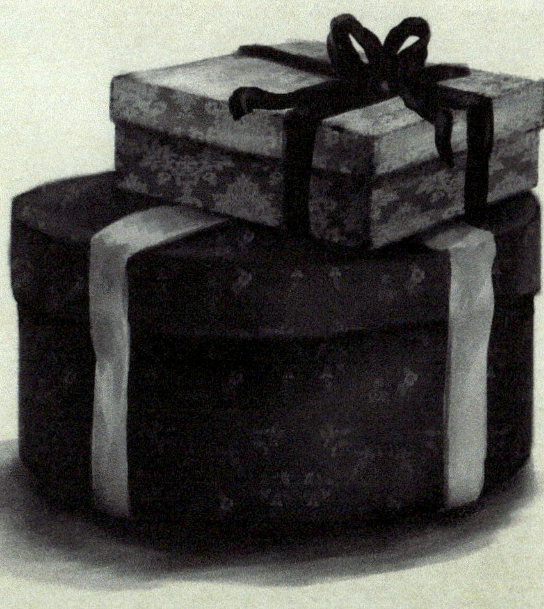

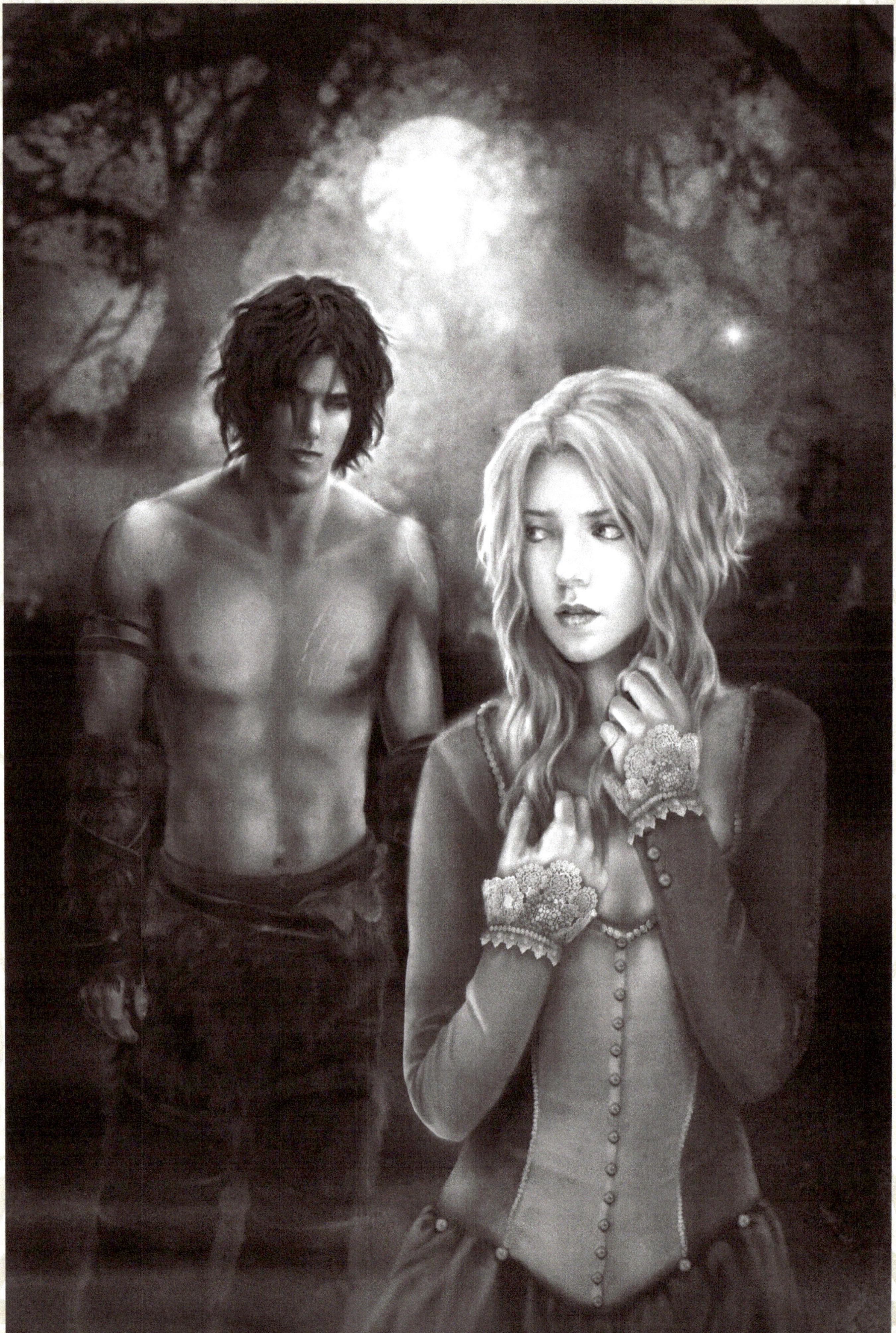

true hero she becomes, Memory is a force to be reckoned with. She is the fresh eyes and ears to discover the worlds through, and also the heart of the story - a broken heart that grows whole again.

And throughout it all, Will was there for her. Her constant point of reference, the only one who truly knew her, and loved her all along no matter what. Not sure what to think of him at first, Memory's love for him grew slowly and surely.

The matching friendship tattoos they made as an act of solidarity between two lonely orphans became a symbol of their unbreakable love. Together forever.

Memory's heart rushed and she bit her lip hard at the thought that overwhelmed her. ***I don't just want anyone to love me. I want Will to love me.***

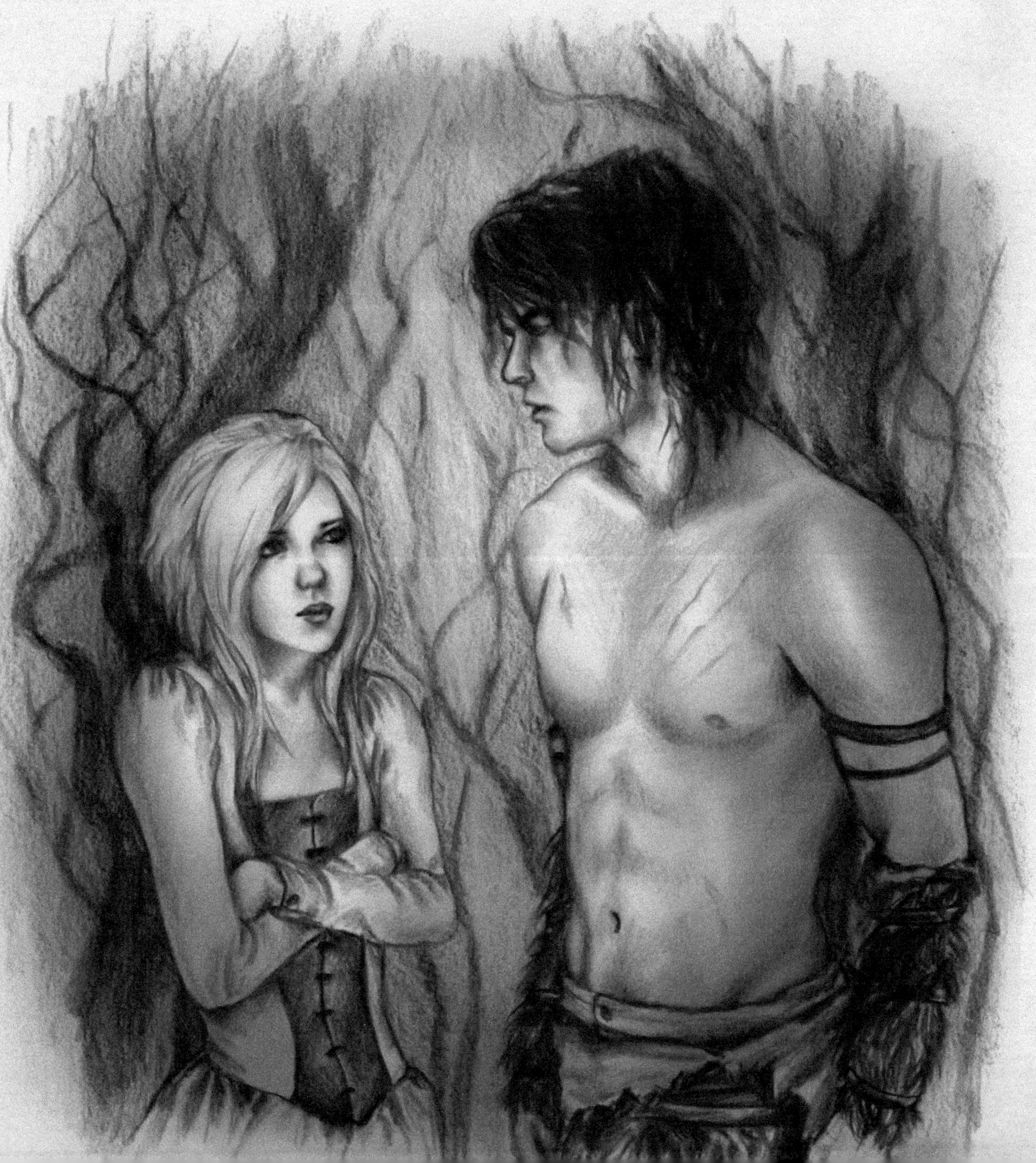

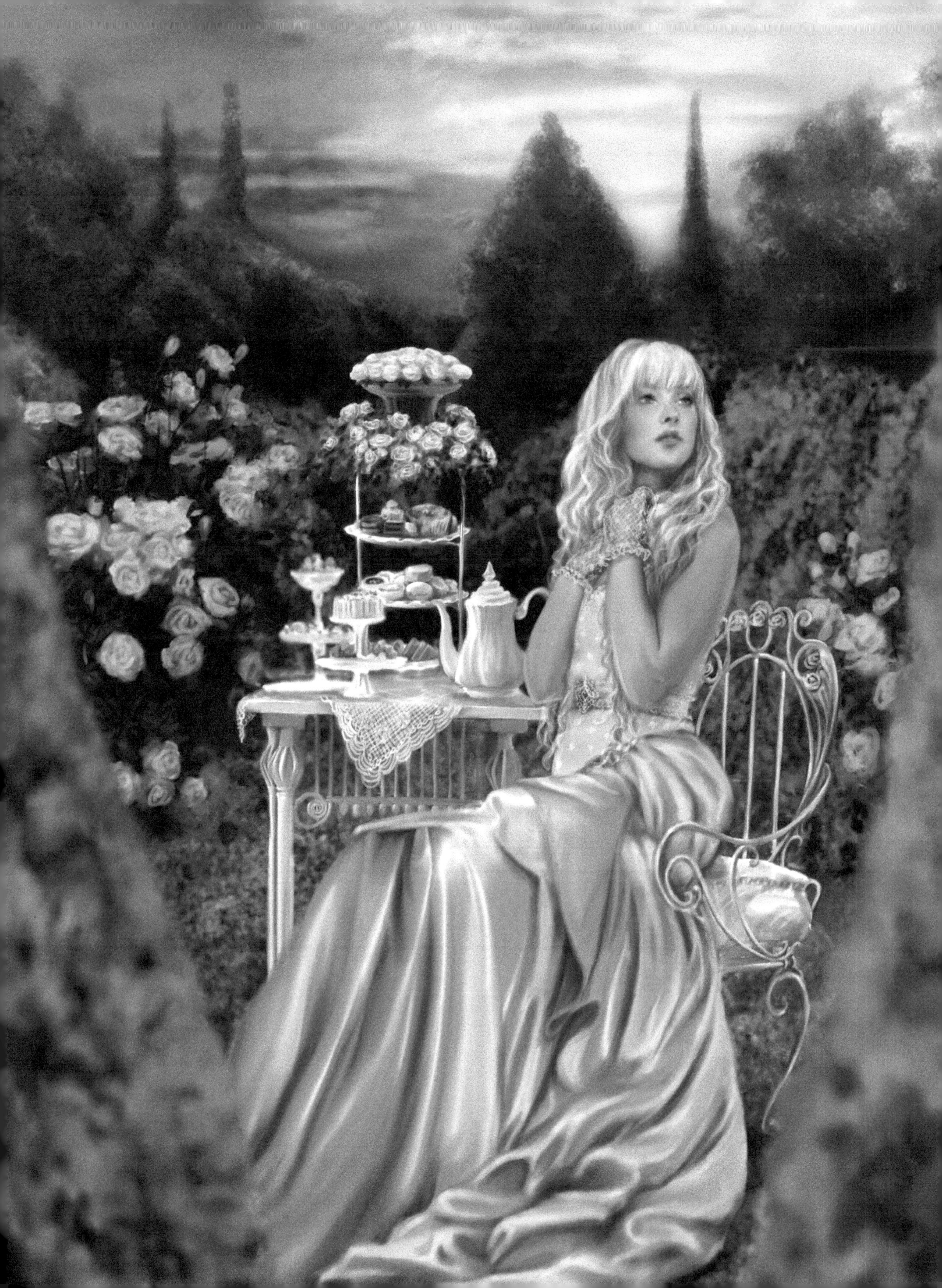

Eloryn

Beside her, another girl crouched on the ground; plump but strikingly pretty, with skin and hair so pale it was almost white against the shadowed woods. The long hair tumbled all around the stranger, making her look like a beautiful, scared ghost.

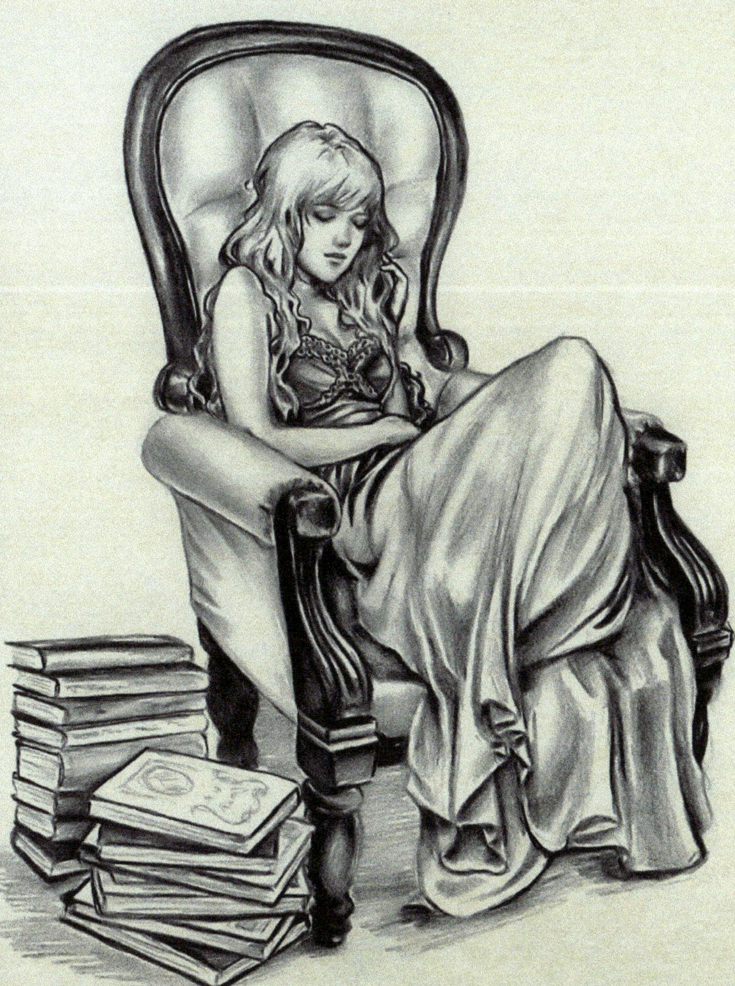

Name: Eloryn Maellan

Aliases: El, Lory

Age: 16-17

Height: 5”

Body Type: soft and slightly plump

Eyes: Jade green

Hair: Pale blonde, long and flowing with fringe

Most prized possession: Her and Alward's collection of books

Flaws: Self doubt, reliance on others for decisions

Strengths: Intelligence, kindness

Skills: Fluency in the magical language and Maellan communication talent allowing for creative and on-the-fly behests

Family: Memory (identical twin sister), Loredanna Maellan (mother, deceased), father unknown

After her twin sister was lost to the other world, Wizard Councillor Alward took the second newborn twin from the scene of Thayl and Providence's ritual and fled. He went into hiding with Eloryn and raised her with a thorough education but little freedom.

A quick learner, and schooled from a young age alongside Alward's other students, Eloryn quickly surpassed her peers and began teaching the local children as well. Her and Alward lived peacefully like this until the wizard hunters found them and Eloryn escaped alone through the faulty veil door.

The twin with the strange hair, name, and behavior was the hottest topic in Avall. The most people gossiped about Eloryn was to say "how lovely" she was.

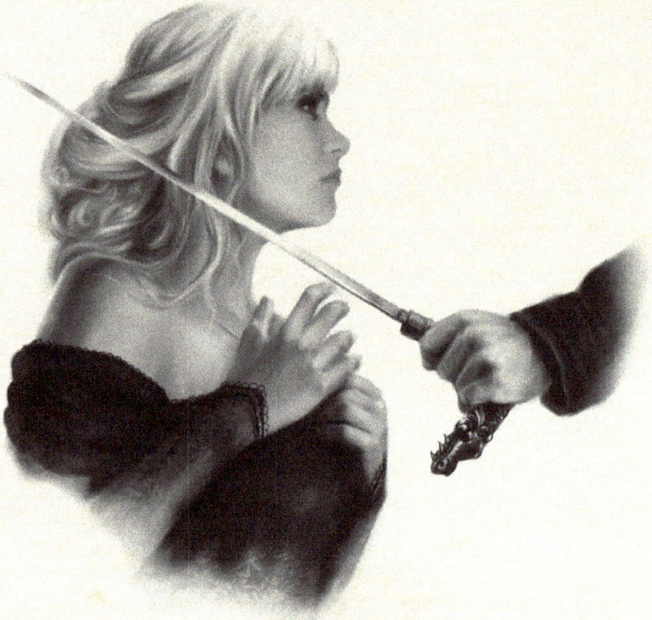

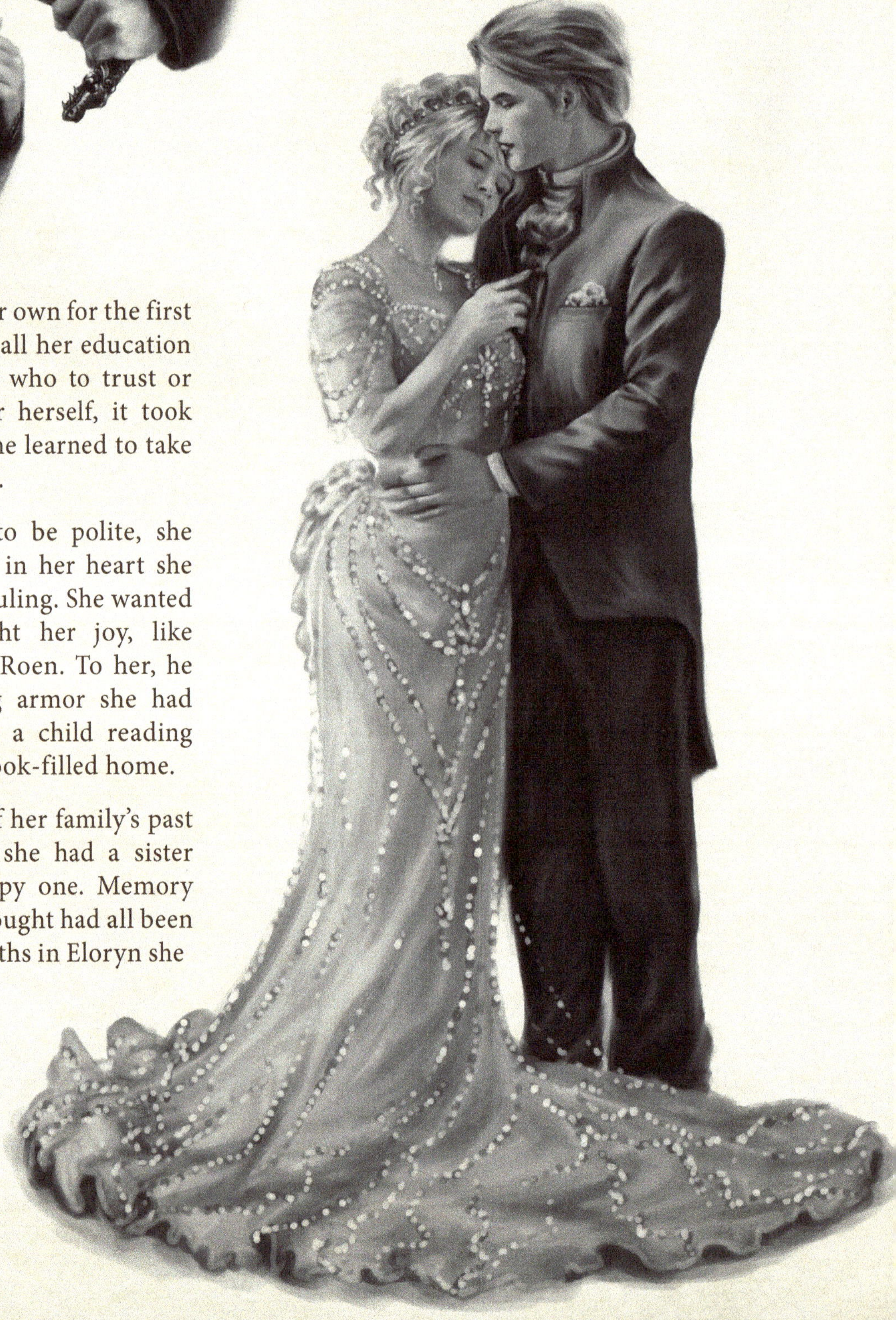

Out in the wide world on her own for the first time, Eloryn felt as though all her education amounted to little. Unsure who to trust or how to make decisions for herself, it took many hard lessons before she learned to take the lead and trust in herself.

Naturally shy and raised to be polite, she always tried to please, but in her heart she never cared for politics or ruling. She wanted simple things that brought her joy, like teaching, and her love for Roen. To her, he was the knight in shining armor she had dreamed of since she was a child reading fairytales in her isolated, book-filled home.

Having been taught most of her family's past from Alward, discovering she had a sister was a surprise, and a happy one. Memory gave Eloryn a family she thought had all been lost, and brought out strengths in Eloryn she never knew possible.

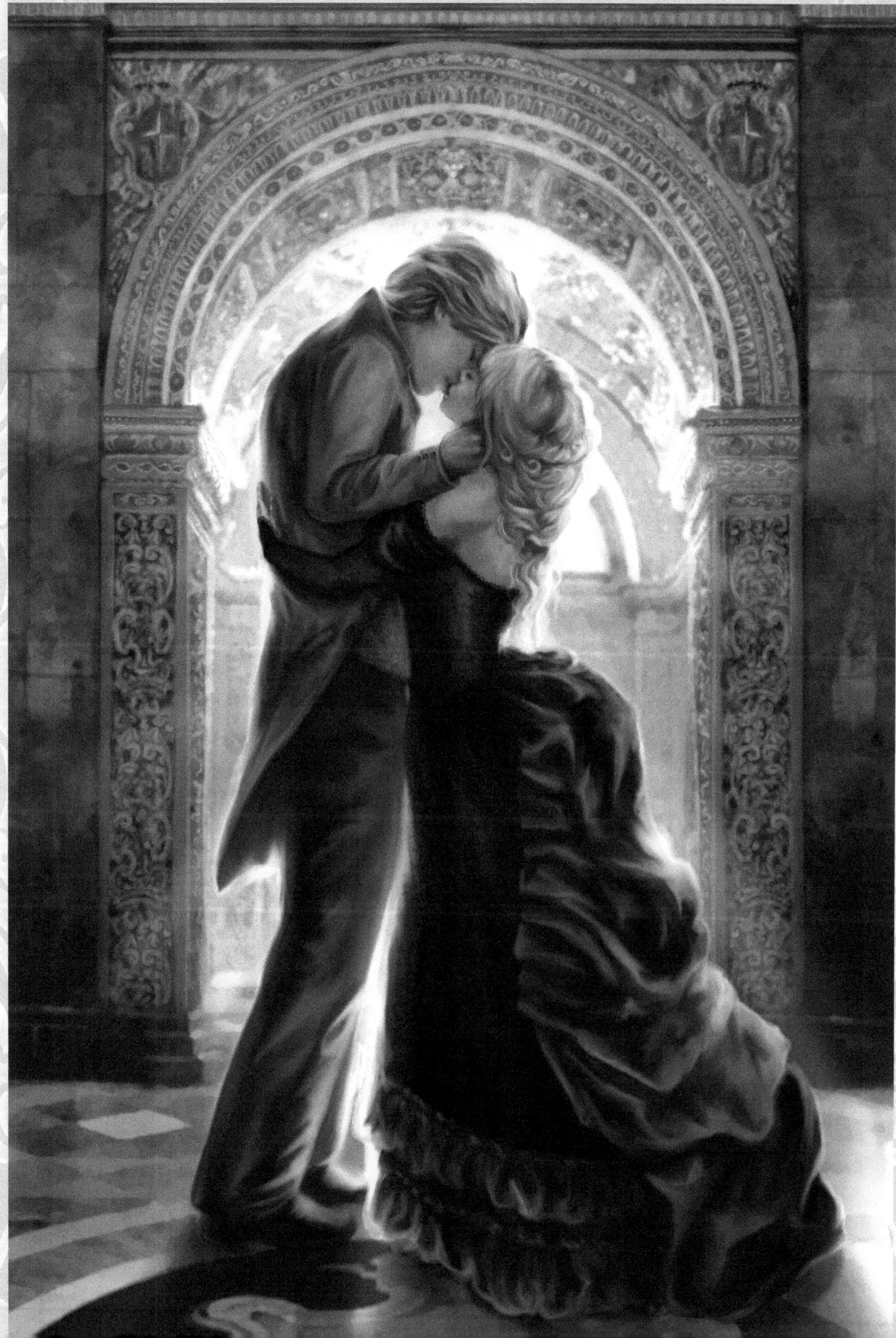

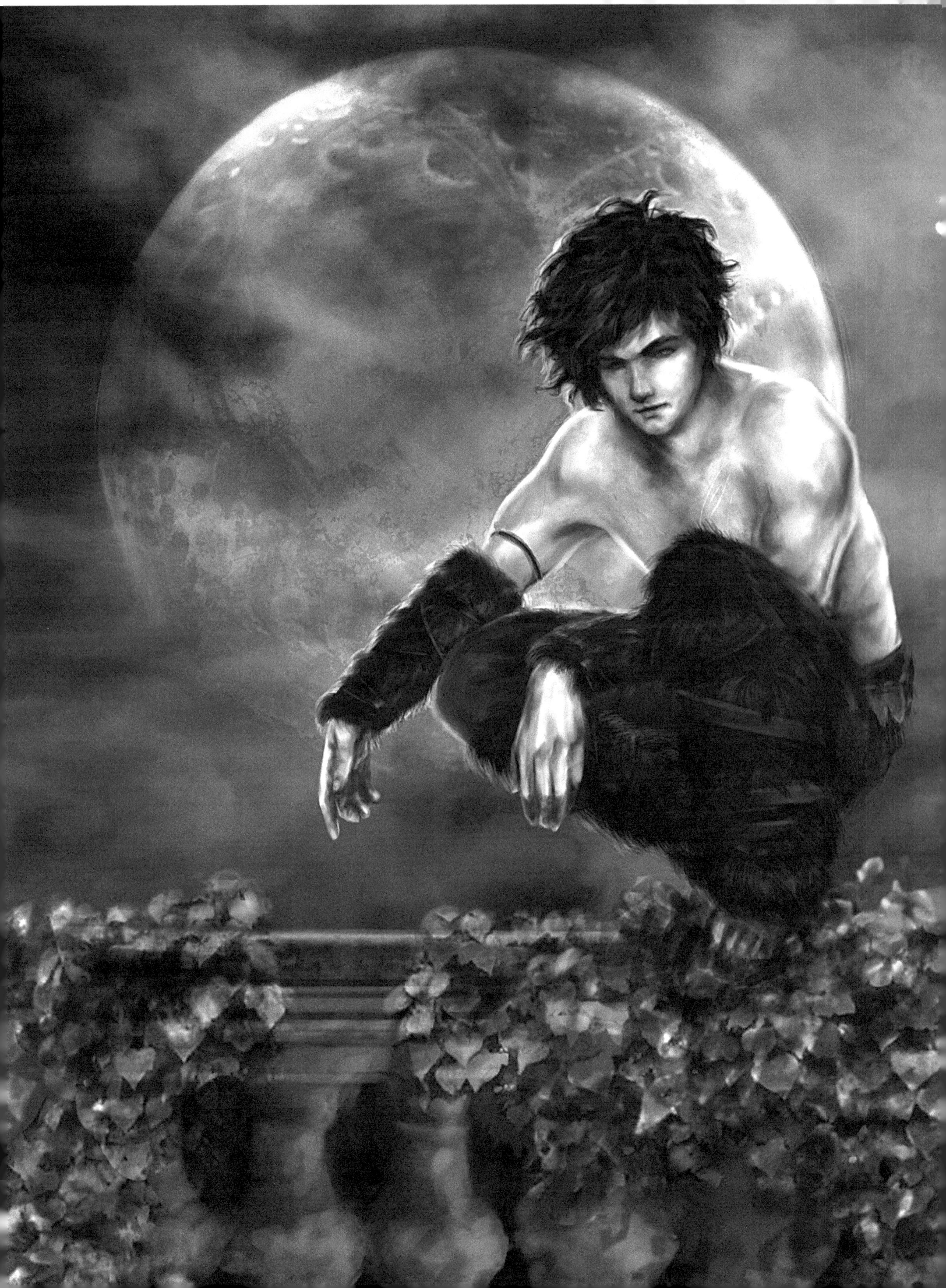

Will

"He's all Tarzan and stuff, like some sort of guardian-angel-cross-savage."

Name: Will

Age: 24

Height: 6'4"

Distinguishing Marks: Scratch shaped scars

Body Type: Muscular

Eyes: Pale blue

Hair: Dark brown, tangled

Most prized possession: Hope's wallet

Flaws: Shyness, removed from society too long

Strengths: Loyalty

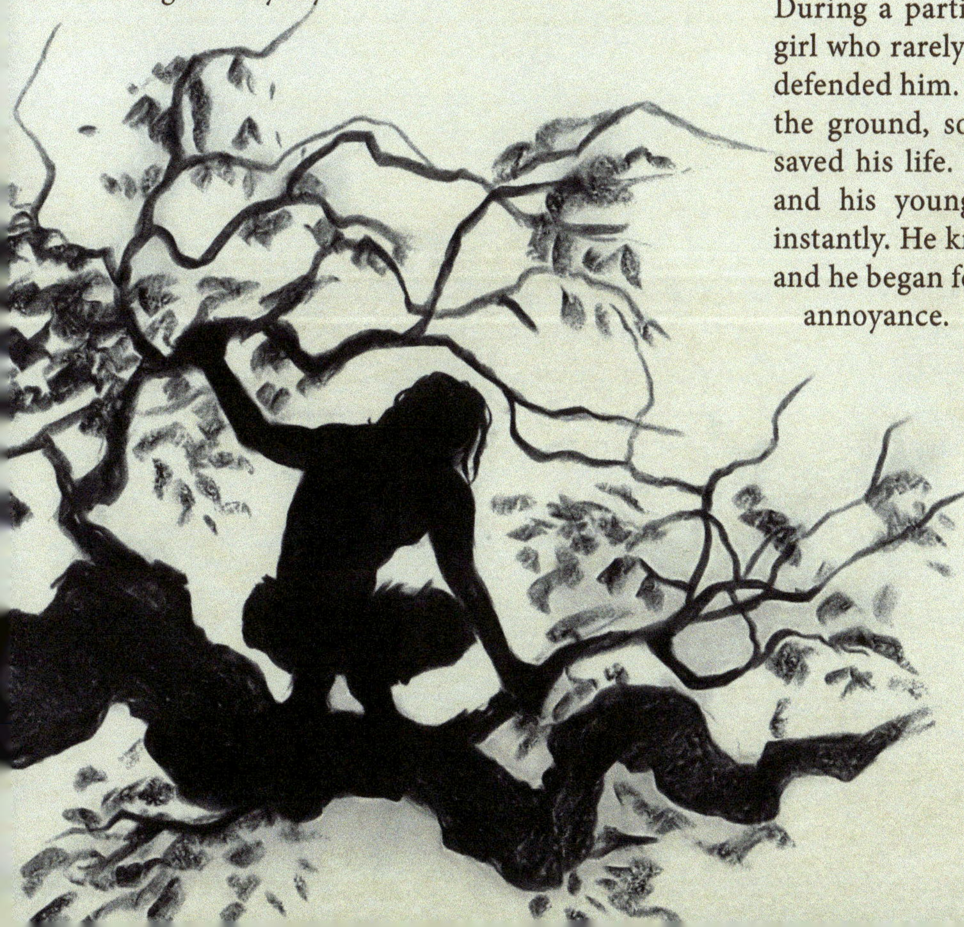

Skills: Swift and stealthy, survival, heightened senses, singing

Family: All deceased

Will's entire family were on holiday together when a landslide flattened their accommodation. Will was the only survivor, trapper under rubble with the bodies of his loved ones for days before rescue. After that, he was sent into group homes and thought there was no longer anything good in the world.

Will was a small and weak boy. He'd never thrived, but his parents had been wealthy and educated and encouraged him to follow pursuits in the arts, including singing. Once in the group home system, his upbringing and talents only brought him more misery as he was mercilessly picked on by other children.

During a particularly vicious attack, the rough girl who rarely talked to anyone, stepped in and defended him. When he looked up at Hope from the ground, sore and bloody, he felt she had saved his life. She was like an avenging angel, and his young boyish heart crushed on her instantly. He knew such a debt had to be repaid, and he began following her around, much to her annoyance.

Soon though, she began to look upon him as her little minion. The rules of their friendship were set:

"First rule- no touching. Second rule- That thing that happens? No talking about it. Ever. Nothing happens. So there's nothing to talk about."

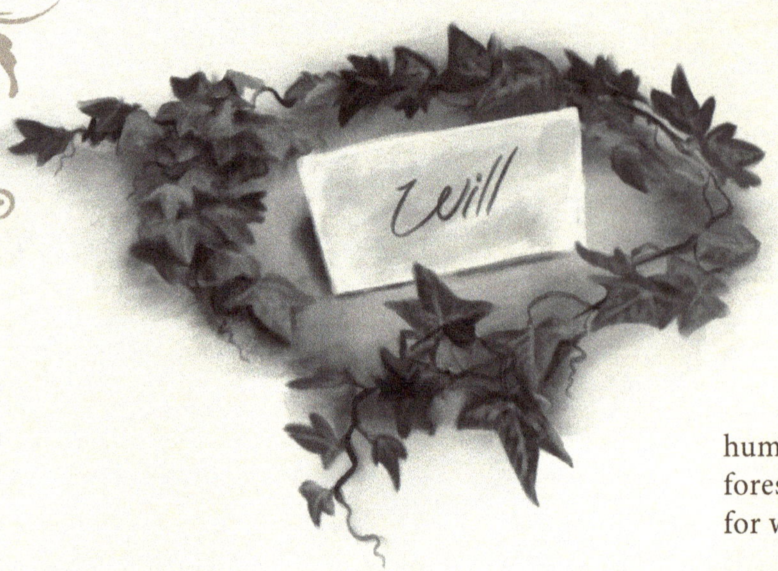

Will. William? William what? He had just been "that animal man". But he wasn't that. He was some normal boy whose life she'd ruined, lost in her own insane world of issues.

But Will did know what happened to Hope, and it hurt him every time she suffered that abuse and he was too weak and powerless to help.

One day he saw Hope running from the group home and noticed she'd forgotten her wallet. It was a small gesture, but following her with it was something he could do. When he discovered her in an alley, looking beaten and with a man draining the life from her magically, he knew he had to act. He'd promised that one day he would save the girl he loved, and he meant it.

But in the confusing moments that followed, he fell into another world and lost her. It would be sixteen years before he saw her again. He almost didn't last that long, lost and starving in the forests. He was saved by the fairy Mina, but was also claimed as her pet. She proved to be a neglectful owner, however, and he grew up mostly alone in the woods, learning to fend for himself. Mina took him to the fairy world at times, and he grew stronger and aged slower than normal for his time spent there.

He could have travelled to live with other humans of Avall, but chose to remain in the forests close to where he'd first arrived, waiting for when Hope would come back to him.

His heart almost broke when she finally appeared and didn't remember him at all.

But he'd already waited sixteen years, dreaming of his first love, the girl who'd saved his life and who he'd promise to protect as well. Now she'd finally returned to him, he could wait a little longer.

Clara studied Will up and down. "Oh my. Now I understand why you leave your windows open,"

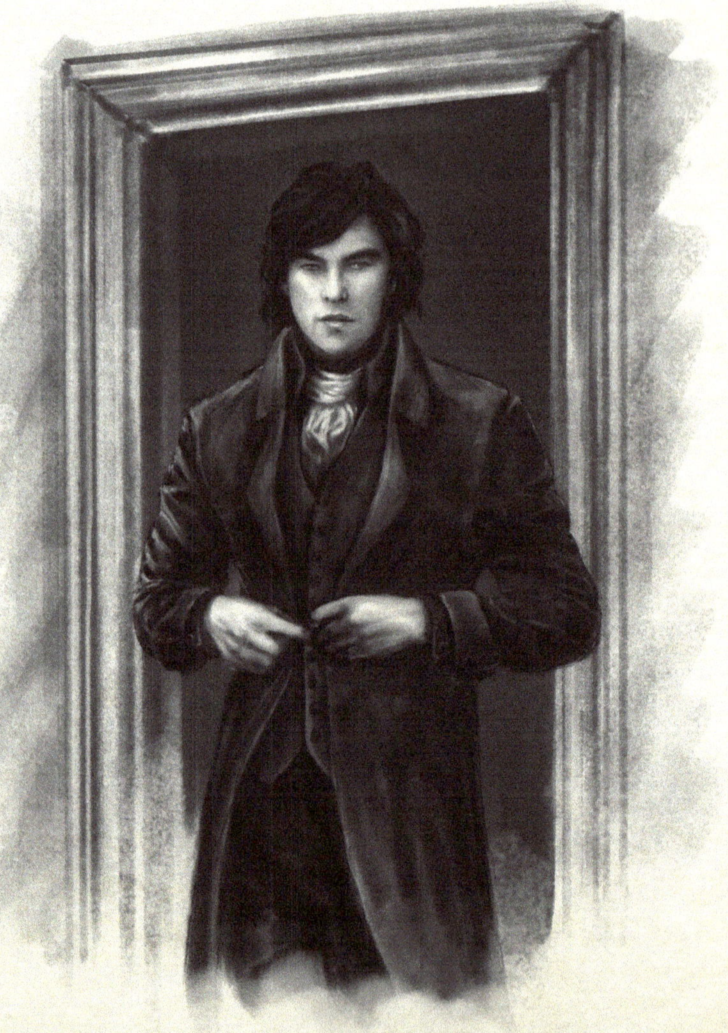

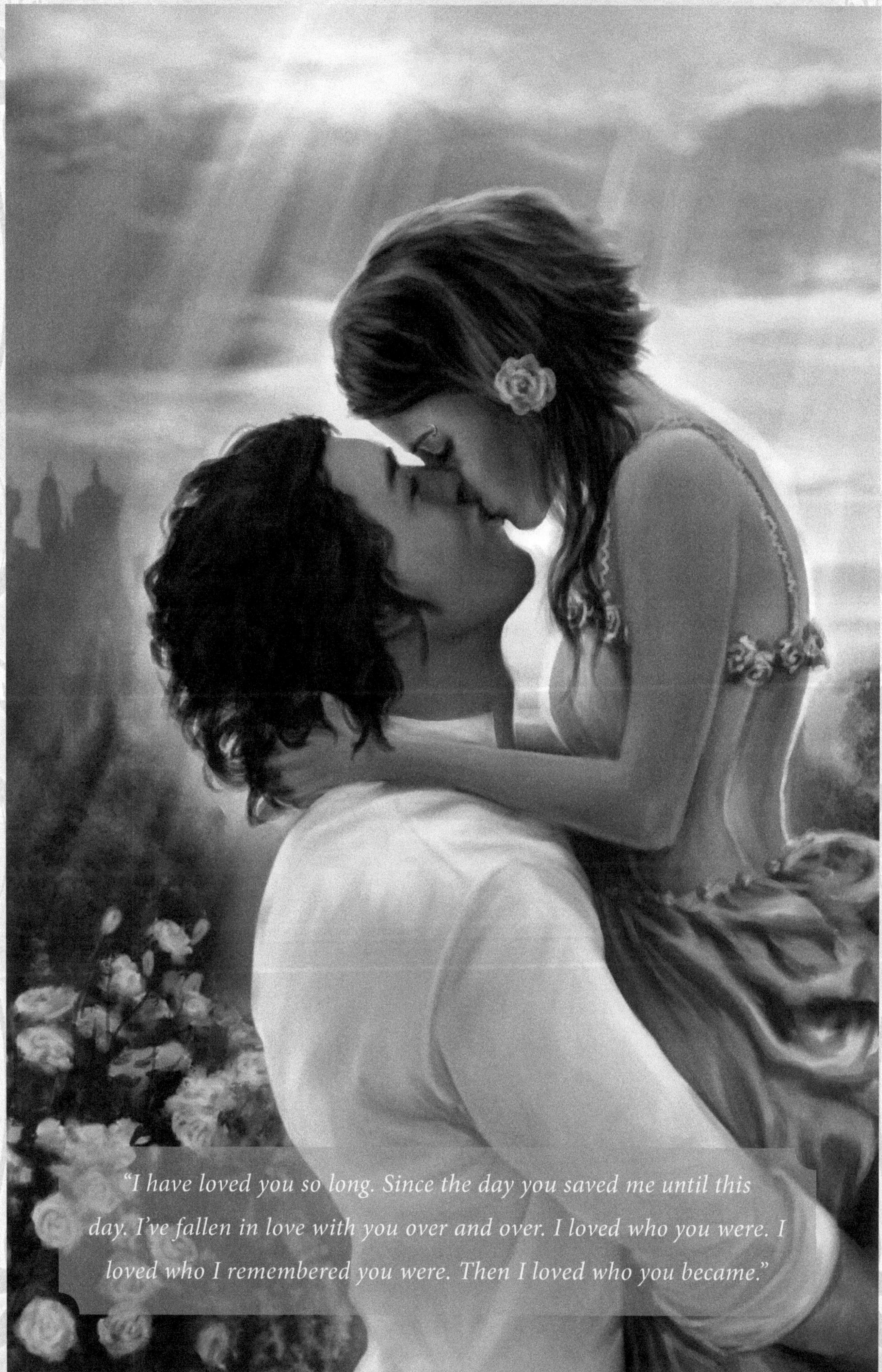
"I have loved you so long. Since the day you saved me until this day. I've fallen in love with you over and over. I loved who you were. I loved who I remembered you were. Then I loved who you became."

"I could just die I love you so much. I've always wanted to be with you, when things are good or bad, no matter what color your hair is or where we are. My home is where you are."

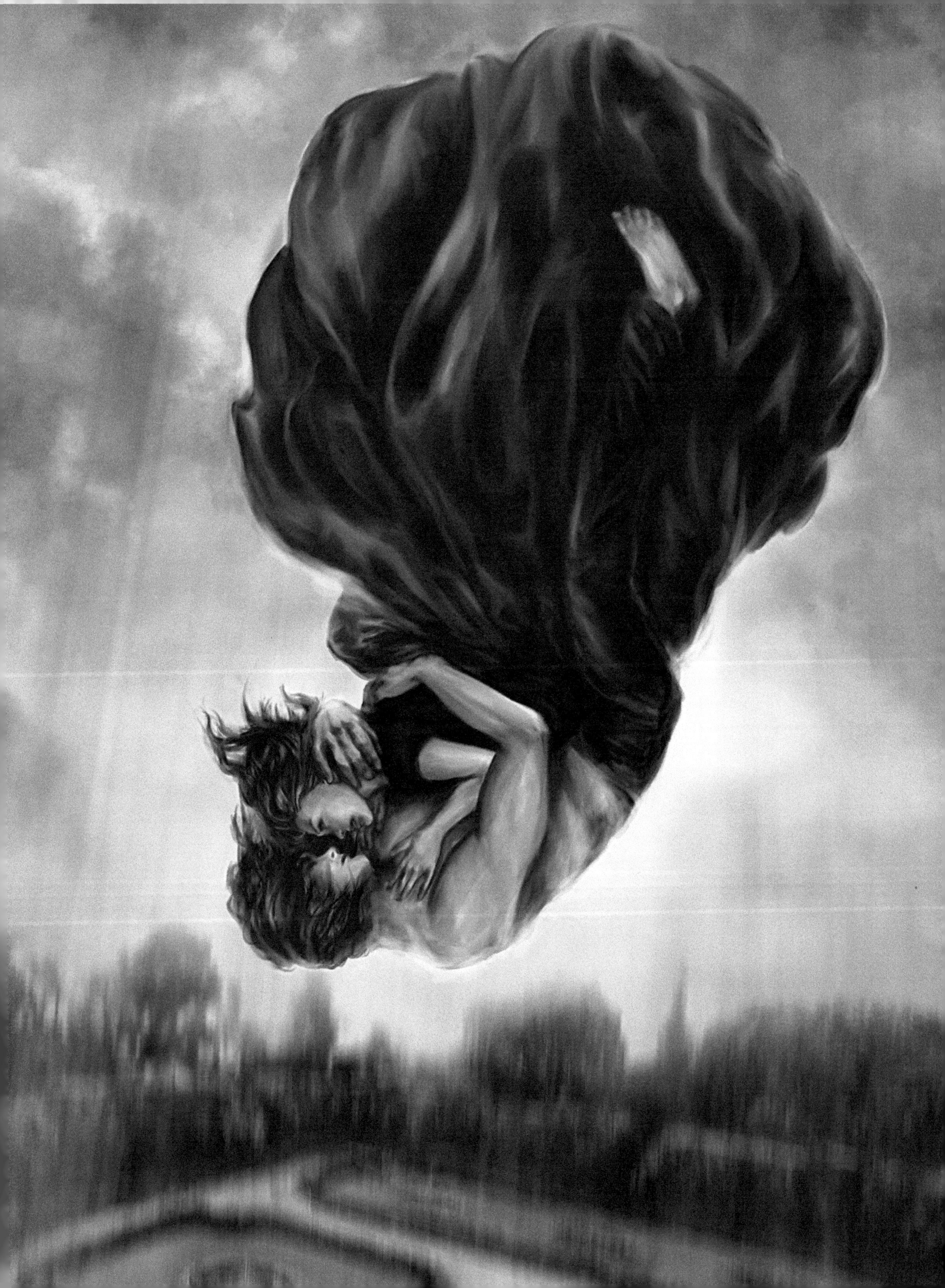

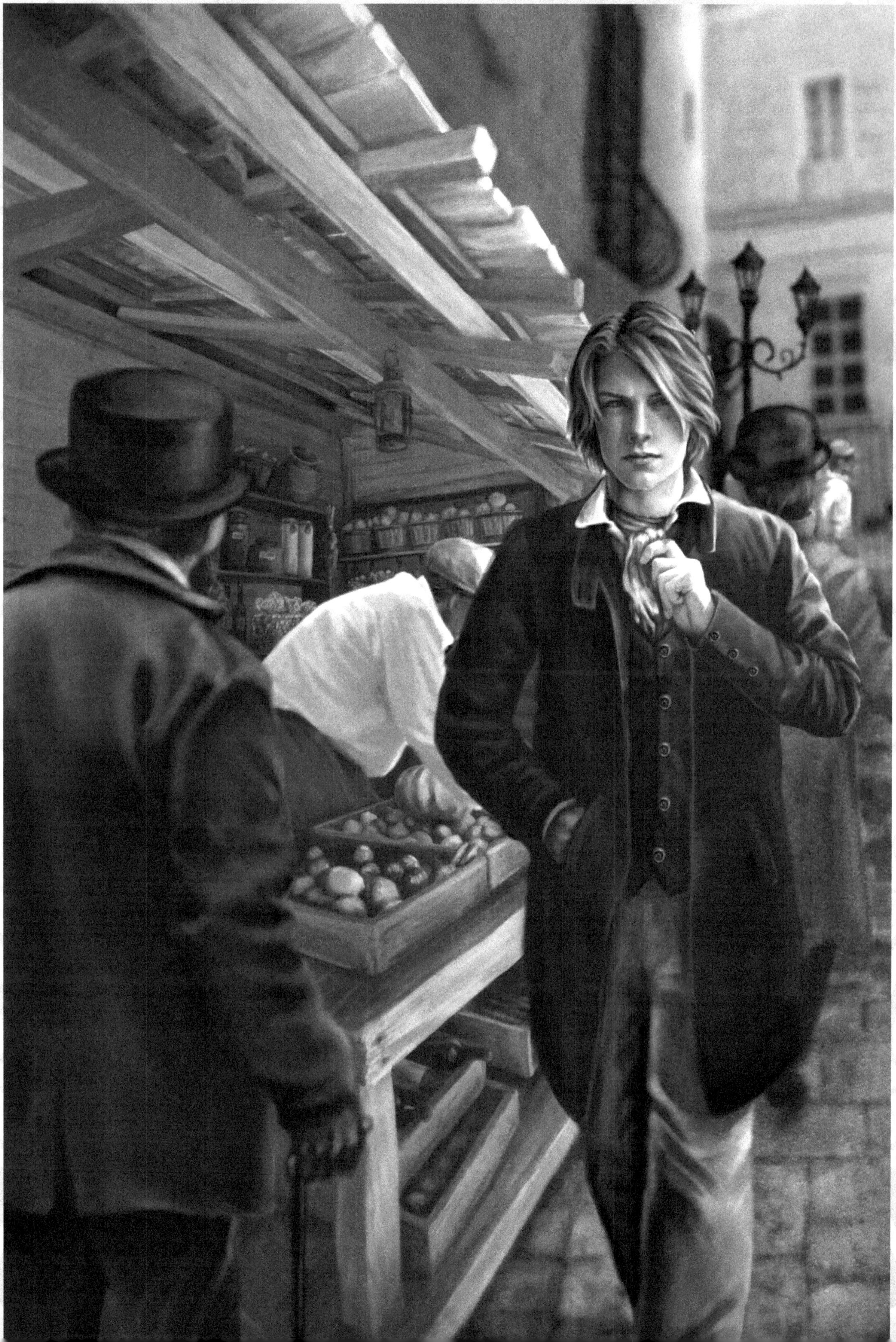

Roen

That was the reality of who he was; criminal, philanderer, sparkless seventh son of a seventh son. A man who had no place by her side.

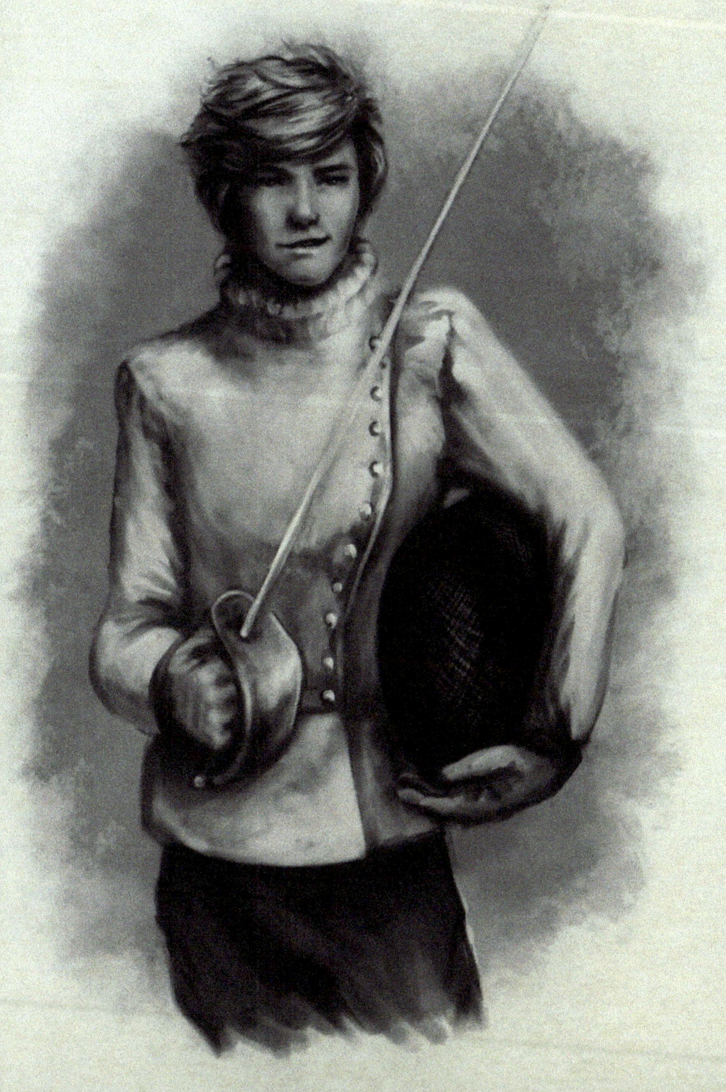

Name: Roen Faerbaird

Age: 18

Height: 5'9"

Body Type: Lightly built, fit

Eyes: Light golden brown

Hair: Caramel blonde

Most prized possession: Eloryn's heart

Flaws: Self hatred for his crimes

Strengths: Charming, selfless

Skills: Sleight of hand, stealth, fencing

Family: Isabeth (mother), Brannon (father), Vaughn (brother, deceased), Jostin (brother, deceased), James (brother, deceased) , Nathaniel (brother, deceased), Tristan (brother, deceased), Dylan (brother).

In Avall, it is a well known legend that the seventh son of a seventh son is born without the Spark of Connection all others have that allows them to connect to magic. They say seventh sons of seventh sons are "blessed and cursed".

When Isabeth and Brannon, who was already a seventh son, had six sons of their own, they never intended to have a seventh child just in case. The seventh pregnancy was unintended and Roen was born without the Spark of Connection.

The Faerbairds were nobles of the highest ranking, Grand Duke and Duchess, and close friends with the Maellan queen. When Thayl

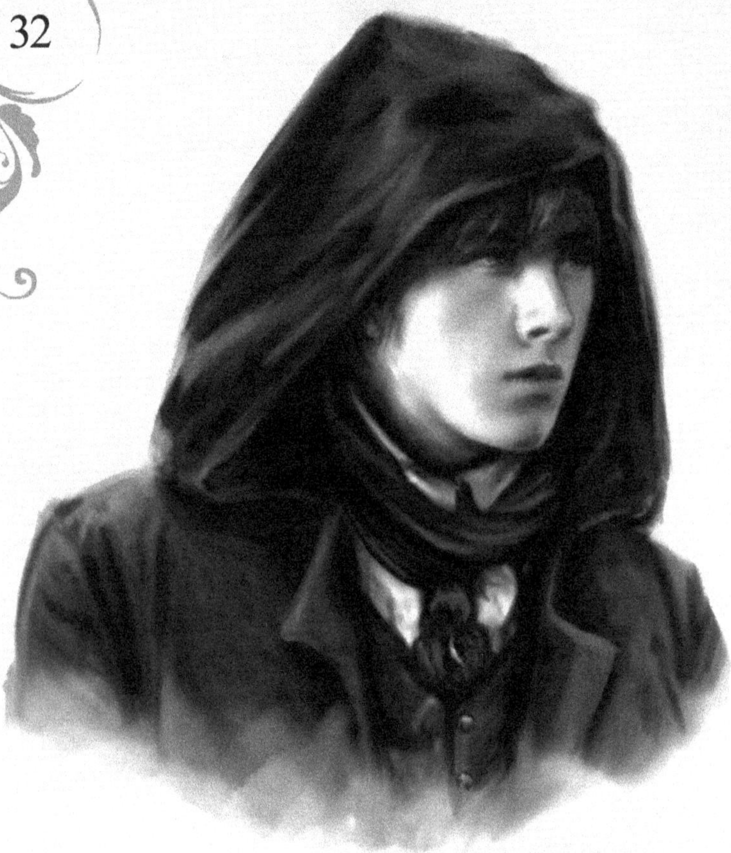

"You are everything a princess should be: kind, clever, brave, beautiful. If I behave differently for you, it's only because whatever I was, whatever I am, I need to be better for you."

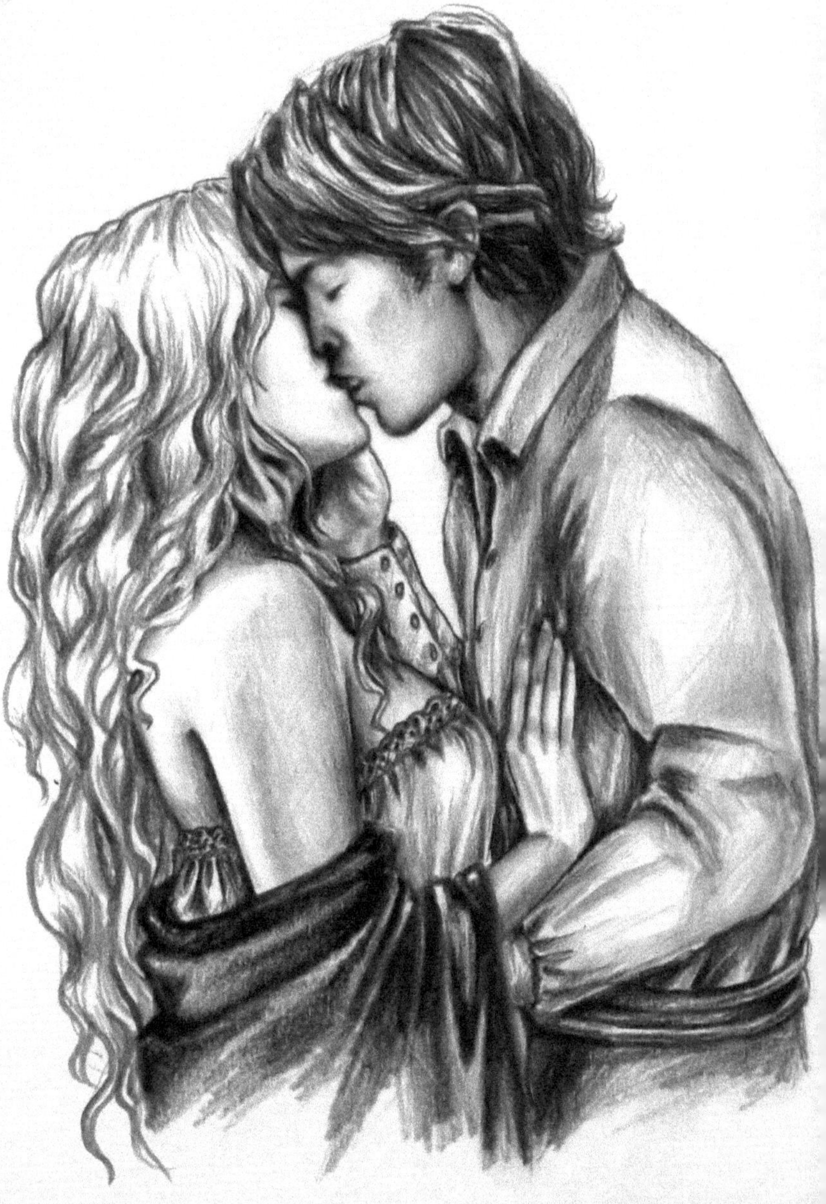

struck, taking rule of the kingdom, the Faerbairds spent the next ten years fighting against him, as many others did. It was futile, and five of their sons were lost in the battles.

The Faerbairds then went into hiding, but Dylan, their second youngest, refused to live in poverty and isolation, turning his back on his family and remaining a noble in Thayl's court- the biggest act of betrayal he could have made against his family.

This left Roen as the only remaining son of Isabeth and Brannon. As they were so recognisable, they remained sequestered while he attempted to make a living for the family without drawing attention to them.

But as a sparkless child with no bearing, he was refused all jobs or trades. It was difficult for him having been raised with noble values to turn to thieving, but he did to keep his family fed when they had nothing left.

Roen knew his birth was an accident, and often felt his presence as a sparkless thief

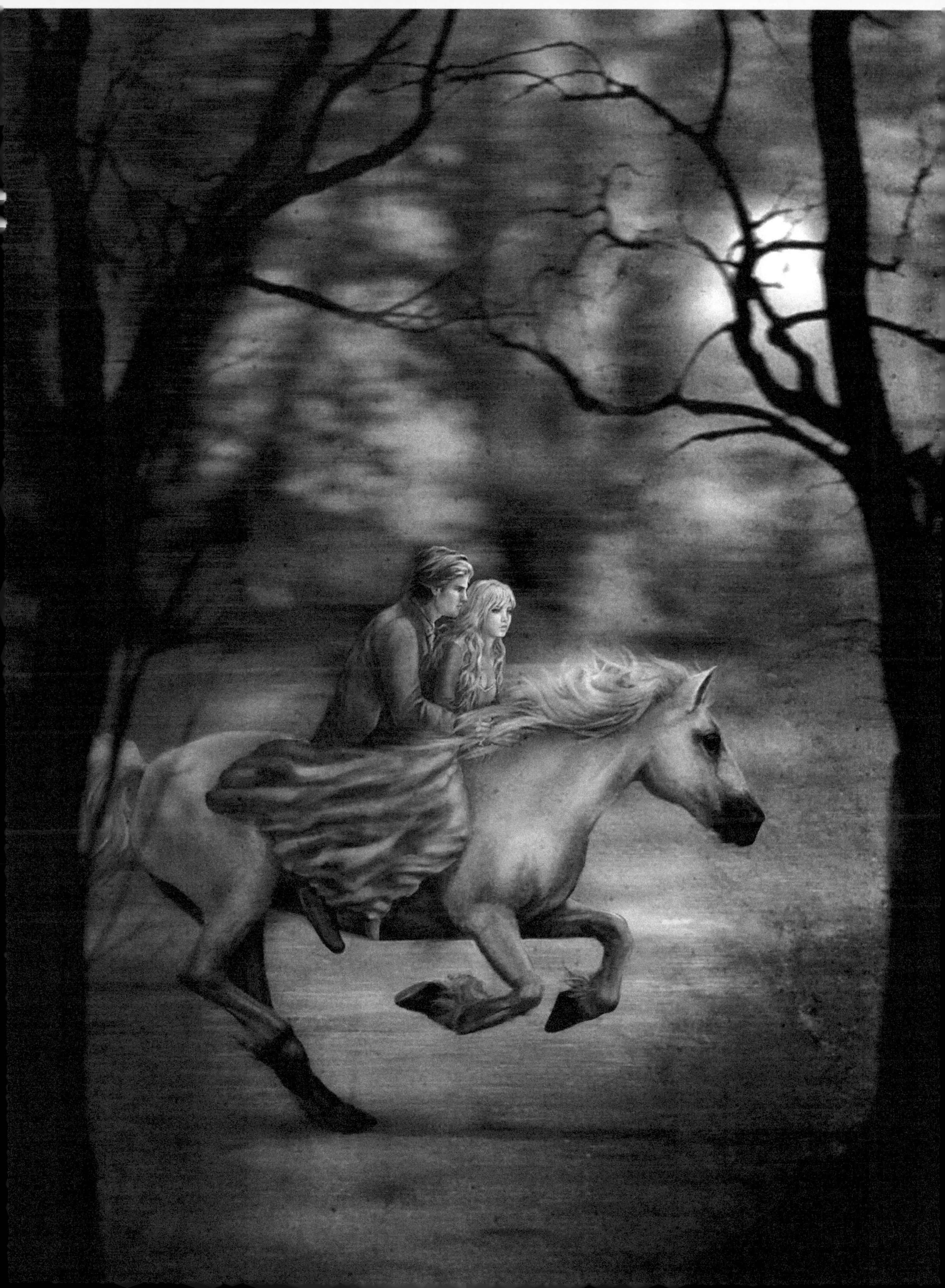

For a moment that he, his parents and so many others had dreamt of for so long, to find this person of such importance, and here he was, throwing the princess into rubbish and manhandling her.

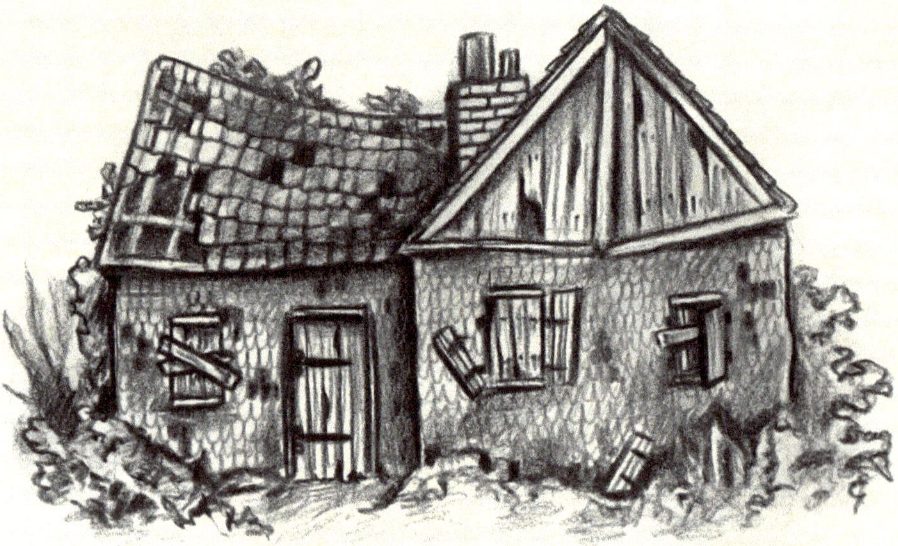

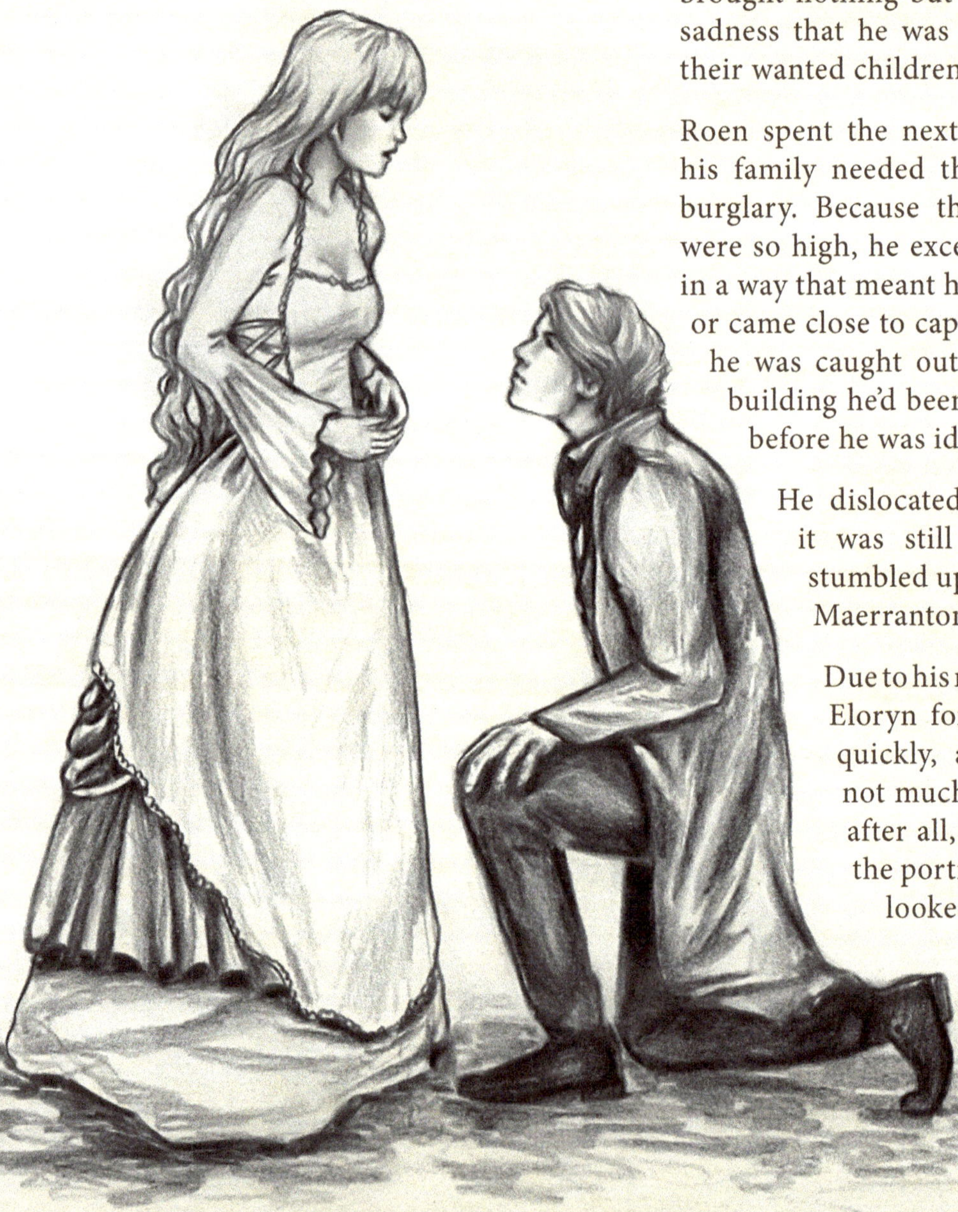

brought nothing but shame to his parents, and sadness that he was all that remained now all their wanted children were gone.

Roen spent the next eight years earning what his family needed through pickpocketing and burglary. Because the stakes of being caught were so high, he excelled at his criminal career in a way that meant he never made any mistakes or came close to capture- until one night when he was caught out on the second floor of a building he'd been robbing and had to jump before he was identified.

He dislocated his arm that night, and it was still troubling him when he stumbled upon Eloryn and Memory in Maerranton markets.

Due to his noble past, Roen recognised Eloryn for who she really was very quickly, and fell in love with her not much longer after that. He had, after all, grown up with a crush on the portrait of Eloryn's mother who looked very much like her.

But his growing love for Eloryn troubled him. As a sparkless thief he felt completely unworthy to be the Maellan princess's guardian, let alone her love.

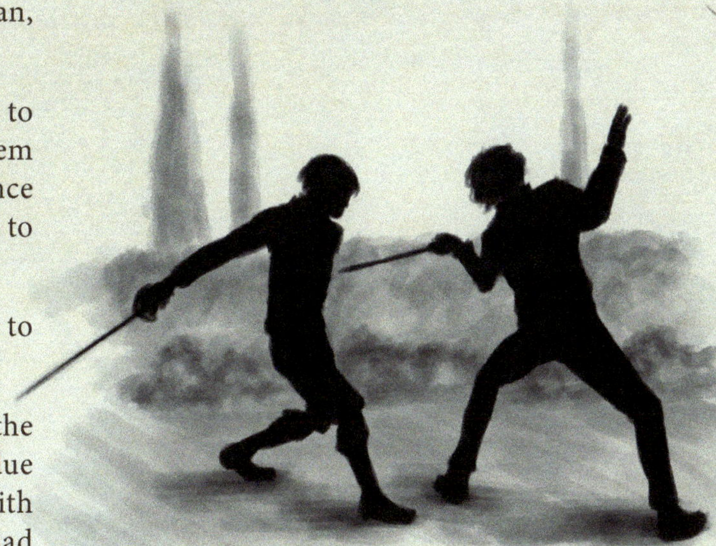

When he finally reveals his criminal side to Memory and Eloryn, he does so expecting them to hate him and abandon him. Their acceptance of him regardless of his past helped him begin to accept himself as well.

During his journey with the twins, he begins to not only accept his past, but to value it.

When he learns Eloryn feels for him as well, the Wizard Council stand in their way briefly, due to their strict rules regarding partnerships with the Maellan bloodline. But Eloryn and Roen had learned from Loredanna and Thayl's mistakes, and refused to let tradition stand between them.

"I love you in a way that should make me a poet, but instead leaves me speechless."

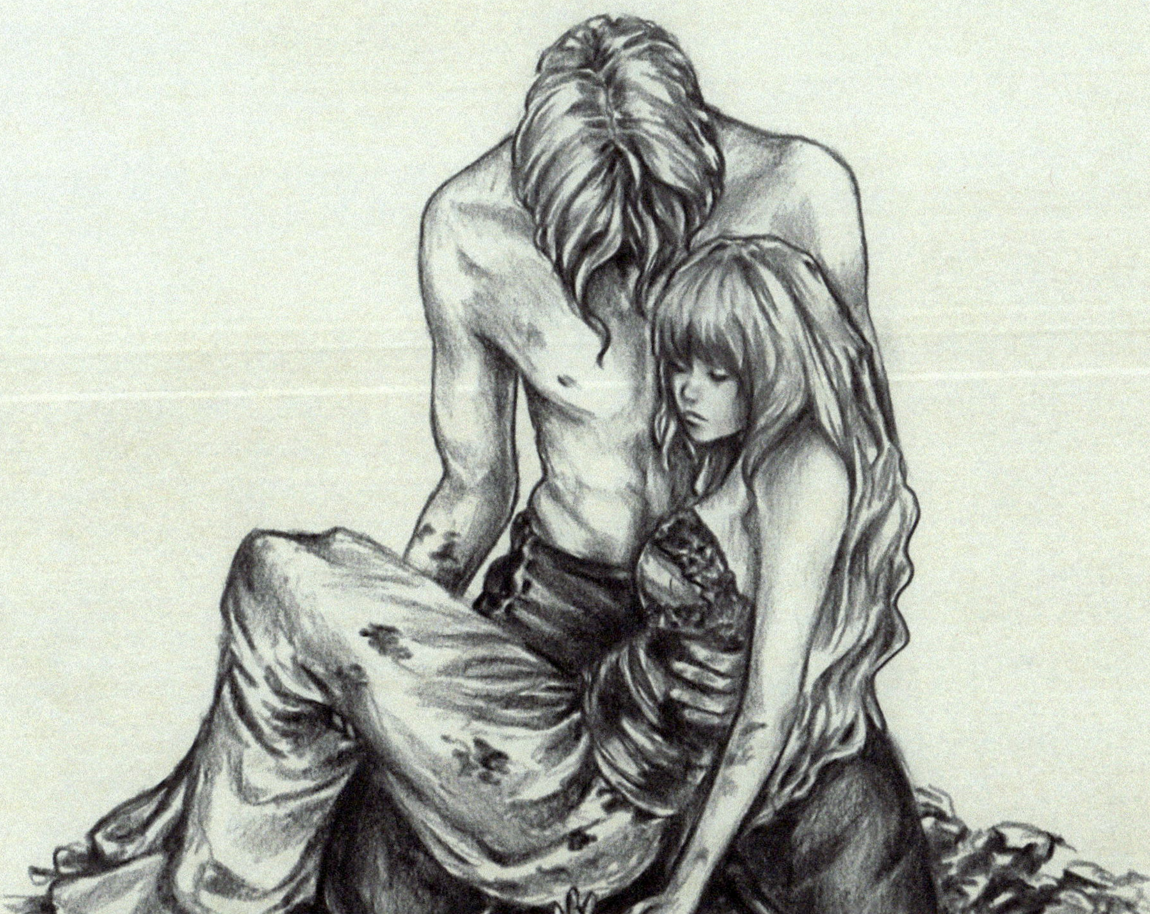

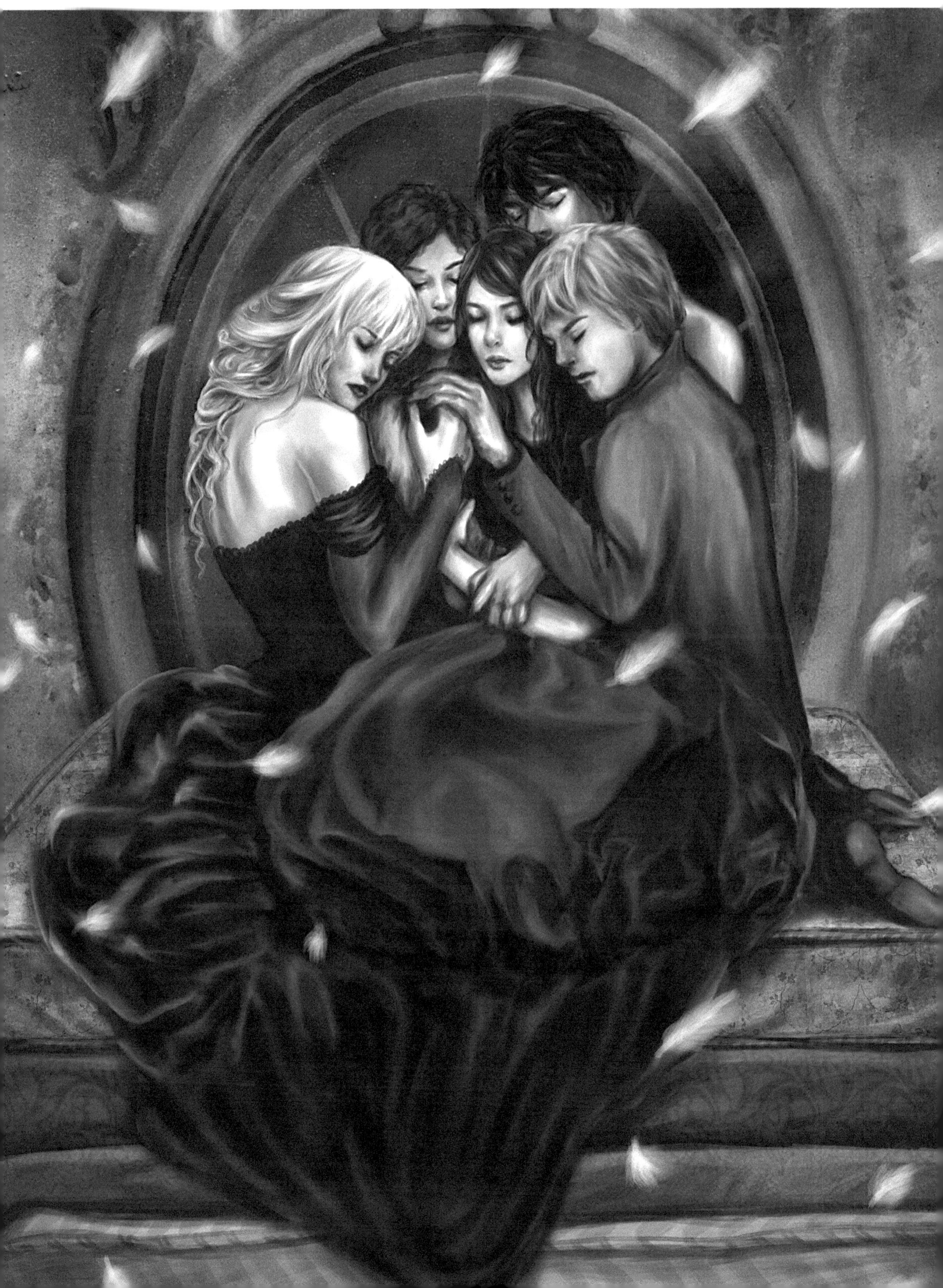

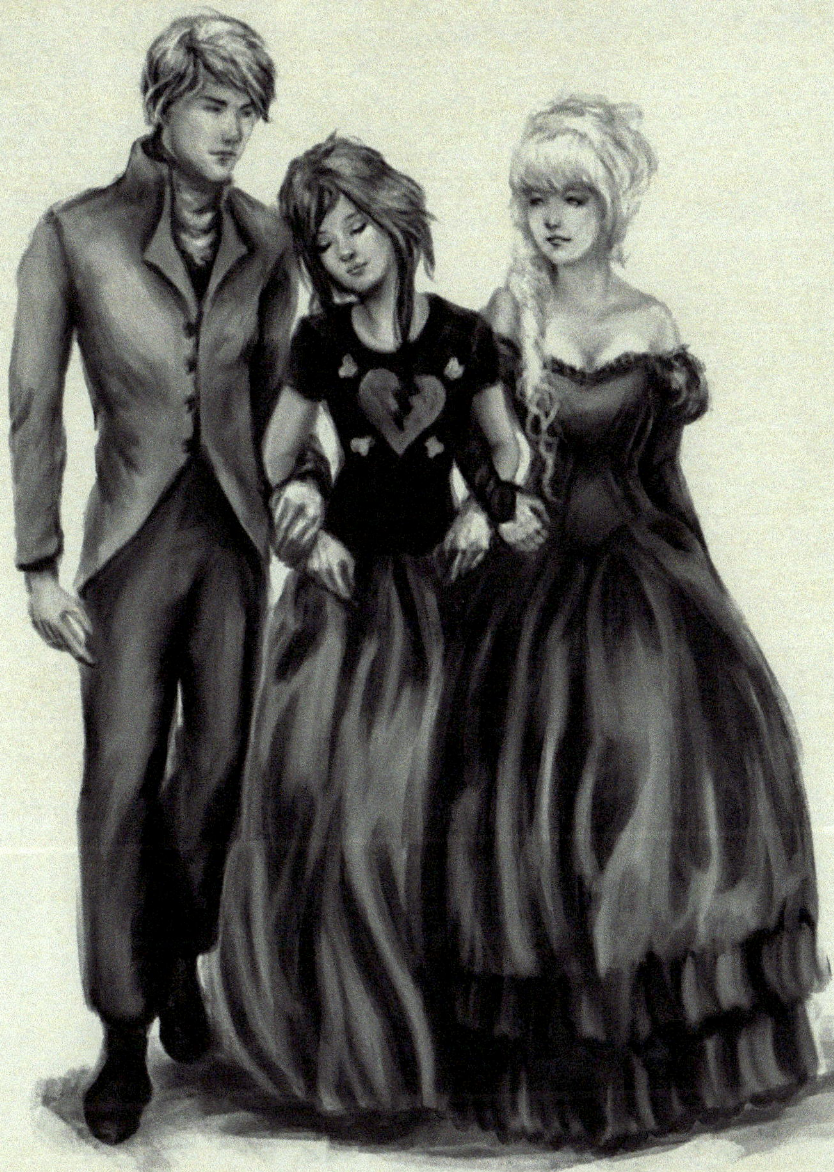

"I know you're hurting. It would be insane if you weren't after everything you've been through. There's no quick fix, but I'll be there for you. And you will be there for me, too, like you always have."

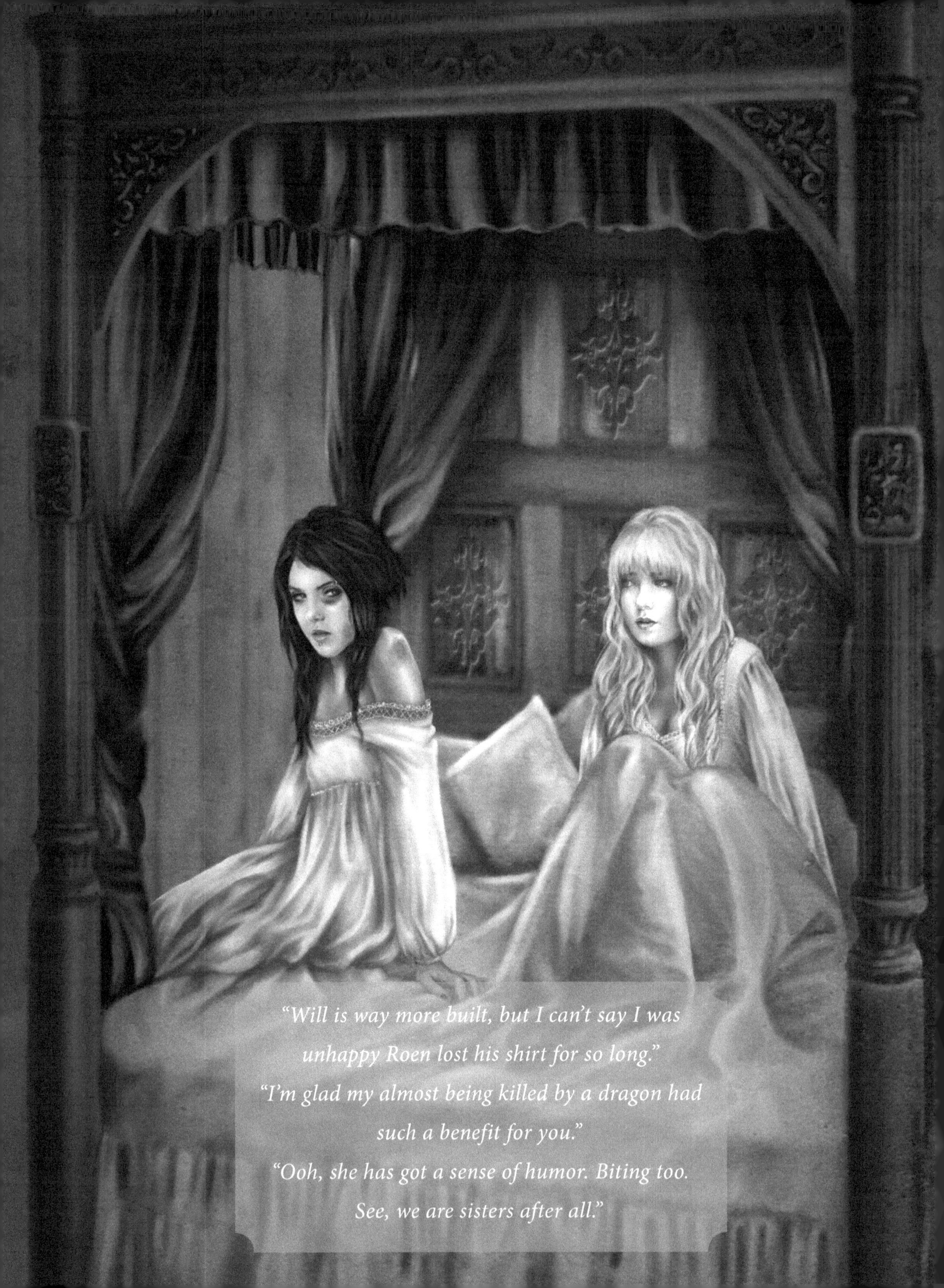
"Will is way more built, but I can't say I was unhappy Roen lost his shirt for so long."
"I'm glad my almost being killed by a dragon had such a benefit for you."
"Ooh, she has got a sense of humor. Biting too. See, we are sisters after all."

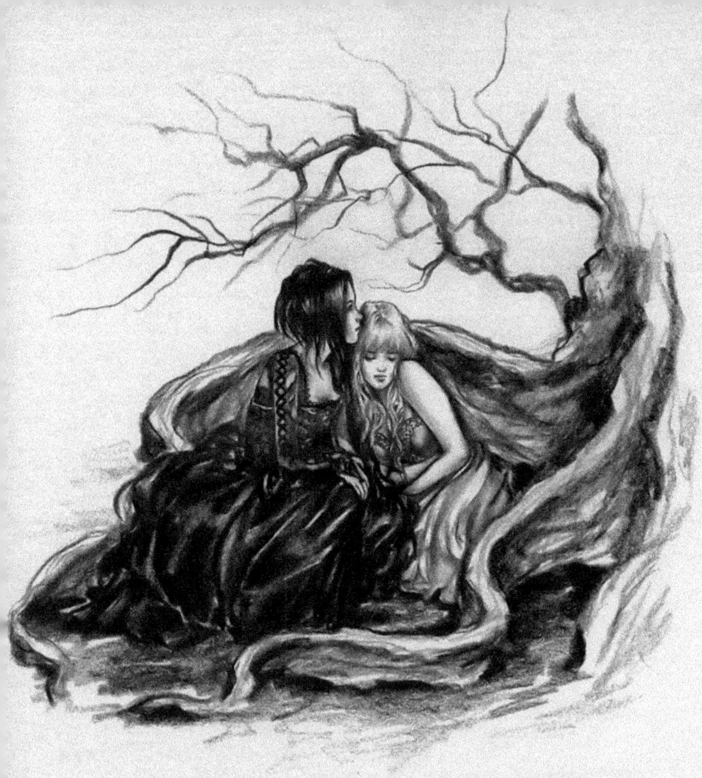

Sometimes Memory looked so much like her it chilled her bones. More often, she was so different – from her angular build to her blunt words – it seemed ridiculous trying to make comparisons.

The Twins

Despite being identical twins, Memory and Eloryn are very different in both personality and appearance.

Apart from Memory's dyed hair, their upbringings caused larger physical changes that hid their similarities. Memory grew up tough, active, and along with an eating disorder it made her build slim and wiry.

Eloryn grew up practically locked indoors, and became soft and slightly plump. When Memory first arrives in Avall her face is also swollen and covered in bruises.

The only similarity they both noticed at first was their matching jade colored eyes.

Personality wise, Memory grew to be rough and sarcastic, while Eloryn polite and withdrawn. As they spend time together, their personalities rub off on each other, bringing out Memory's kindness and Eloryn's sense of humor.

The twins never learned who their true father was after discovering Loredanna's husband may not have been. Even Thayl did not know.

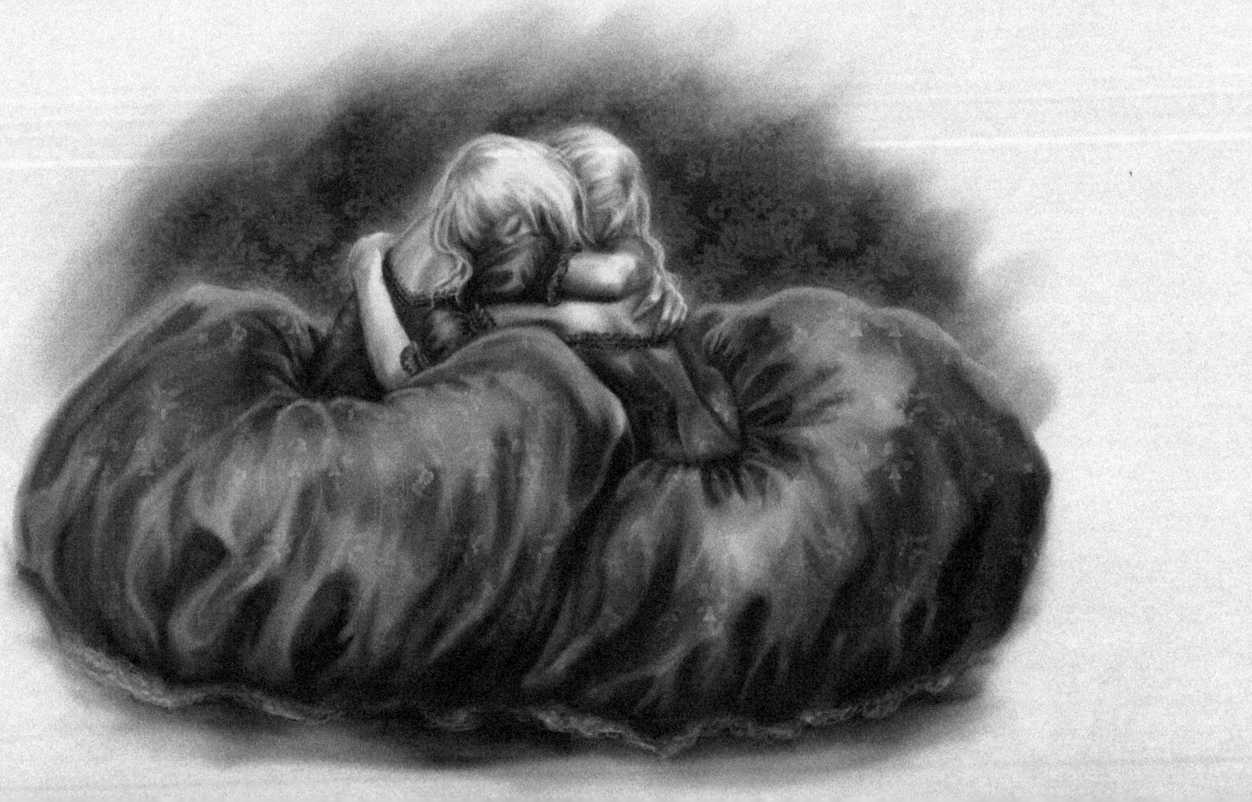

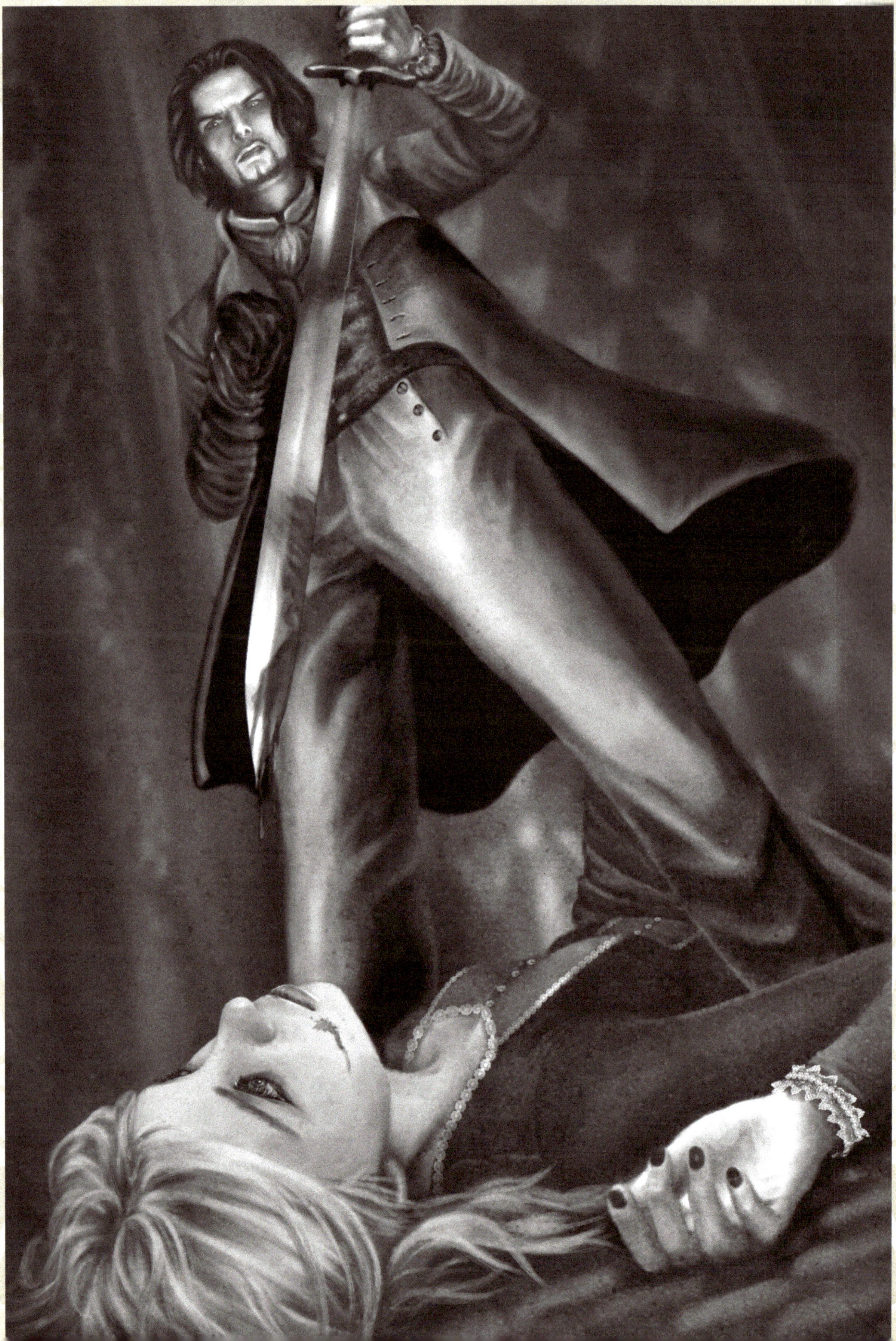

Thayl

Name: Thayl Vaircarn

Age: 38

Distinguishing Marks: Hand covered in rune shaped scars

Eyes: Troubled

Hair: Rich brown

Flaws: Jealousy, vengeance

Strengths: Driven

Skills: Magic without behests

Family: Isode (sister, deceased)

The son of a minor noble, Thayl had only met Queen Loredanna by chance, but the attraction between them was instant and mutual. She was still very young and new to her role as queen, her parents having died tragically at sea and leaving her the sole Maellan heir.

Marriages for the Maellan line have always been arranged by the Wizard's Council, choosing partners that are deemed strong at magic to maintain the inherent talents of the Maellan family. Thayl was not considered a worthy partner, and another man was chosen. Deeply upset, but feeling helpless, Loredanna agreed to the marriage and said goodbye to Thayl. But Thayl wasn't willing to give up so easily.

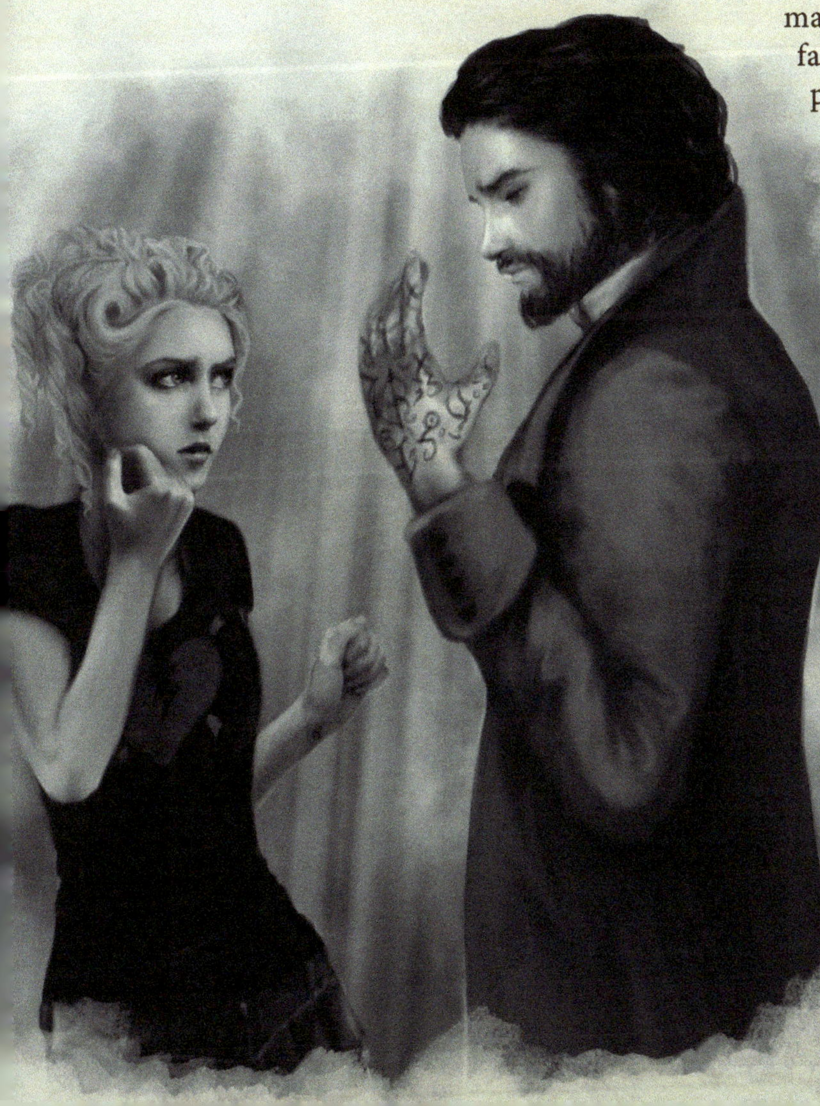

Not long after being publicly humiliated trying to fight for Loredanna's love and being turned away, Thayl was approached by Providence, who appeared to him as an old woman, wise in the magical arts. She told him she could provide everything he needed to get revenge on the Wizard's Council, for a price. He agreed too quickly.

Loredanna and her chosen husband had been married, and her pregnancy was announced not long after. She was heavily pregnant when on the night of a lunar eclipse, Thayl went to her

"But! What? He couldn't have her, so he killed her? That's crazy person logic! What kind of story was that?"

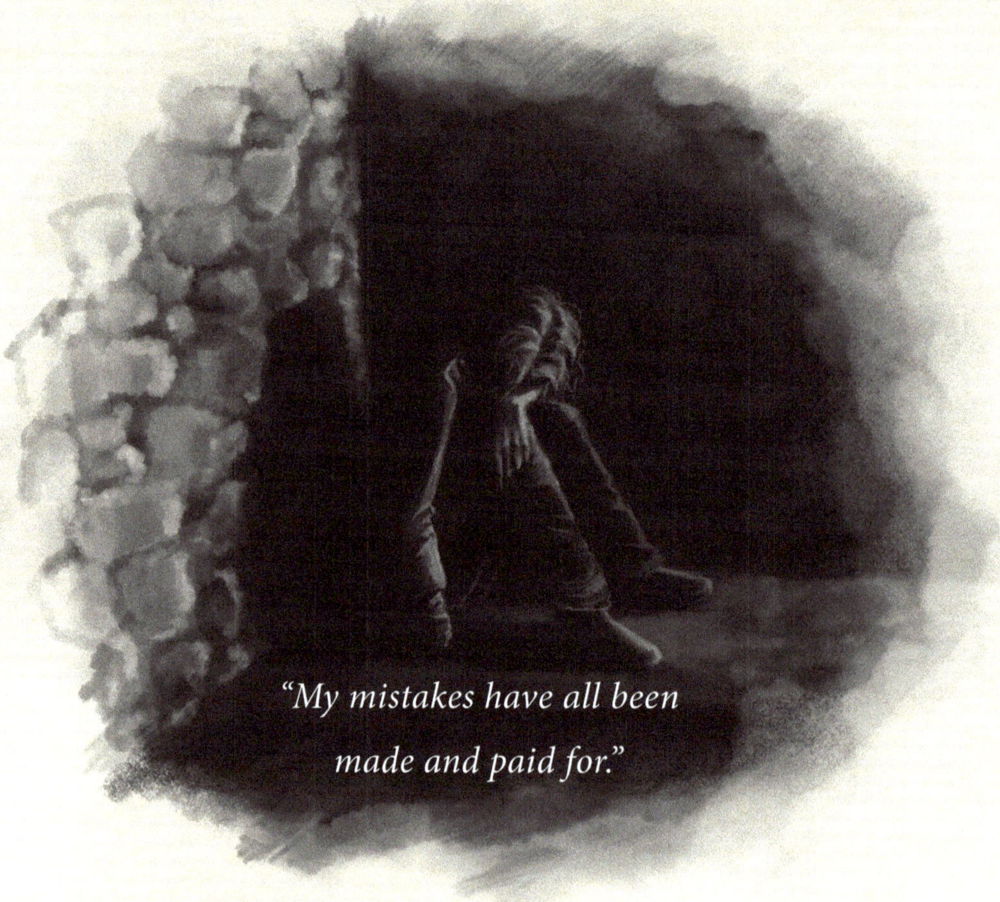

and asked her to run away with him. She agreed, wishing she had from the beginning. They ran, but he took her instead to Providence and induced her labour so they could use her child as part of their ritual. Thayl had imagined he could simply remove the child he believed to belong to the other man, then take his Loredanna and his revenge. But the birth of a second infant, Loredanna's refusal to leave without her children, and the interference of Alward, changed everything. A spell of death meant for Thayl struck Loredanna instead. As she died, she helped Alward escape with the second born child.

In the confusion of misery that followed, Providence continued the ritual, sacrificing Thayl's younger sister to allow him to travel across time into the future of the other world and reap the magic from the now grown infant they'd just sacrificed. But again, there was interference, with Will stopping him.

Without that interference, without suffering the grief of losing Loredanna, Thayl may have been strong enough to have defeated the entire Wizard's Council when he then attacked the capital with his new magic. But instead, some managed to flee and survive in hiding. With them alive, his debt to Providence never came due.

After sixteen years of trying to hunt the remaining wizards, and growing wiser as to Providence's true motives and identity, the child he sacrificed came back into his world. She would change him in more ways than he'd ever imagined.

"You think I planned it all? Think child, what magic did I have, before I stole yours? I had help."

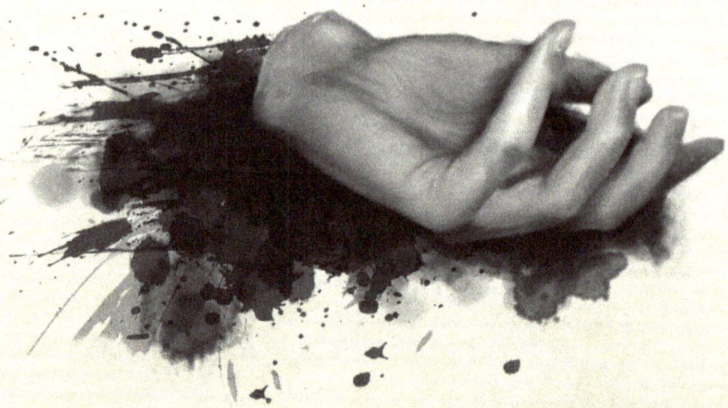

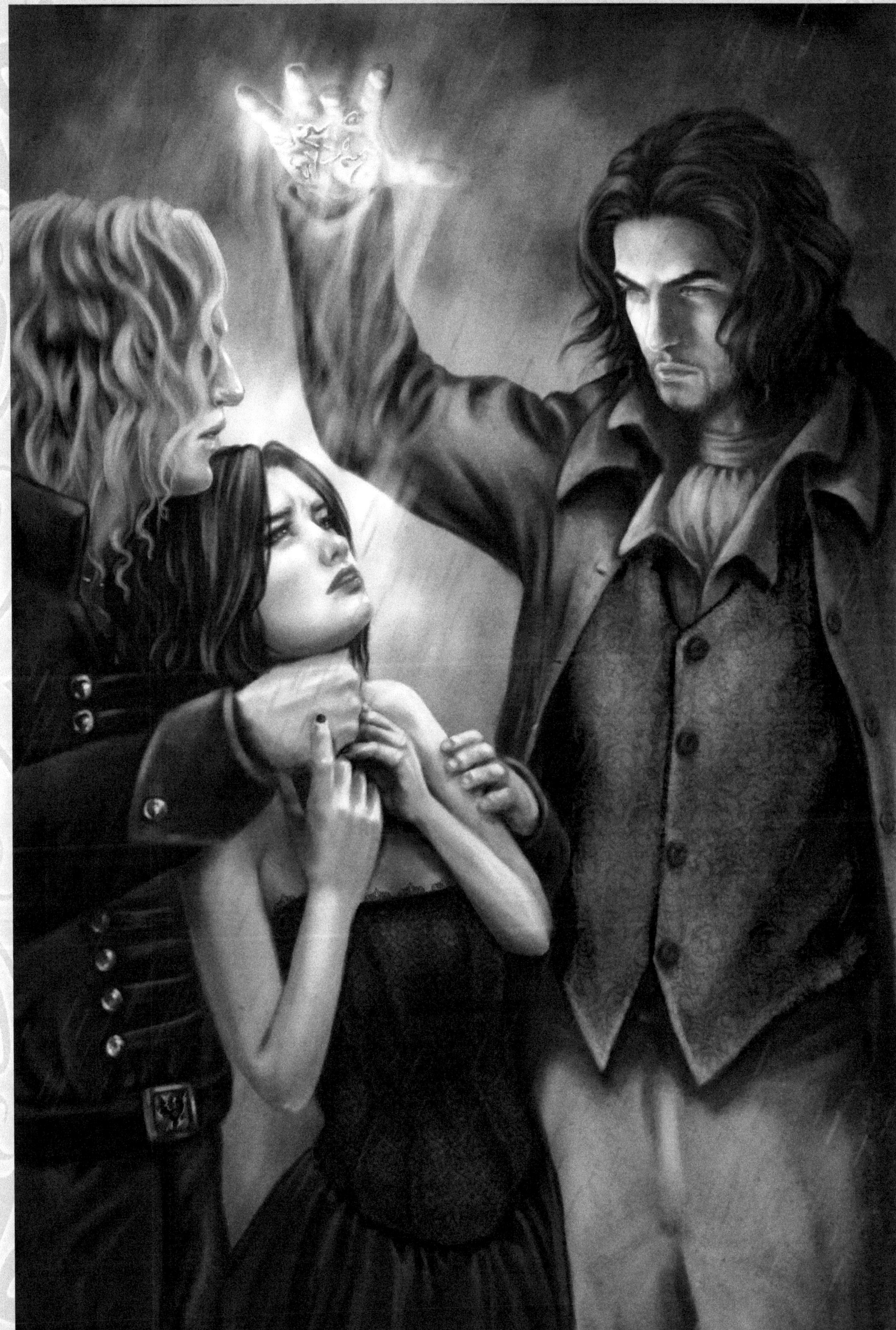

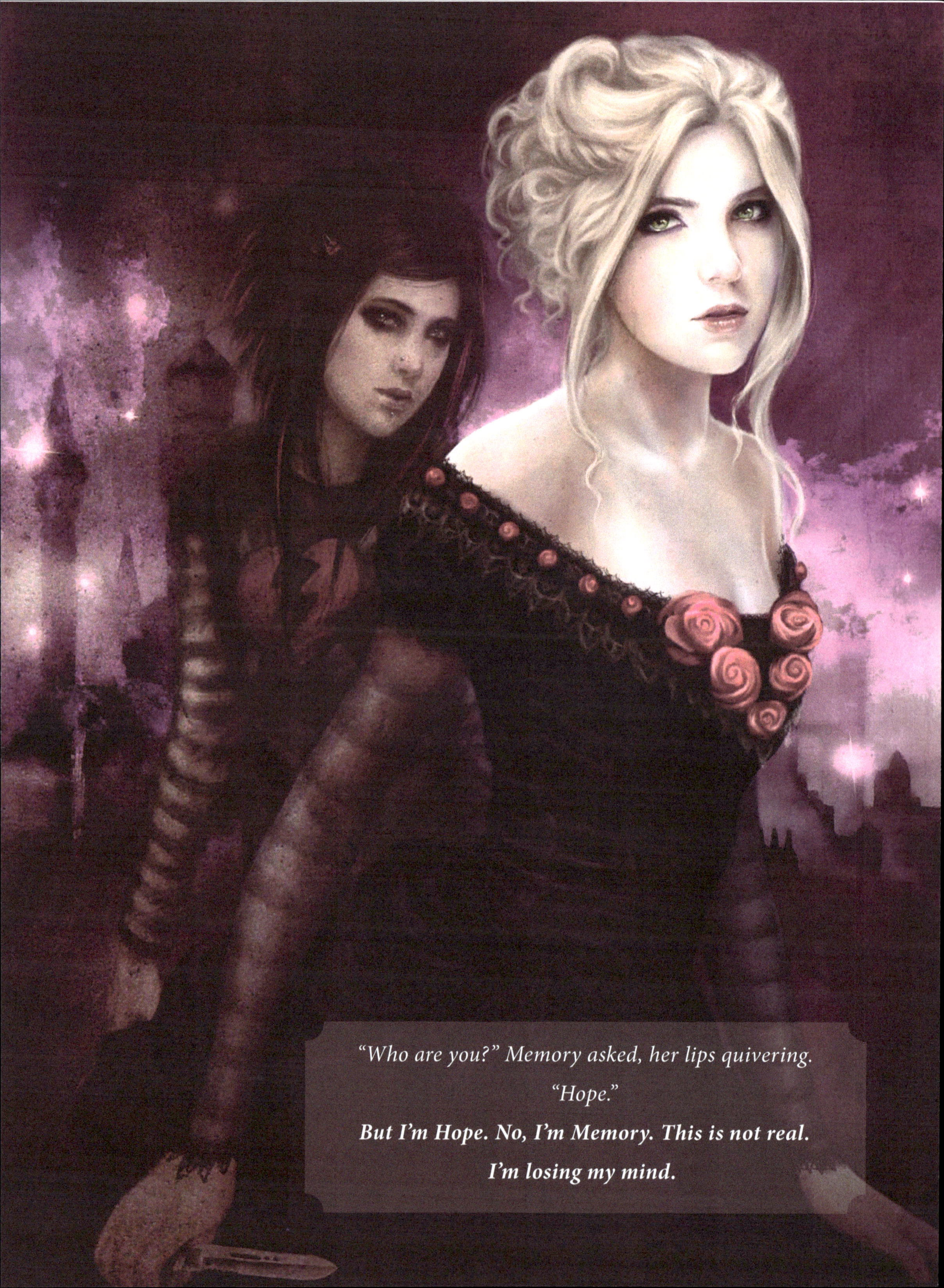

"Who are you?" Memory asked, her lips quivering.

"Hope."

But I'm Hope. No, I'm Memory. This is not real.

I'm losing my mind.

Nyneve

No, Nyneve wasn't insane. She had planned so carefully and so cleverly for so long. She never seemed insane. If anything she just seemed deeply sad, and hurt.

Name: Nyneve

Aliases: Providence, Hope, Nimue

Age: Ancient/Immortal

Height: 6'6" as Nyneve

Complexion: Silver scales

Eyes: All black unseelie eyes

Hair: So black it reflects no light

Flaws: Species prejudice, grudge holding

Strengths: Deception, manipulation

Skills: Highly skilled in human magical language

Family: Finvarra (father), Oonah (mother)

Despite the taboo of him being a half fae/half human, Nyneve loved Myrddin. He loved her, too, but held a greater, unrequited love for

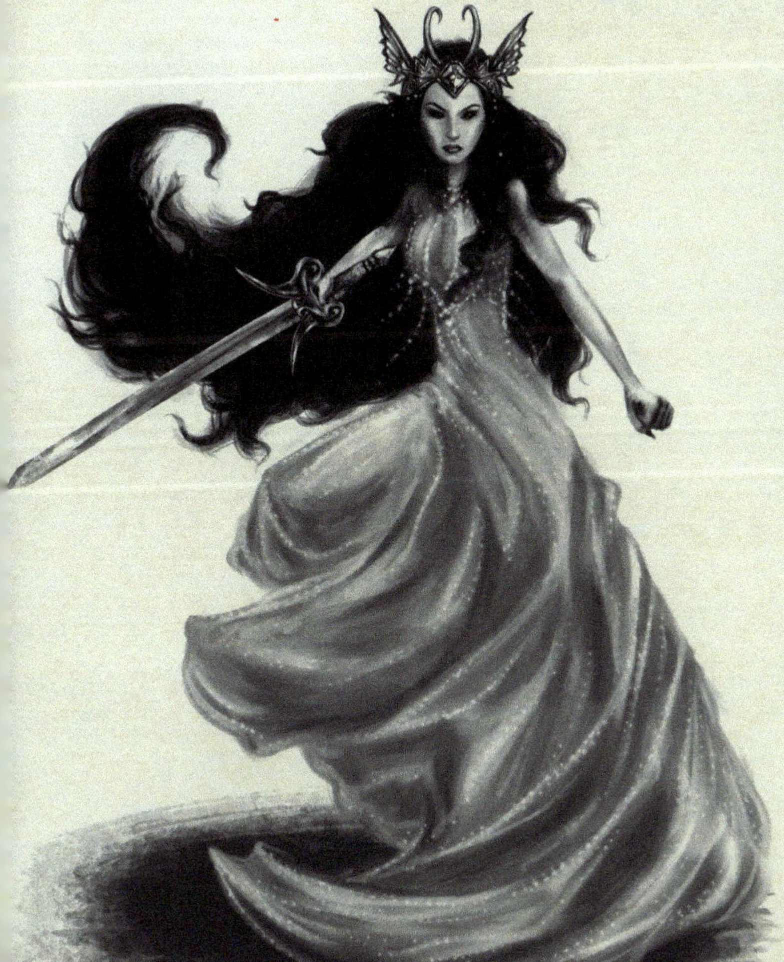

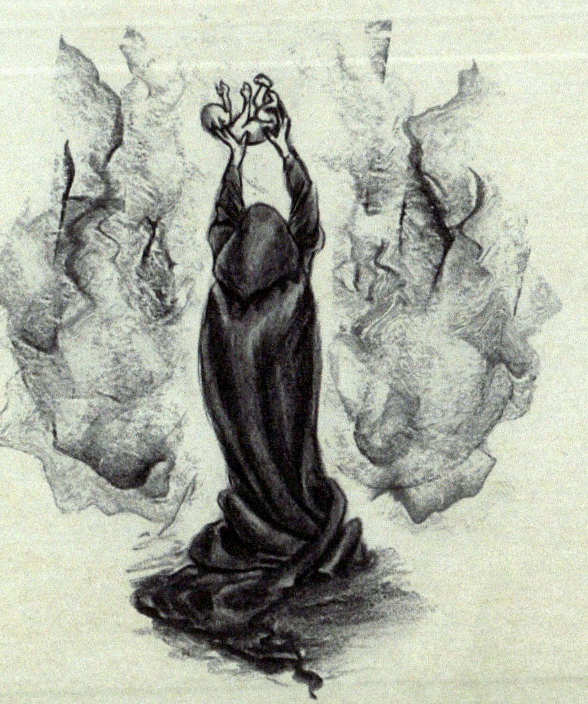

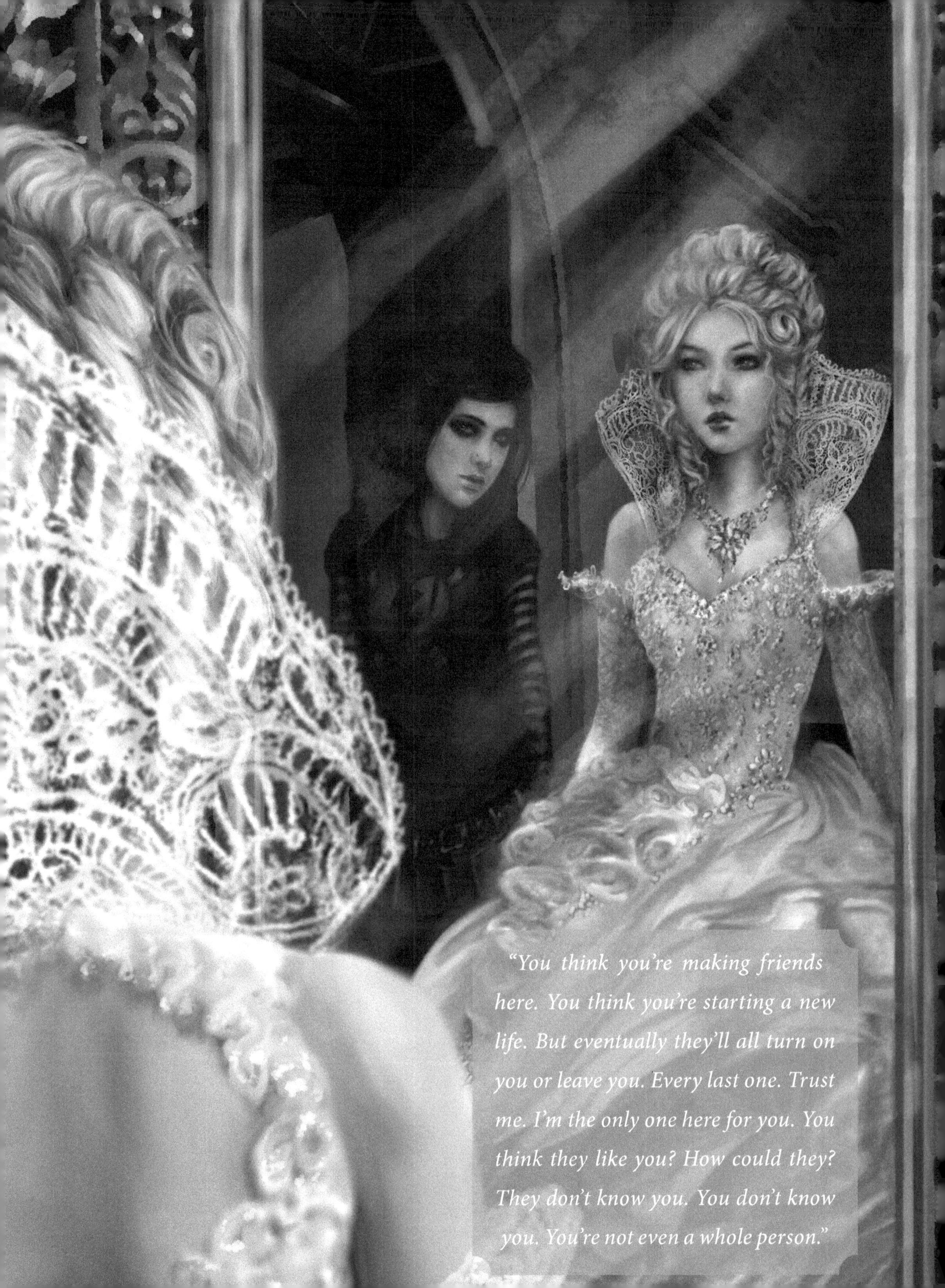

"You think you're making friends here. You think you're starting a new life. But eventually they'll all turn on you or leave you. Every last one. Trust me. I'm the only one here for you. You think they like you? How could they? They don't know you. You don't know you. You're not even a whole person."

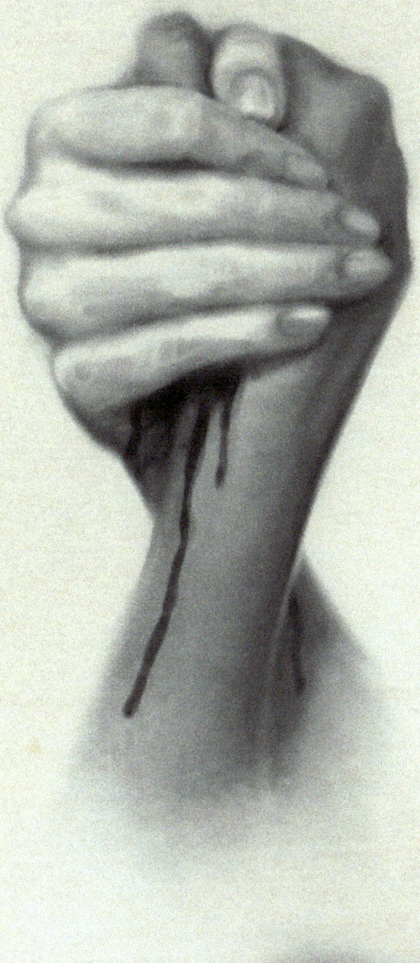

the human Arthur Maellan. For that, Nyneve hated Arthur, and she hated him more when he arranged Branding to be part of the Pact. Myrddin helped Arthur develop the magical language the inhabitants of Avall would use for behests, and while most fae spurned the practice as being tainted by humans, Nyneve learned this magic from him as well.

After Myrddin's disappearance, Nyneve's jealousy and grief drove her descent into dark magics. She turned to violent rituals, sacrificing Myrddin's fae father to bring Myrddin back from the veil. Discovering he was Branded and losing him to that Brand soon after broke her completely. It was then she began making her plans to turn the people of Avall into a blood farm and return Avall to the rest of the modern world, reaping her revenge on all humankind. She attempted to use Thayl to kill her father, Finvarra, and bring the Pact to an end, then turned to Memory when Thayl was gone.

Nyneve is almost always seen wearing mourning colors. She has never stopped mourning the loss of Myrddin, and mourning the loss of anything good within herself at the same time.

"Love is a poison that has no antidote."

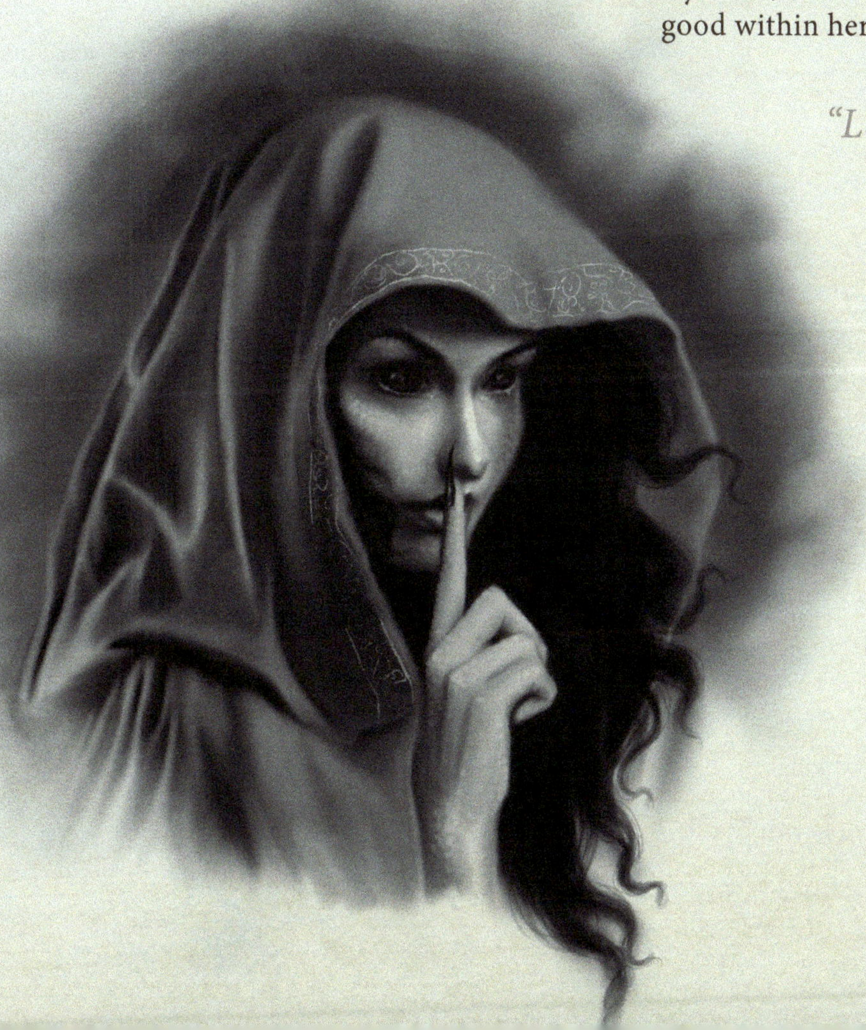

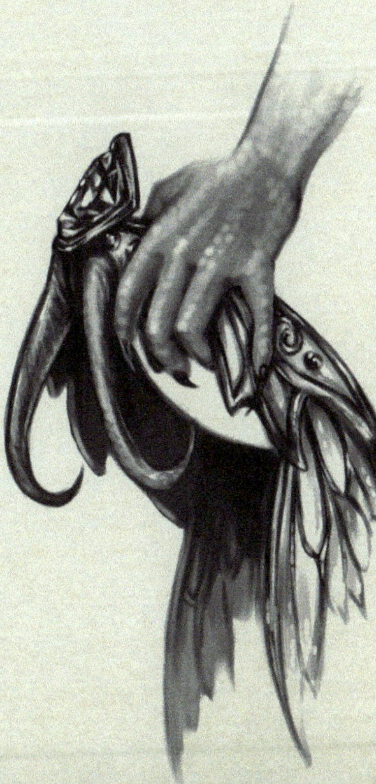

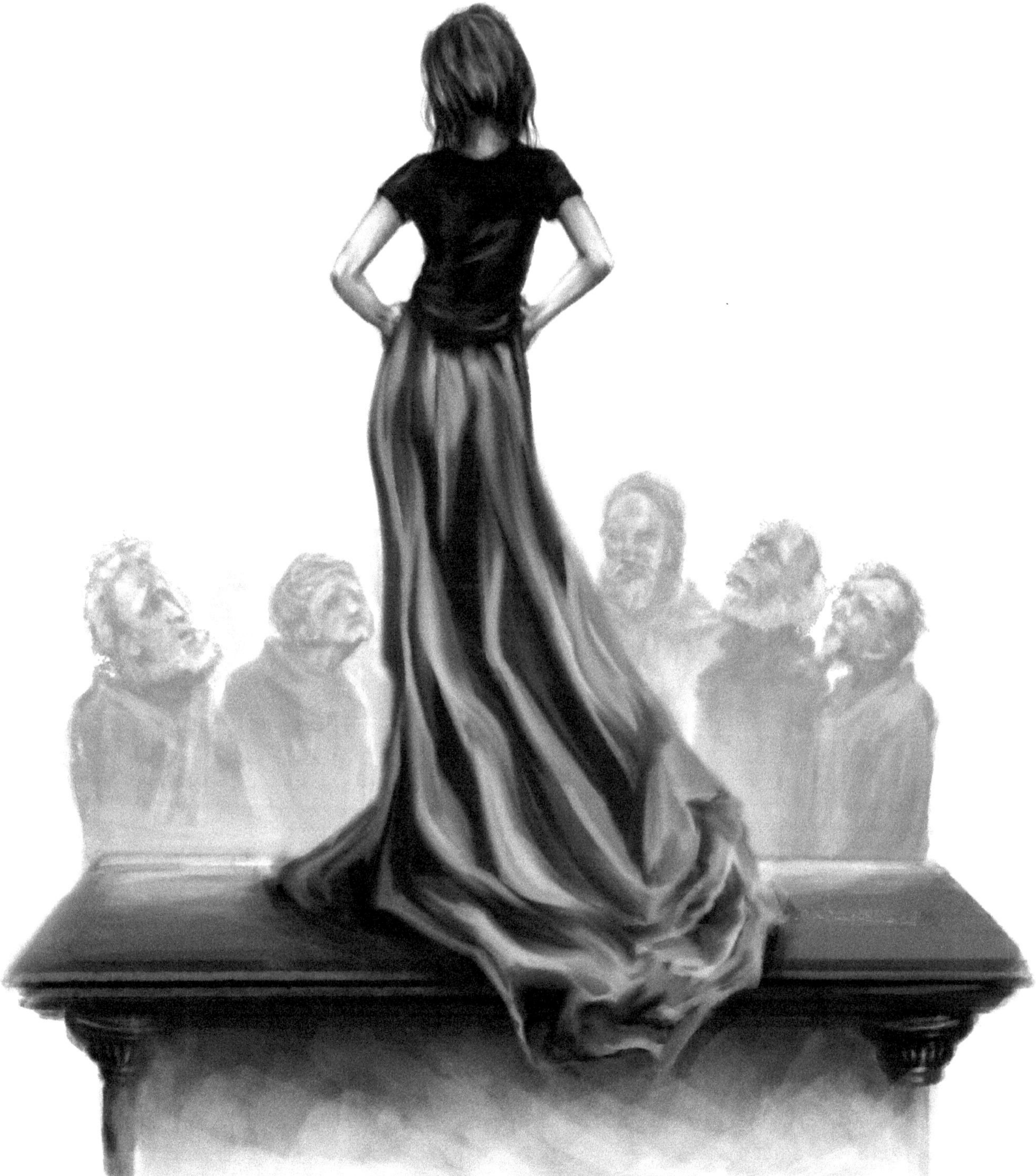

Wizards Council

They were old. Really old. The kind of old that's misshapen with bitterness and arrogance.

Known Members: Alward, Hayes, Waylan, Bedevere, Bors, Madoc, Lucan

Just before Thayl's strike against them, the Wizard's Council numbered nearly fifty council members. Their primary duty was to the magic of Avall - researching it, maintaining it, teaching it. Arranging and approving marriages for the Maellan line was also one of their primary duties.

They ran a large university where they trained noble males in magic of functional forms, to send them back into the community in roles such as healers, communications providers, and metal workers. The best of their students could be selected to become new council members.

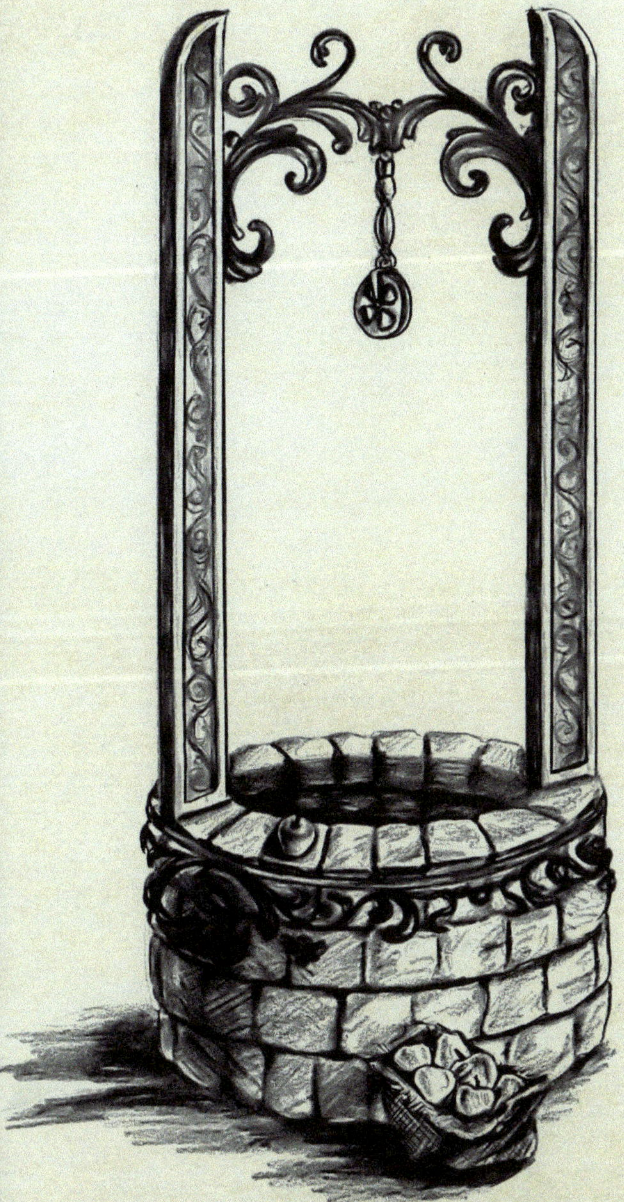

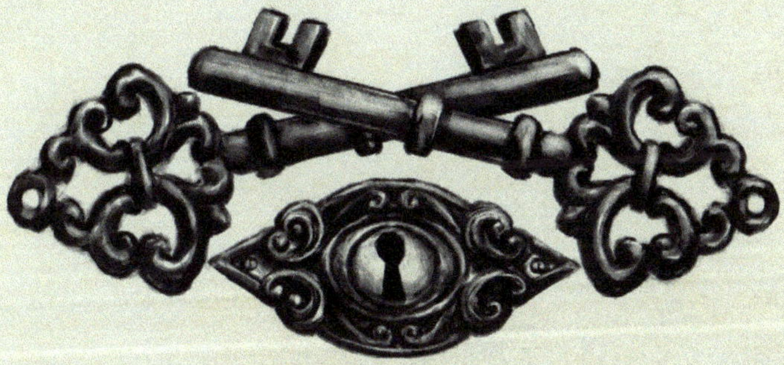

Hayes, Alward, and Lucan were all among the newer members of the council, the last to be signed in before Thayl began his quest to destroy them all. After Thayl's first assault, fewer than fifteen original council members remained alive.

Hayes quickly took control of the remaining council in hiding. His cleverly planned strategies and harsh methods kept them alive for many years in hiding, but he remained harsh, manipulative, and ambitious once the council were returned to power again.

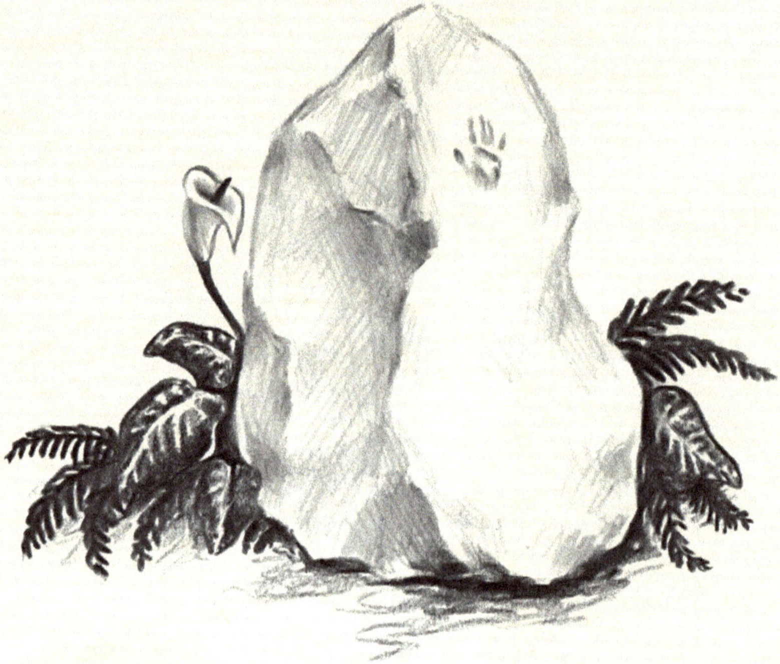

Alward

Alward's voice echoed in her head, the words he would speak each night before kissing her forehead and dousing the lights,
Always, always, keeping the princess safe.

Originally known as Pellaine, this young Wizard Council member took the name Alward when he went into hiding with Loredanna's surviving newborn. Having witnessed the ritual and seen what happened to the other child, along with his deep guilt for the fate of Loredanna and her magically powerful dying request that he save her children, Alward devoted his life from then on to nothing other than protecting Eloryn and recovering the lost twin.

When he and the newborn escaped the ritual through Loredanna's veil door, they arrived back at the estate she had been staying at, not far from the ritual site. Alward quickly gathered up everything he could before fleeing, including the Maellan crested medallion and the estate's speaking mirror.

He knew Thayl saw them travel through the veil door, so Thayl could have believed him anywhere. So he didn't flee much further, choosing to remain near the estate and site of the ritual. He found a monastery of a dying religion, and hid there. As the last of the priests also died, Alward took over the property and raised Eloryn there. He earned what they needed by teaching local children, and spent all his time educating her and researching the veil, trying to find explanations for the ritual and a way to bring the lost child back. He would even travel out into the forest to the site of the ritual for experiments. He kept this all secret from Eloryn, not wanting to burden her with the knowledge of even more pain in her past.

Clara

"You've got the poor girl working triple shifts."

"Oh, she loves it. Besides, it keeps her out of trouble with the guards."

"She's in trouble with the guards?"

Memory wriggled her eyebrows.

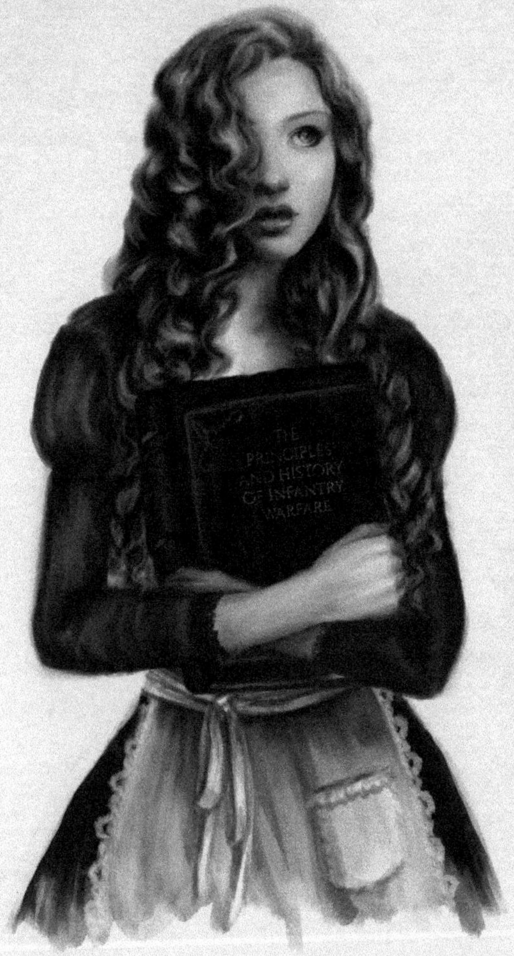

Flirty and joyful, Clara enjoyed the simple things in life, and helped Memory do the same. Although she worried she could not fight or be brave or heroic like her friends, she never truly understood her value in what she gave to Memory. She was almost a mother figure to her.

When the unseelie fae attacked Caermaellan, Clara only entered the battlefield as fighting ended to find Eloryn so they could do what they could for Memory. It was then she saw the unseelie knight attempt his final revenge on the princess. Clara had never felt like a hero, but in that moment she knew, for Memory, she would do anything to save Eloryn's life. So she threw herself between the blade and Eloryn's body.

Her death was quick, but she will be remembered by her friends and by Avall for a very long time.

Dylan

"I kissed the princess and made her vanish. If I didn't find you, I would have been in trouble!"

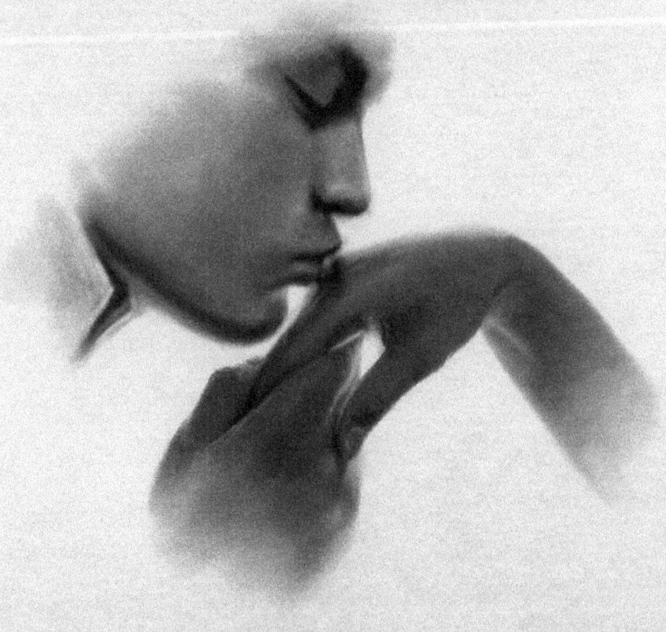

The selfish older brother of Roen, Dylan is brought into Memory's life by Hayes, who feels she needs a distraction to fill her time and keep her compliant. Dylan is extremely charming, but his selfish nature showed through when he complained he deserved more than the strange one of the twins. He showed his greed again when he murdered Hayes for ruining his chances at a wealthy and comfortable life.

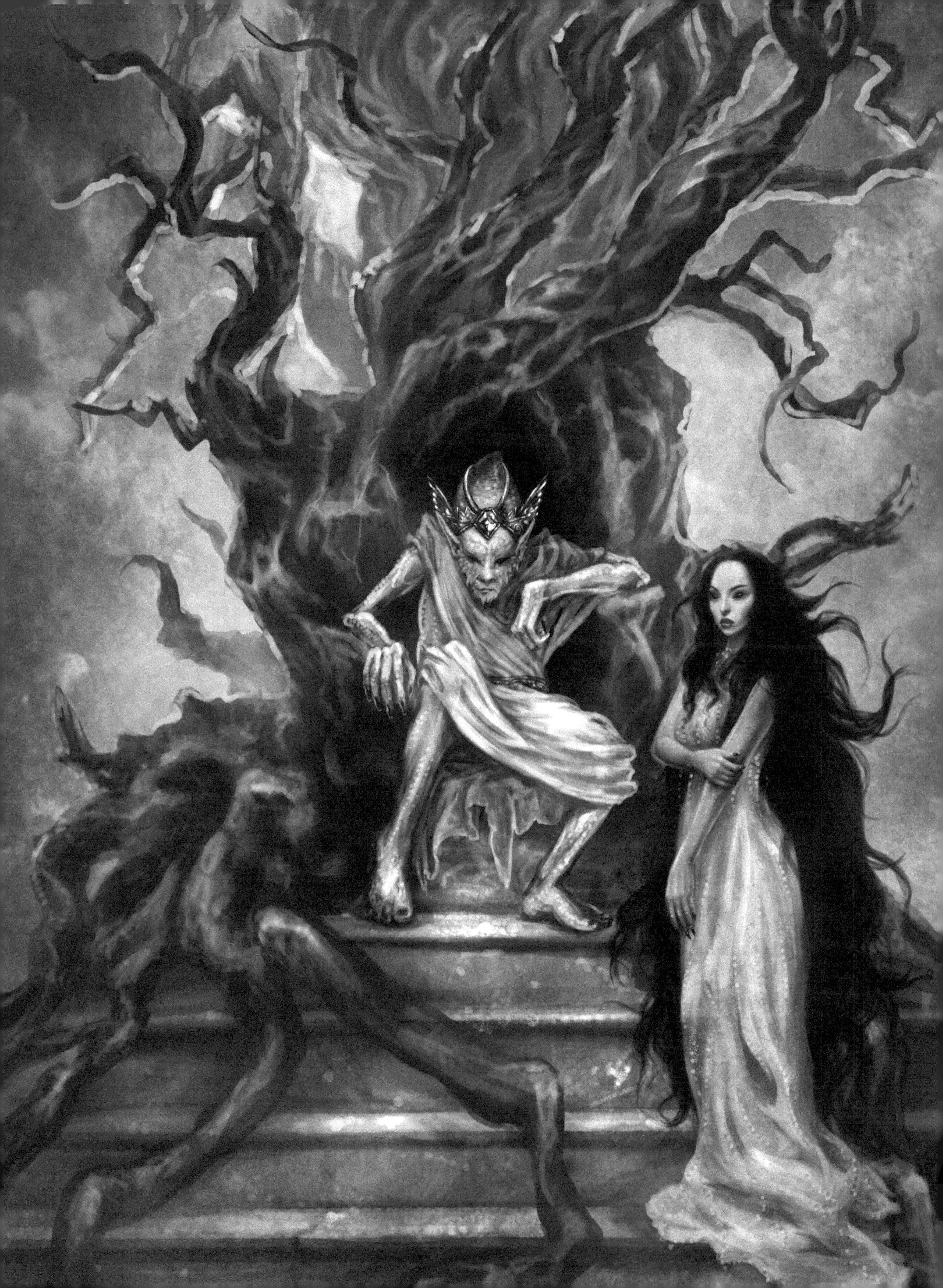

Fae Royalty

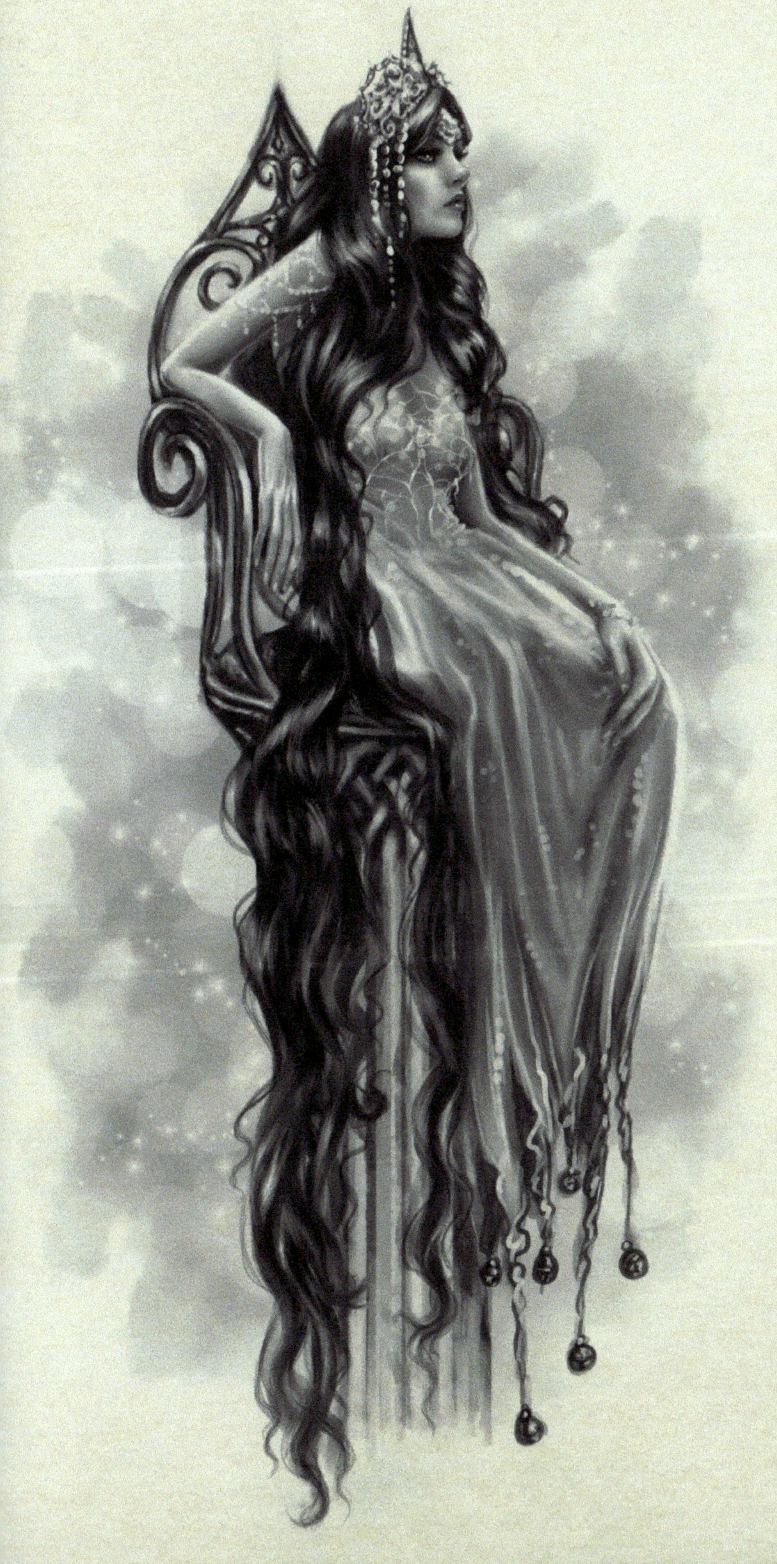

Aine

Aliases: Seelie queen, Summer queen

A vision of perfect beauty and warmth, with sparking honey skin and rich auburn hair, the seelie queen proves to be as cold of heart as any unseelie fae.

Lugh

The seelie queen's human consort. Lugh is rumored to be centuries old, but no longer ages due to fairy food, and spending all of his time with the fae in the summer court.

Finvarra

Aliases: The winter king, King under the hill.

Ancient, twisted, and possibly suffering a form of dementia, Finvarra is all anger and spite. Only his daughter, Nyneve, can calm him, as he loved her dearly - which is ironic when it is her who had secretly been plotting his assassination.

When the Pact was signed, Nyneve disagreed with Branding being part of it. She saw her father as weak for allowing the humans to force such a cruel agreement, and for fearing the humans and desiring Branding himself for protection. She never forgave him for that.

As he grew older and more insane, Nyneve had no hesitation in planning his downfall to make herself ruler of the Unseelie court.

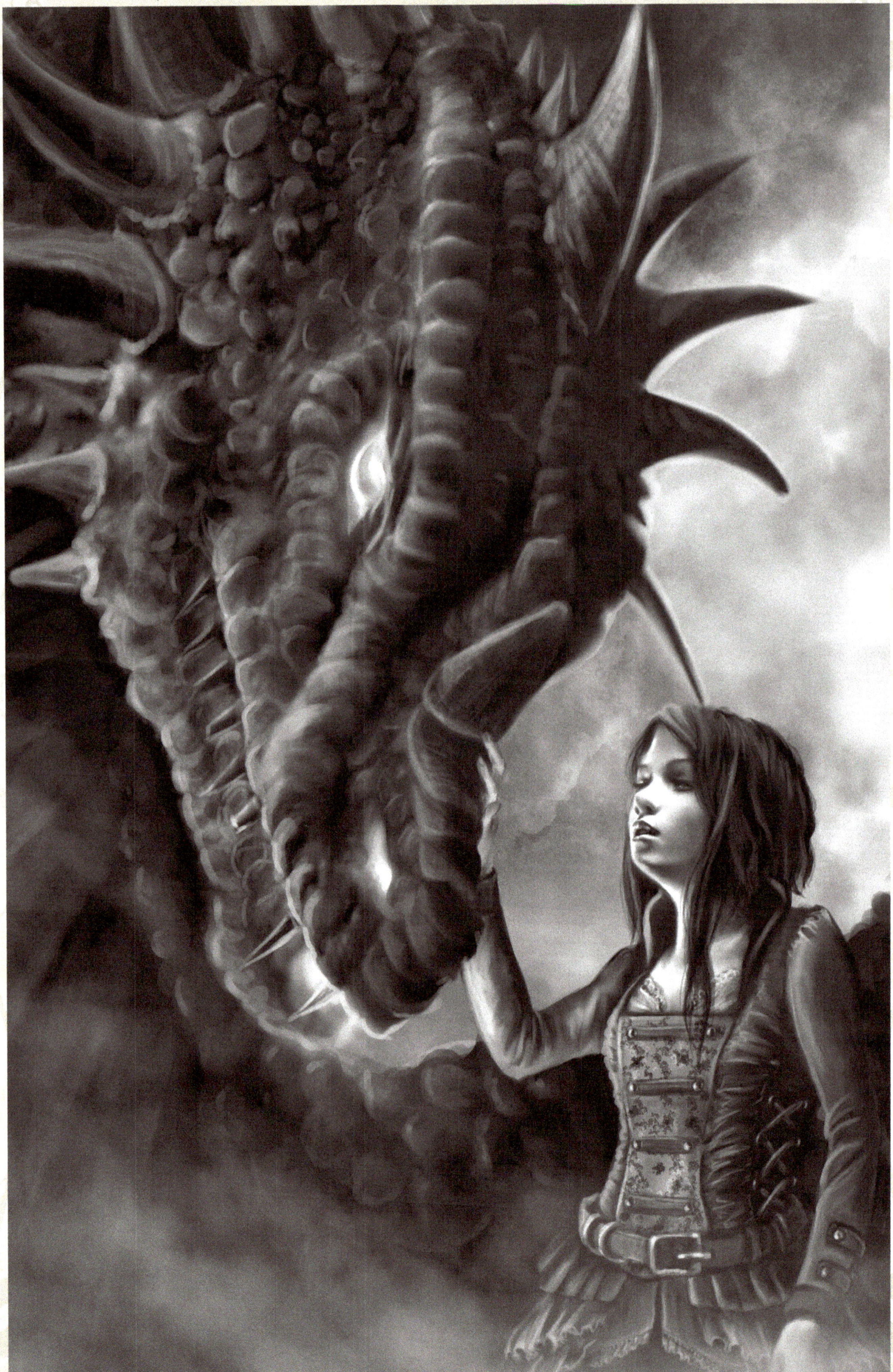

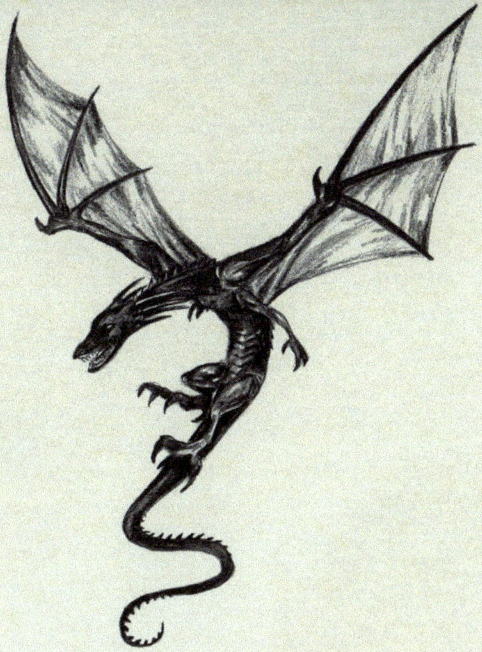

The Dragon

Dragons are a thing of legend, even in fairy filled Avall. Technically part of the Seelie court, dragons generally remained removed from the other fae and their petty politics and mischiefs. They preferred instead to explore the reaches of time and space in a way only such a powerfully magical creature can.

The dragon of the story is now the last of his kind. His soul mate, already weakened but the lack of life-magics, was killed by the group of wizard hunters. The flute they made from her bone allowed them to take control of him, using him as a hunting dog, until he was freed by Memory.

The vast size of the dragon meant the lack of magic in Avall and Tearnan Ogh affected him more than smaller fae, his imminent death visible in his crumbling body. Seeing him this way brought home the truth to Memory that the fae really were dying, all of them.

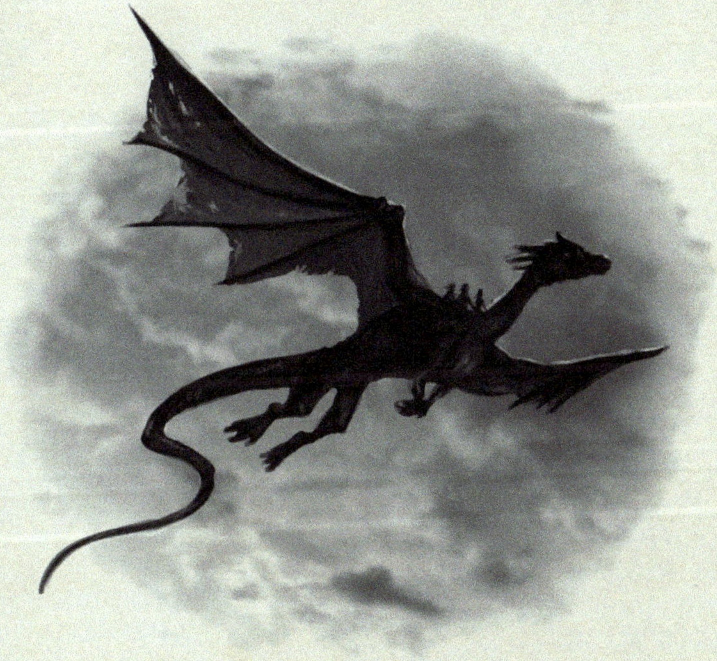

The creature lowered its glittering head down to their level. He spoke without movement, in a low growl that reverberated through their bodies.

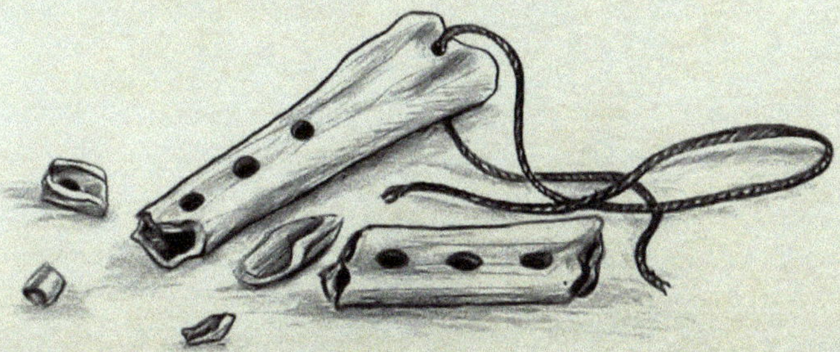

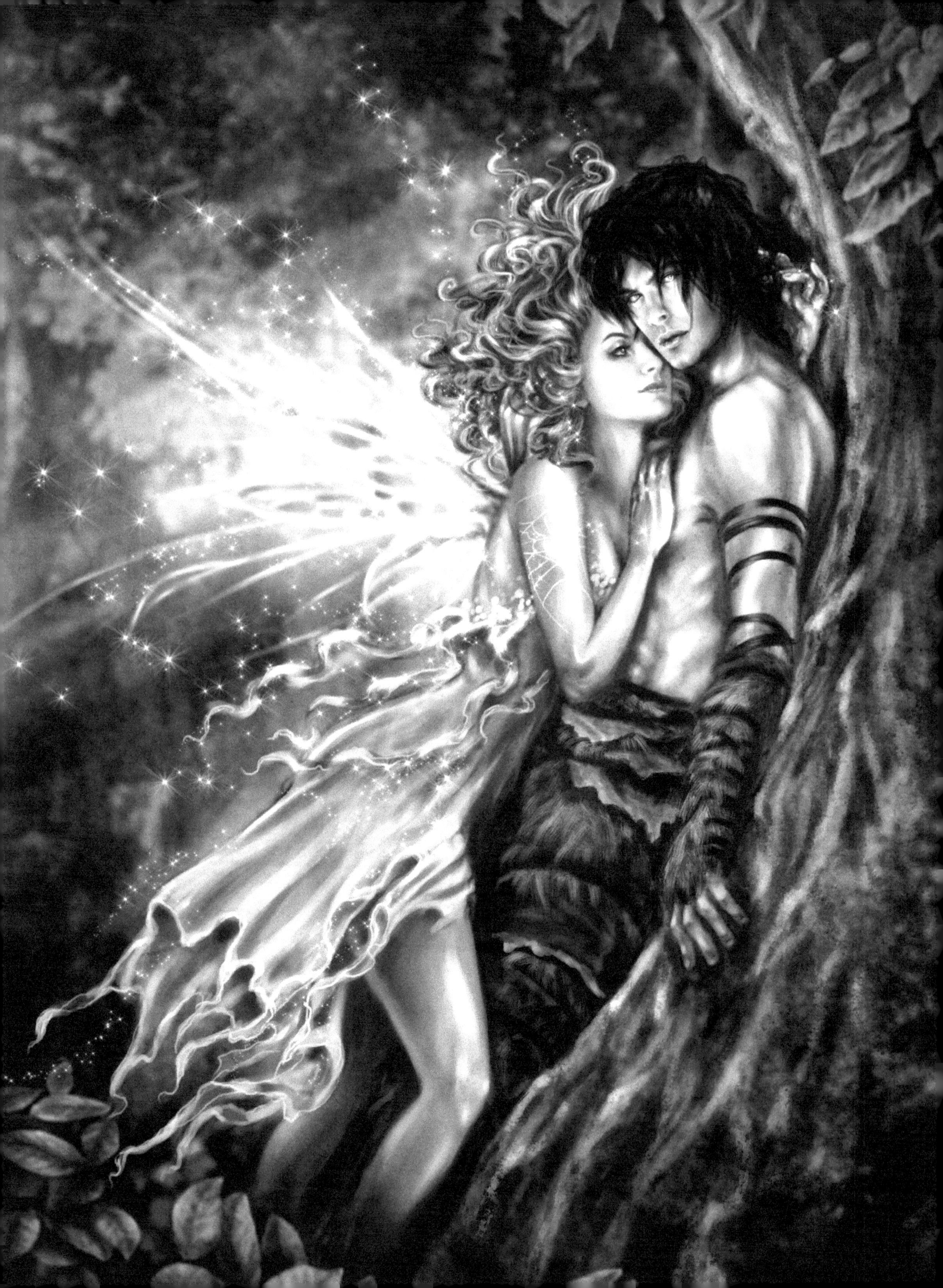

Mina

This temperamental sprite was the first fae creature to stumble upon the human boy Will as he roamed the forests of Avall alone and starving. She saved his life, but also took ownership of him then. It tickled her to have a human pet of her own, as few fae did anymore, as the inhabitants of Avall were generally wise to fairy tricks.

But this boy didn't seem to understand fairy ways. She was disappointed when she discovered he didn't have a Spark of Connection, as it meant he wouldn't be as much fun. She often grew bored of him, leaving him to his own devices in the forests of Avall for long stretches until she decided he might be fun again.

As he grew up he spoke sometimes of a girl named Hope that he waited for, but Mina had little interest, until that girl appeared in Avall. Memory drew Will's attention away from Mina, and for that Mina grew increasingly jealous.

But owning Will had also changed her. Seeing his dedication, loyalty, patience and kindness originally angered and confused her in the way looking upon something terribly cute can make you want to squish it. When she lost him, she turned violent, but then realized she still wanted to be part of his life one way or another. She risked her life to hold Caliburn and defend him, and for that she was given a second chance. A chance to not be his owner, but to be his friend.

Shonae

Black eyes… does that mean unseelie fae? But she's so beautiful.

As nearly immortal creatures, the fae have extremely long lifespans, and very rarely have offspring. Most fae are very old, but Shonae is one of the few younglings. Still potentially more than a century old, she is young by fairy standards, and had a greater fear of death than many of the older fae.

Guiding Memory through Tearnan ogh, she learned about Memory and her goals, and decided some things were worth dying for- things like a human willing to look upon the unseelie fae, who have been villainized for millenia, and choose to save them too.

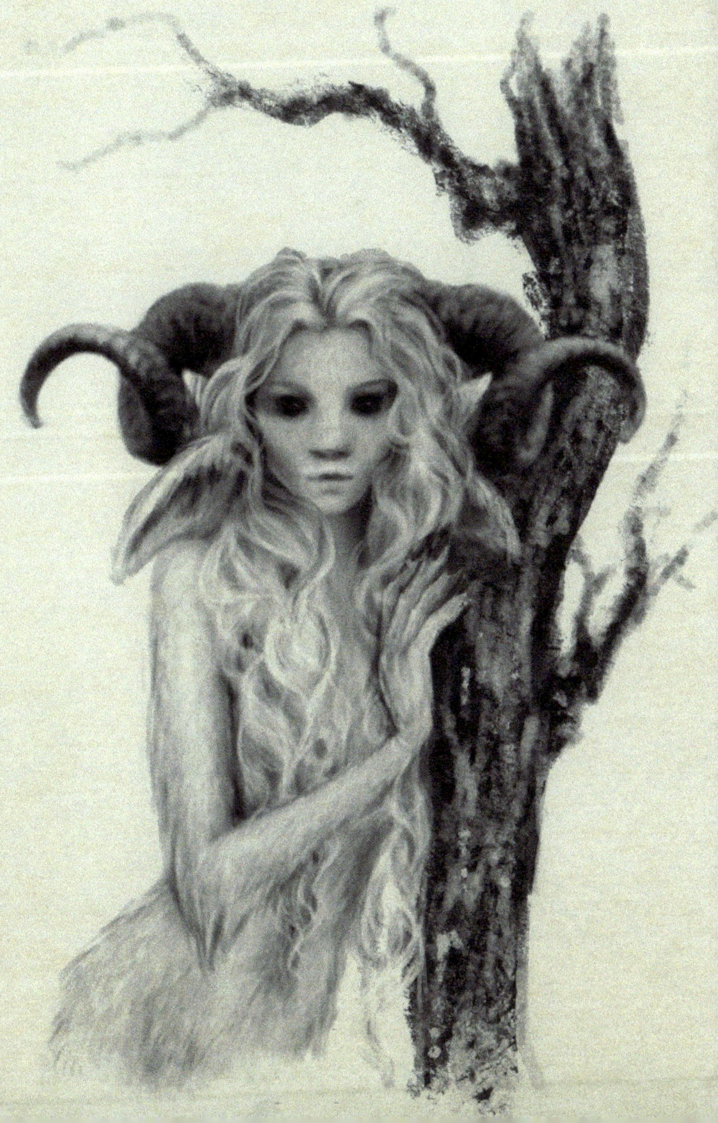

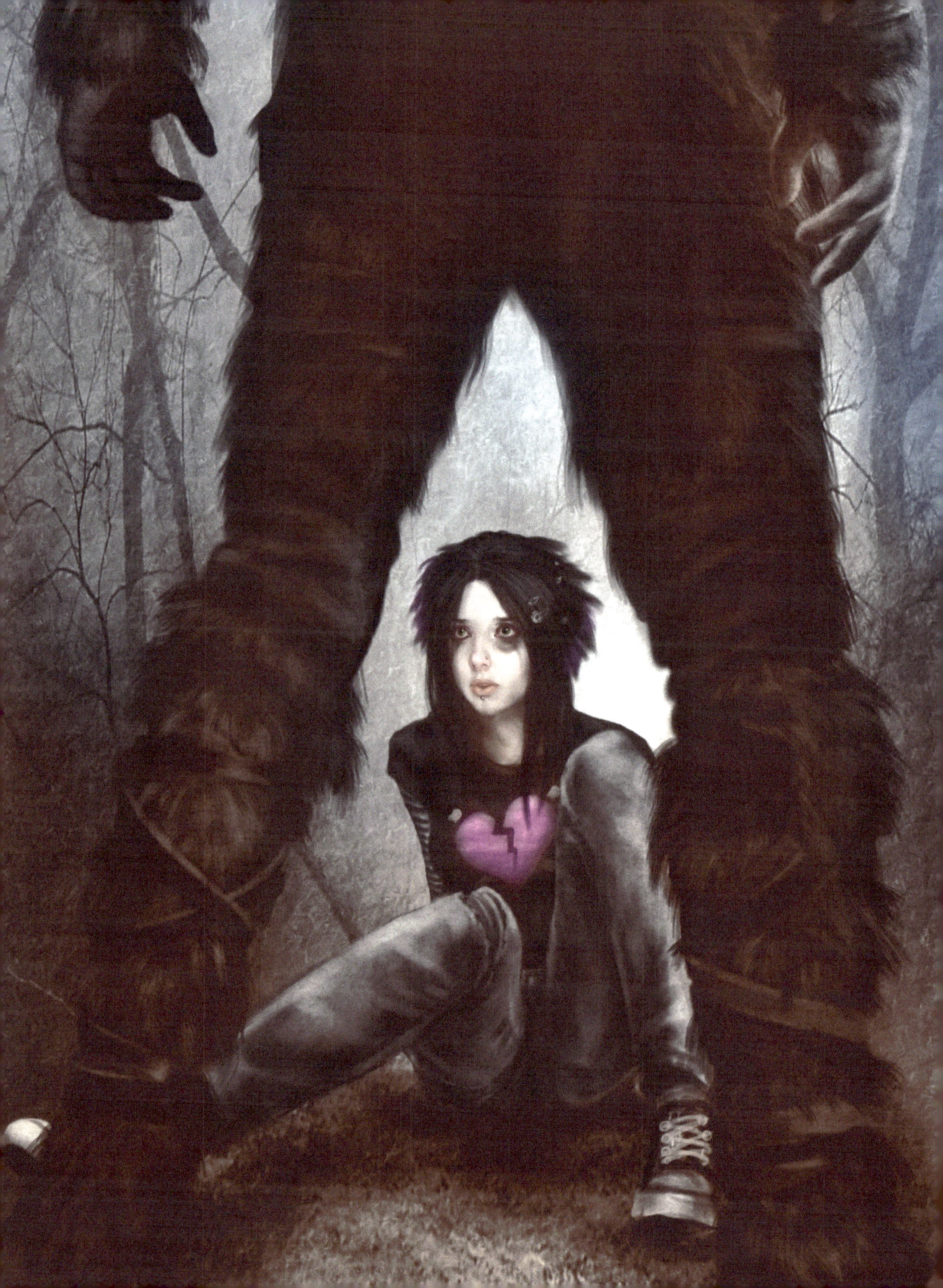

Locations

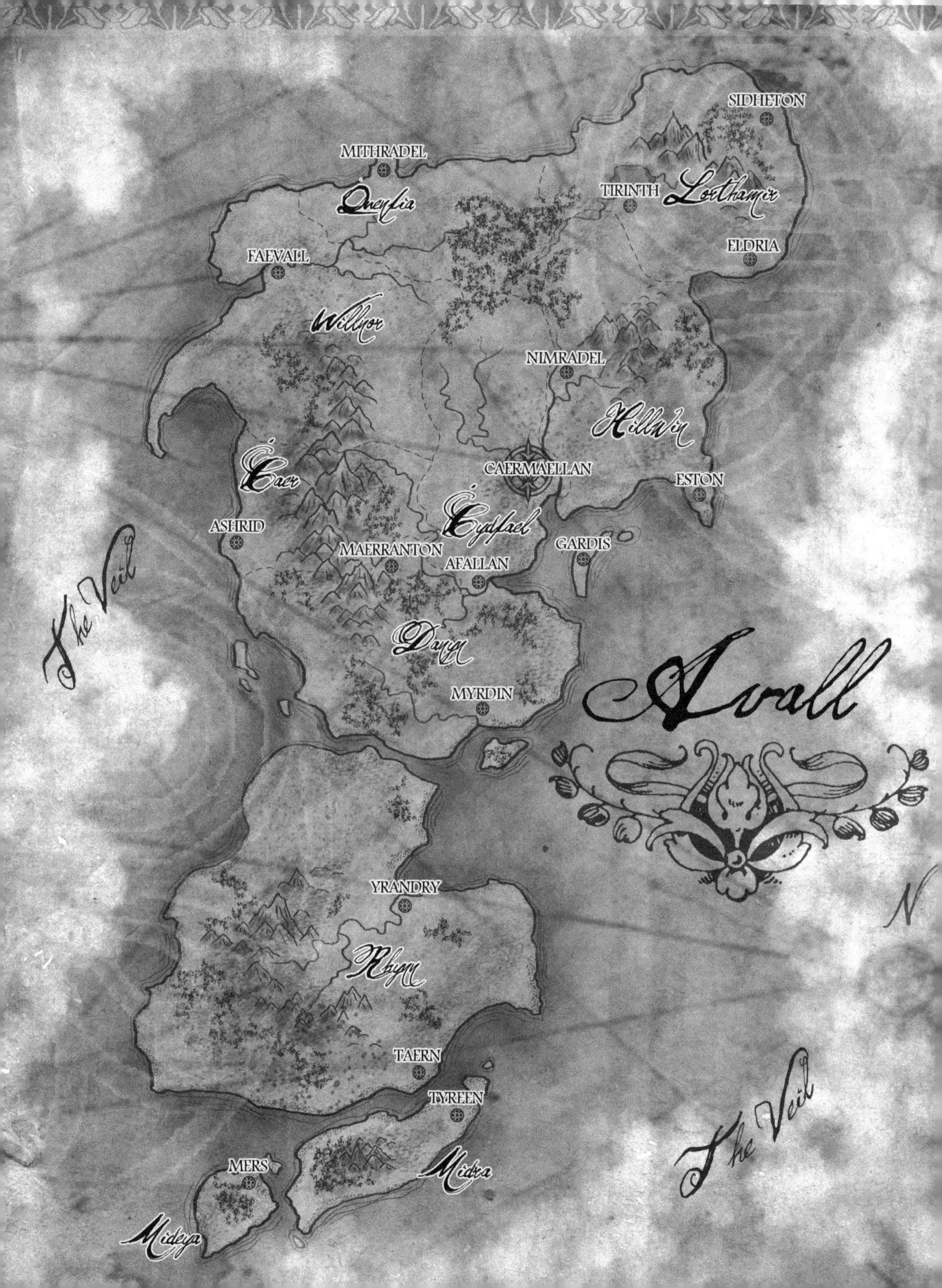
Avall
The Veil
The Veil
N
MITHRADEL
SIDHETON
TIRINTH
ELDRIA
FAEVALL
NIMRADEL
CAERMAELLAN
ESTON
ASHRID
MAERRANTON
AFALLAN
GARDIS
MYRDIN
YRANDRY
TAERN
TYREEN
MERS

Avall

Once upon a time in a beautiful land, surrounded by seas, man and fae lived side by side, peacefully, under the Pact.

Avall was once a barren and hostile environment with freezing temperatures and harsh ocean winds. The human population was small, and struggled, mostly relying on fishing and trade, but also mercilessly preyed upon by neighboring countries.

In approximately 500 A.D., the fae approached the human ruler Uther Aurelianus, through their chosen diplomats Arthur and Myrddin. They told of a hell that would engulf the whole world, and that not only could they save Avall from that hell, they could make the land rich with life, comfortable, and prosperous.

Uther could easily believe in a hell coming to beset humankind, due to the suffering his people had already endured. The lure of making Avall a land that could sustain his people comfortably was enough for him to agree to the terms of the Pact. The humans of Avall would share their land with the fae, and forever be separated from the rest of the world and all other humans.

Uther had no heir of his own, so he chose Arthur Maellan to be his heir. The Maellan family ruled Avall since that time until Thayl took control.

Author's Insight

Selina always imagined Avall to have originally existed in the North Atlantic Ocean, above Iceland and similar in size.

Even before the Pact, the people of Avall generally accepted and believed in the fae, much like the Irish culture have. They know the Seelie fae are "good" - if mischievous and dangerous they are still to be revered. Unseelie Fae however were always seen purely as monsters to be avoided or hunted.

Imports the fae brought from the rest of the world into Avall continued to influence the land, making its progress similar although slower than the rest of the world. When imports ended completely, around the time of the industrial revolution, Avall's culture and fashions didn't progress much further beyond that point.

By the end of the story, the people of Avall have learned that the rest of the world didn't become hell, and have a way to once again travel there. It will mean big changes for Avall.

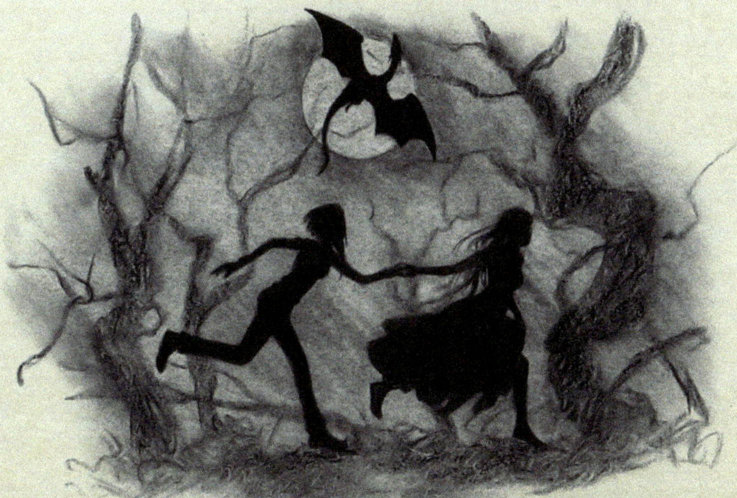

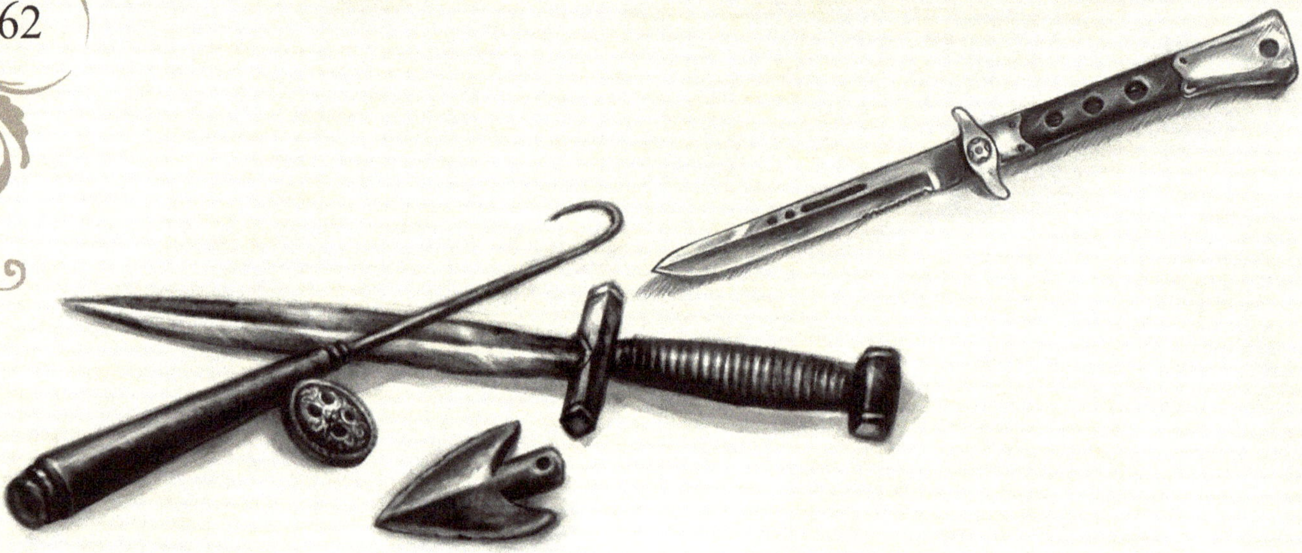

"This metal is poison to the fae. I don't know how you could have this. There should be no iron in Avall."

Iron

Raw iron, as an element, channels the magical energies of life. The earth's core is molten iron, almost all living things need iron to live, in their bodies and blood, channeling the magic of nature. Iron ore that has been worked by man into "cold iron" is changed, and becomes a stronger channel for magical energy, affiliated to humans, bringing the magic into them. It also steals a fairy's life force, channeling the life-magics out of them- that's why it's poison to them.

One of the terms of the Pact was the removal of all iron from Avall. A great undertaking to remove all forged iron began, leaving only the barest few iron items which became valuable artifacts, used by powerful wizards. In order to prevent any further creation of forged iron, Arthur and Myrddin magically extracted all raw iron ore from the land and forged it into the magical sword Caliburn.

Thayl's antimagic darts were created with forged iron that had been magnetized and then behested by Nyneve with ancient runes to steal the victim's spark of connection.

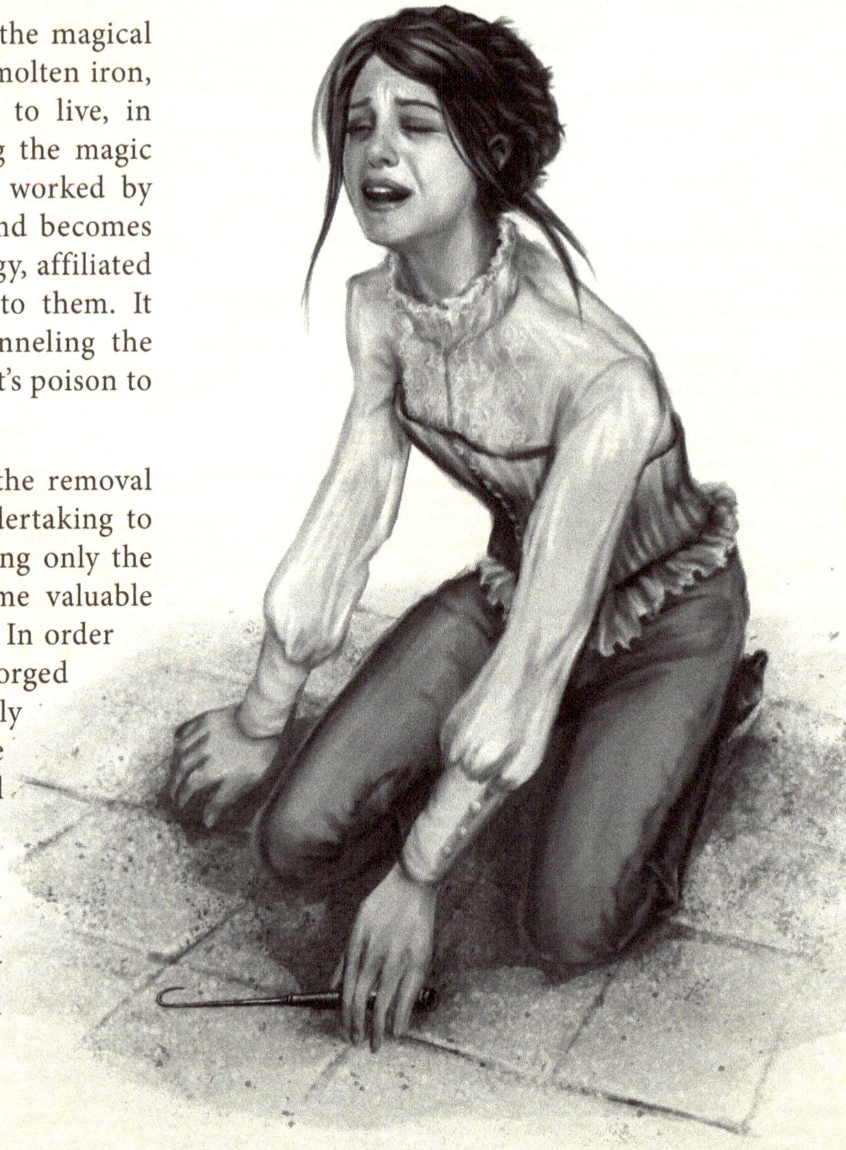

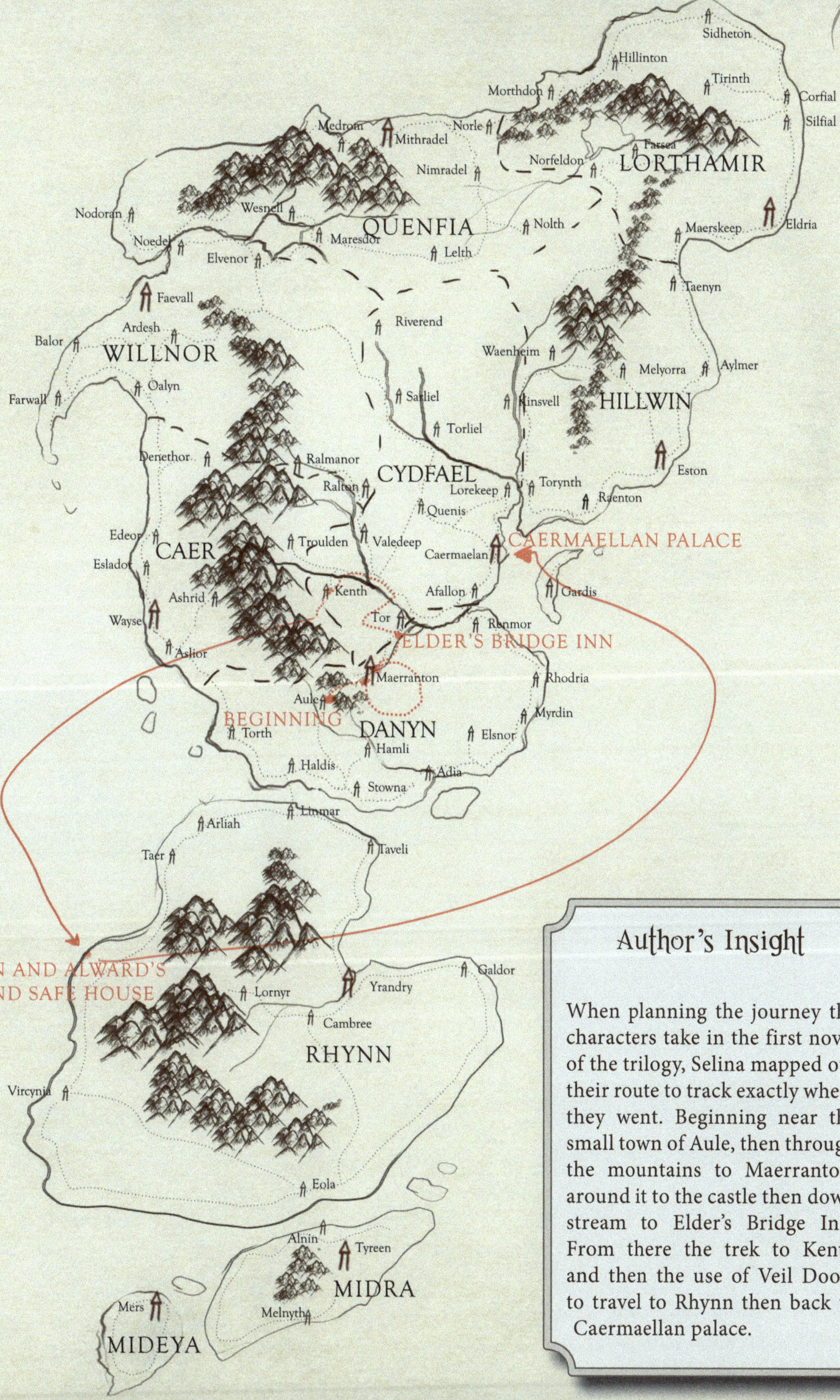

Author's Insight

When planning the journey the characters take in the first novel of the trilogy, Selina mapped out their route to track exactly where they went. Beginning near the small town of Aule, then through the mountains to Maerranton, around it to the castle then down stream to Elder's Bridge Inn. From there the trek to Kenth and then the use of Veil Doors to travel to Rhynn then back to Caermaellan palace.

Fashion

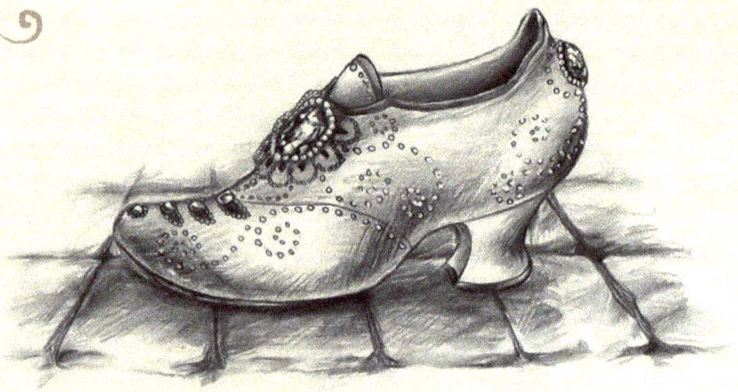

Avall's fashion is similar in style to earth's fashion of the 1800's. Men wore full suits, often with waistcoats, cravats, hats, and coat tails. Women were generally corseted, with large skirts built up with layers, hooped petticoats, and bustles, but empire waisted dresses were also in fashion and considered acceptable.

With women's rights still behind the rest of the world, more similar to the 1800's too, it's considered improper for a woman to show her legs. The bicycle was never introduced in Avall, which in the rest of the world was a major turning point for women's rights- including the right to wear pants and attire suited to riding.

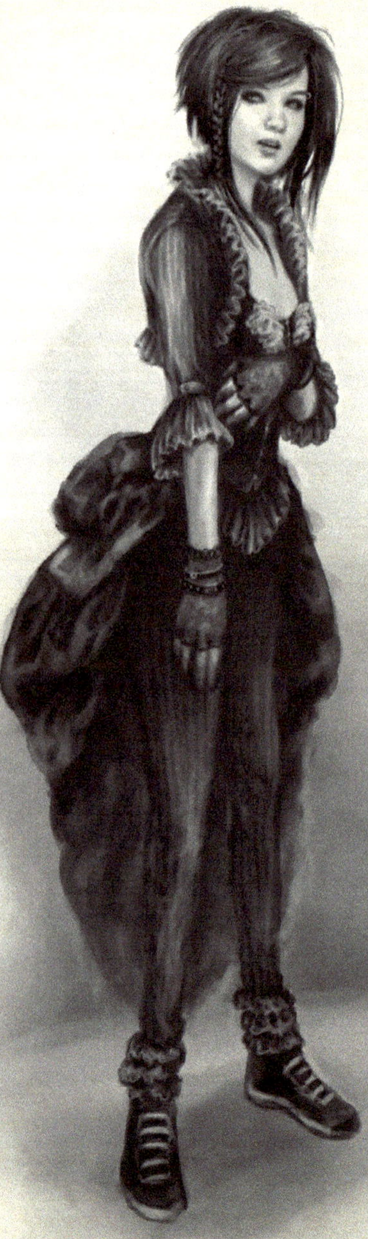

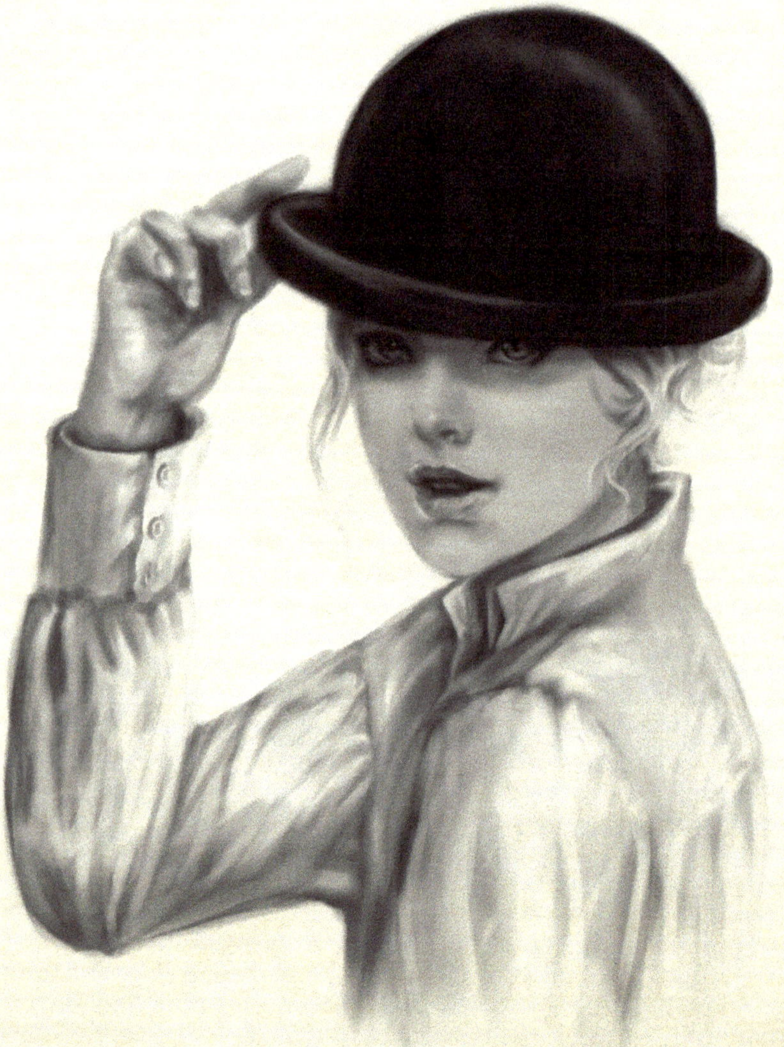

Food

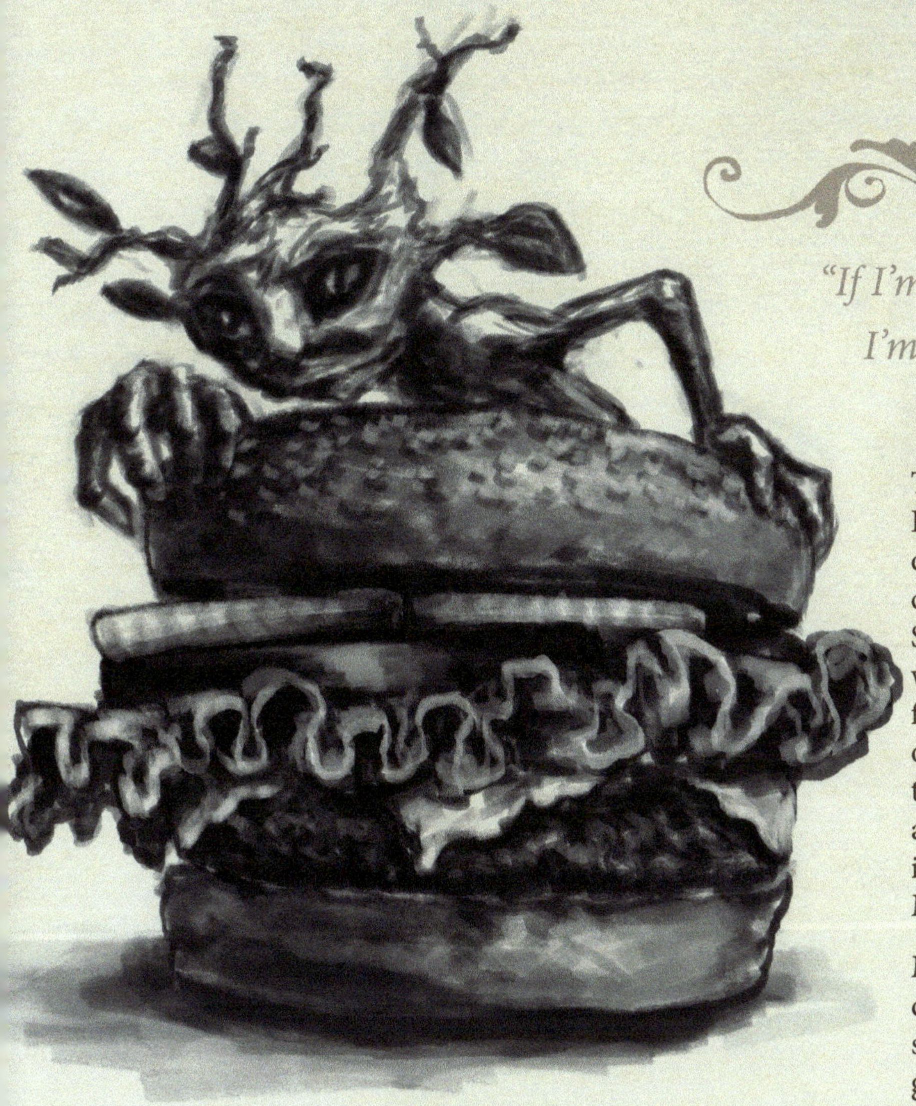

"If I'm going to save the worlds, I'm going to do it on a full stomach."

The food of Avall is similar to older English and European cuisine, with dishes such as crepes and hearty casseroles appearing in the story. Spice, tea, fruit, and vegetable plants were among the more popular items for the fae to import, so Avall has many of the same ingredients as the rest of the world- all except coffee, which although there were attempts to grow it, the trees wouldn't thrive, much to Memory's dismay.

Memory grew up with an eating disorder, but when she forgot her past, she was simply a hungry, growing, teen girl on an adventure who wanted to eat all the time. Her appetite throughout the story can be closely matched to her psychological well being.

Fairytale References

Throughout the trilogy, there are numerous references to fairy tales, as though Avall were the place all fairy tales originated and were once all true.

Speaking mirrors are a reference to Snow White.

Memory refers to herself not feeling like "the fairest of them all".

Memory loses a shoe like Cinderella at Palace de Montreduer.

How many more can you find?

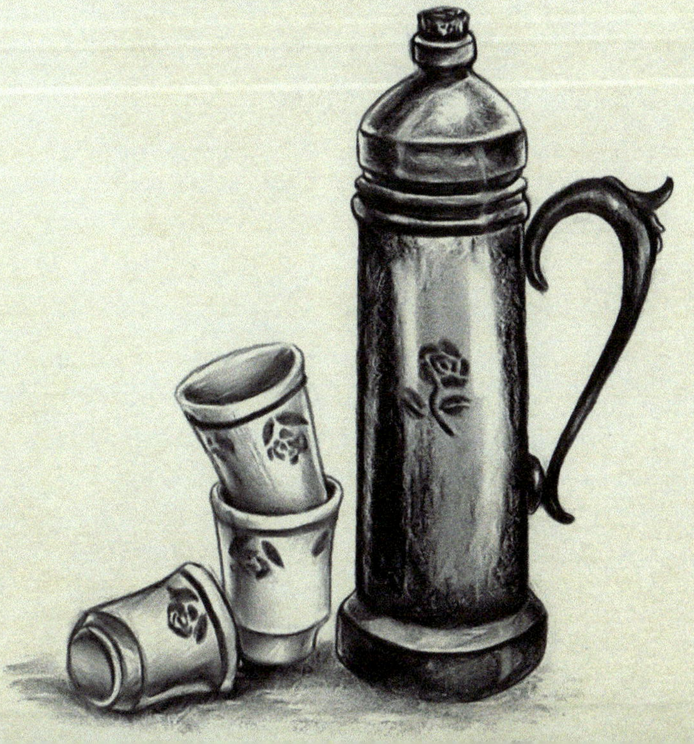

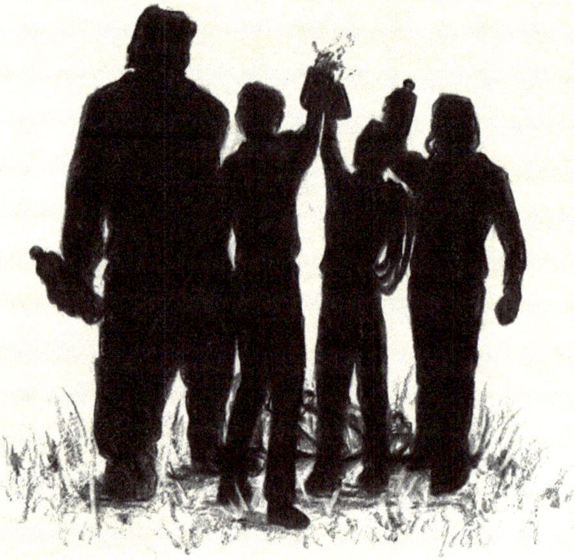

Crime and Punishment

Avall had a mostly peaceful history. Due to the prosperous land, few were left wanting or in need and everyone thrived. There was little need for crime or warfare.

But in any population there will be those with violent natures, and the land always had a small police force and royal guard to maintain the high level of peace.

Because there was little crime, any that was committed was treated very seriously. Executions were public, barbaric, and commonplace for even minor offenses.

As the fae began dying and leaving the land, Avall's prosperity declined, and that caused hardship for parts of the population. Given its history, Avall was completely unprepared to deal with the rise in crime this brought, nor were they prepared to provide aid to those who were suffering when all they'd been used to was having enough for everyone.

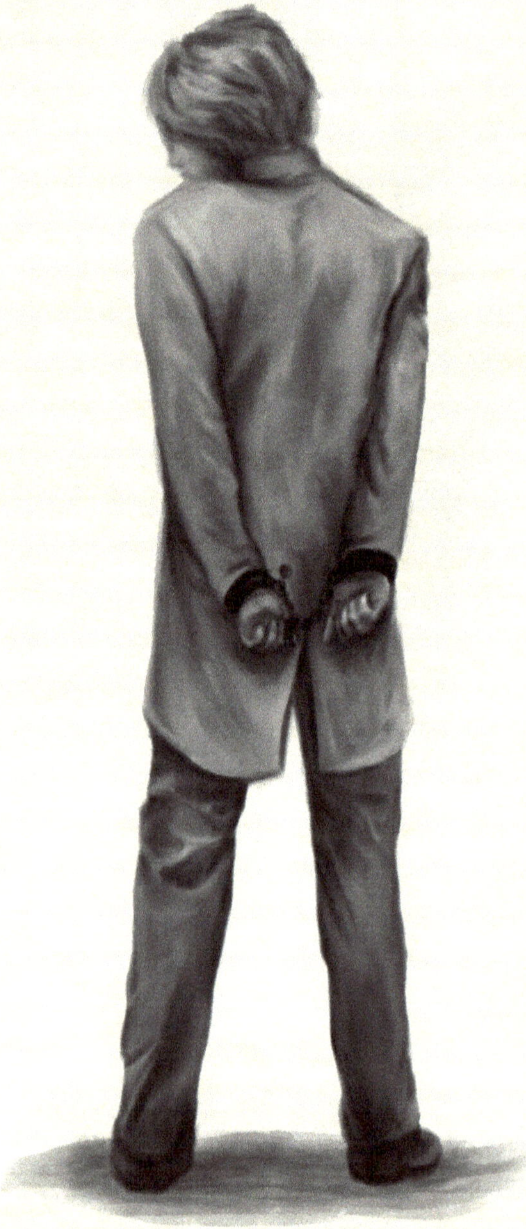

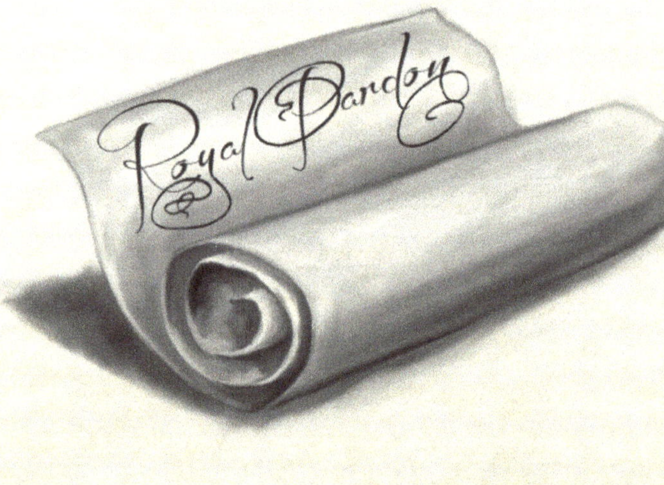

When the small police force became inadequate for dealing with the increase in crime, victims began turning to illegal bounties to seek punishment against criminals.

Thayl, never truly suitable for or interested in ruling, ignored the problem and it grew worse.

Hayes took a hard line against the issue once he was in power. He aggressively increased the police force, militia, and used the royal guard to round up anyone even considered suspicious, which often meant the people who were living rough and poor.

Hayes even turned to hiring the many small groups of bounty hunters in Avall for his militia. These hunters, violent by nature, were among those sent after Roen by Hayes in an attempt to remove Roen from Eloryn's life.

When Memory became Queen, she abolished all death penalties and presented a more compassionate response to the poor of Avall.

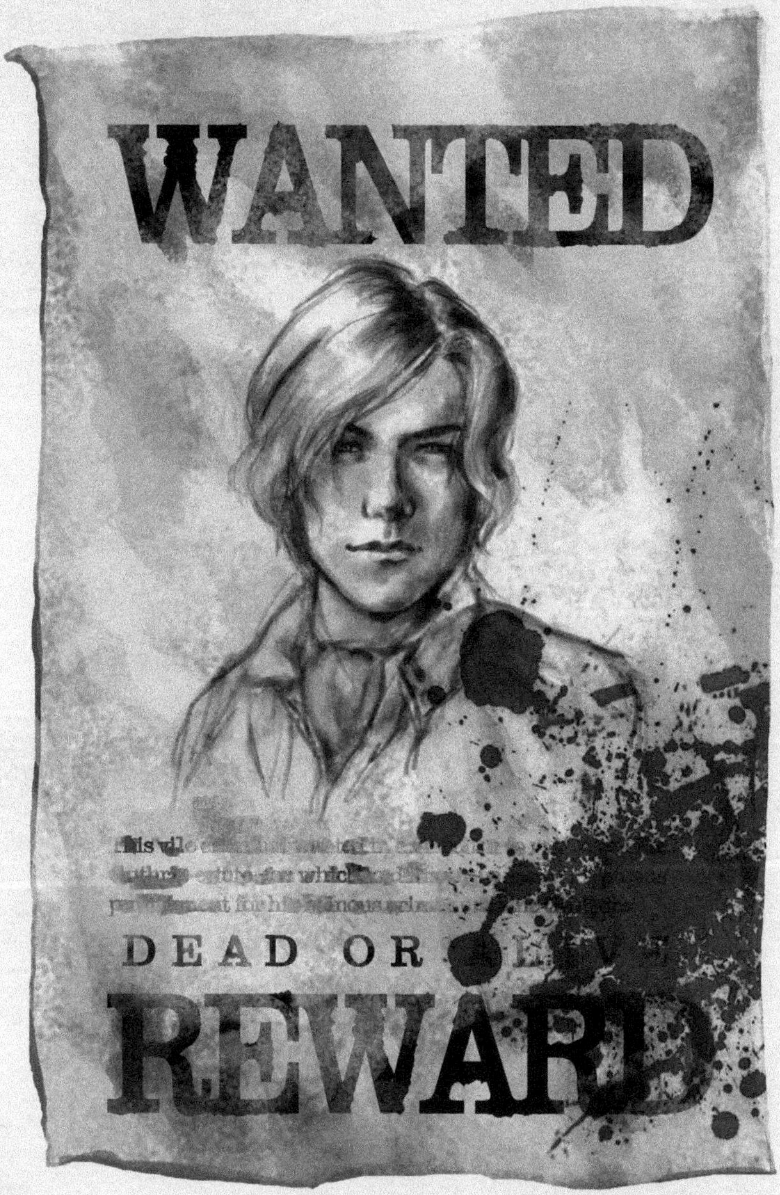

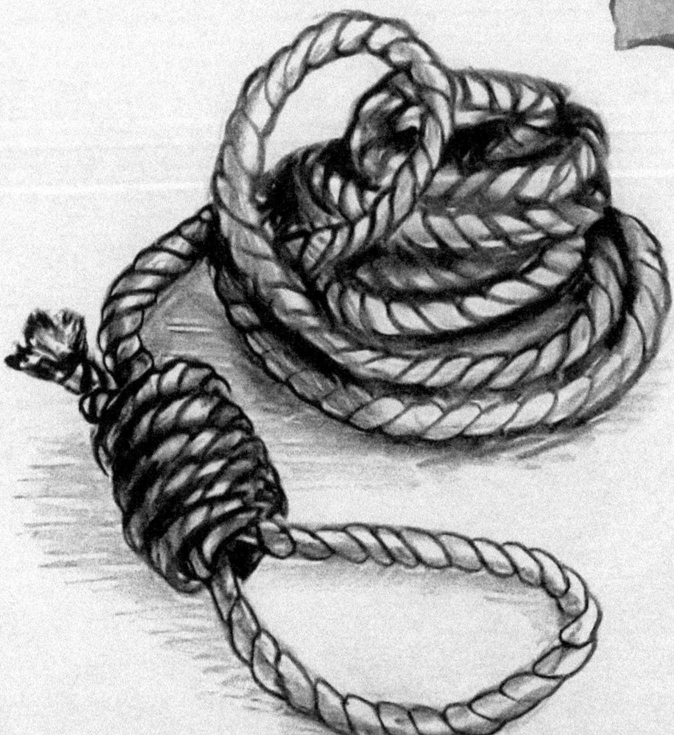

"You're using the words executed and celebrations in the same sentence here. Have I just gone to crazy land?"

"Crime in our lands is treated very seriously, perhaps unlike in the lands where you have been."

Education

Surely there were more important things for them to be learning than how to bend perfectly at the waist.

Higher education in Avall generally meant university level science, math, history, philosophy, and magic for men, and finishing school for women.

Women were expected only to receive education in those arts which made them more suitable wives and mothers. Still even this level of education was reserved for nobles only, with common folk only receiving a primary school education at best, and then normally learning a trade.

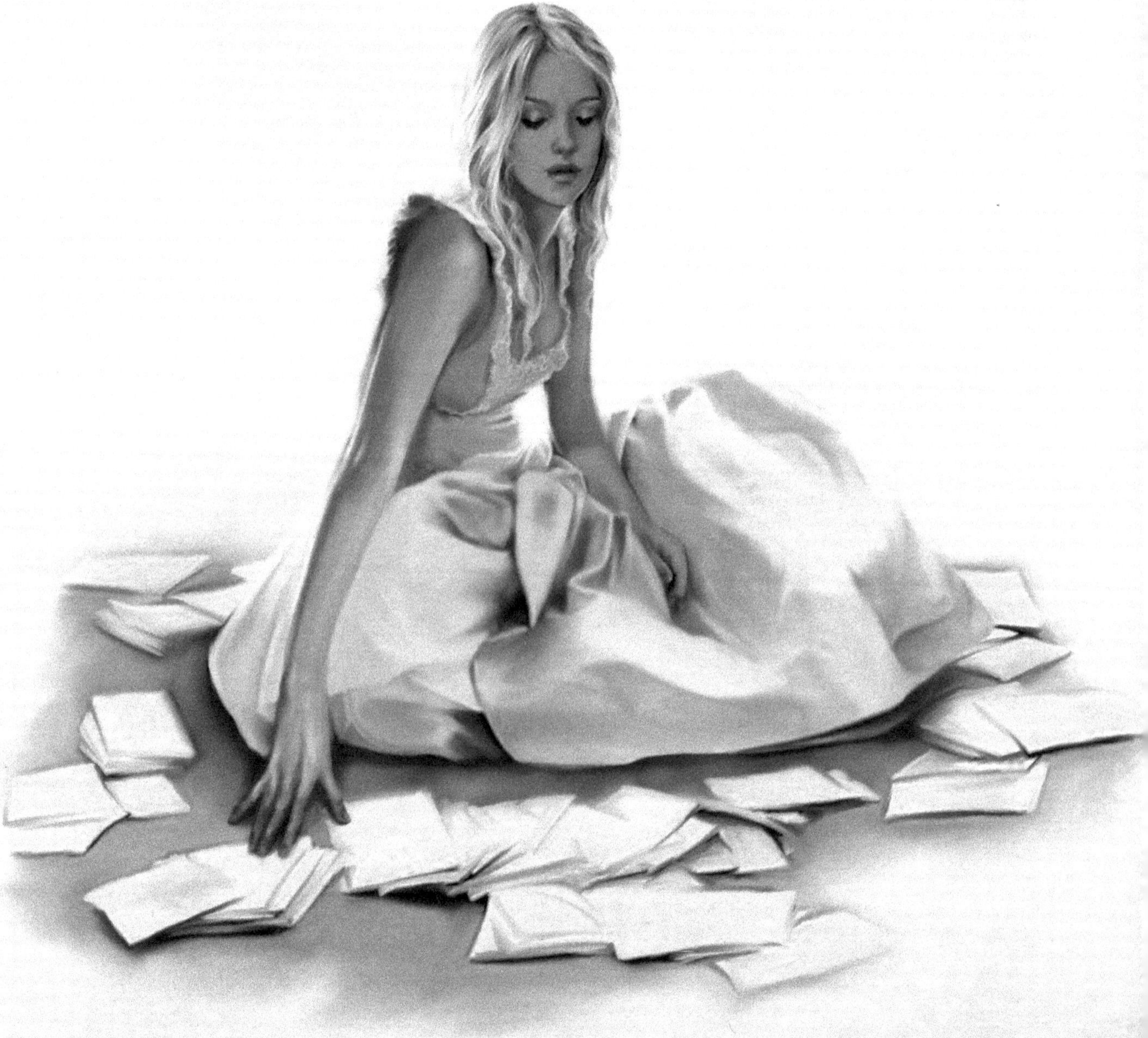

"You have classes for sword fighting? This is so unfair! Men get to do all the cool stuff. I hate to talk down on my kingdom, but there are some funny ideas here about the positions men and women should have."
"Don't look at me, I think women should be able to take any position they want." Roen paused a moment then laughed. "That was a little risqué even for me."

During the sixteen years of Thayl's rule, there was no wizard's university or the education it had provided. Without new people being trained in the magical arts of healing, correspondence, and metal work (the magical hardening of softer metals since there was no iron to use), the community soon began to suffer from a shortage of these trades.

Memory's very first regained part of her past was about school. She remembered hating it. It then comes as a surprise to her just how much she begins to enjoy learning once she throws herself into it.

While her etiquette classes do still bore her, she is eager to learn all she needs to learn to be a good ruler for Avall. Sneaking away from her womanly classes and into the classes with the boys is her first taste of real learning. From there on, she doesn't turn back, learning from all possible sources at any chance she has.

"So I was reading this book," Memory started.
"Since when do you read books?"
"Since shut up."

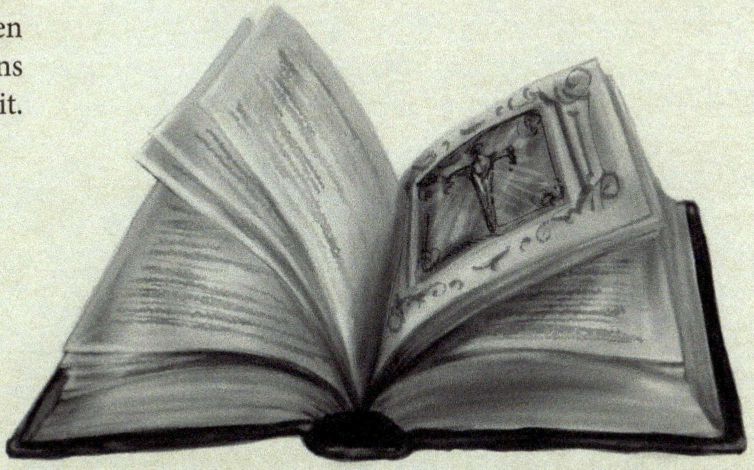

Weather

"They say this is the first snow to fall in Avall since before the Pact."

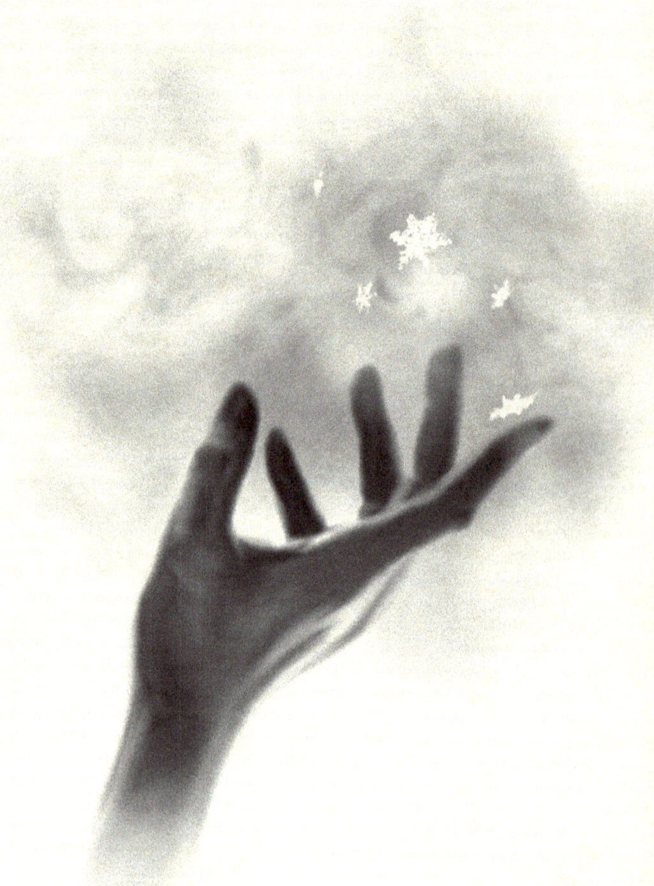

The weather in Avall is directly affected by the fae in the land. While it was part of the rest of the world, its geographic location meant it was an icy and barren land. It is the very presence of the fae in the land, and the removal of Avall into the veil, that brought abundant life to the islands.

The climate became warm and the earth became rich with life. As the story of Memory's Wake progresses, the weather becomes increasingly colder. It is the passage of autumn into winter in the story, but it is the most bitter winter Avall has known since the Pact, as the diminishing number of fae in the land mean it is reverting to its cold and barren origins.

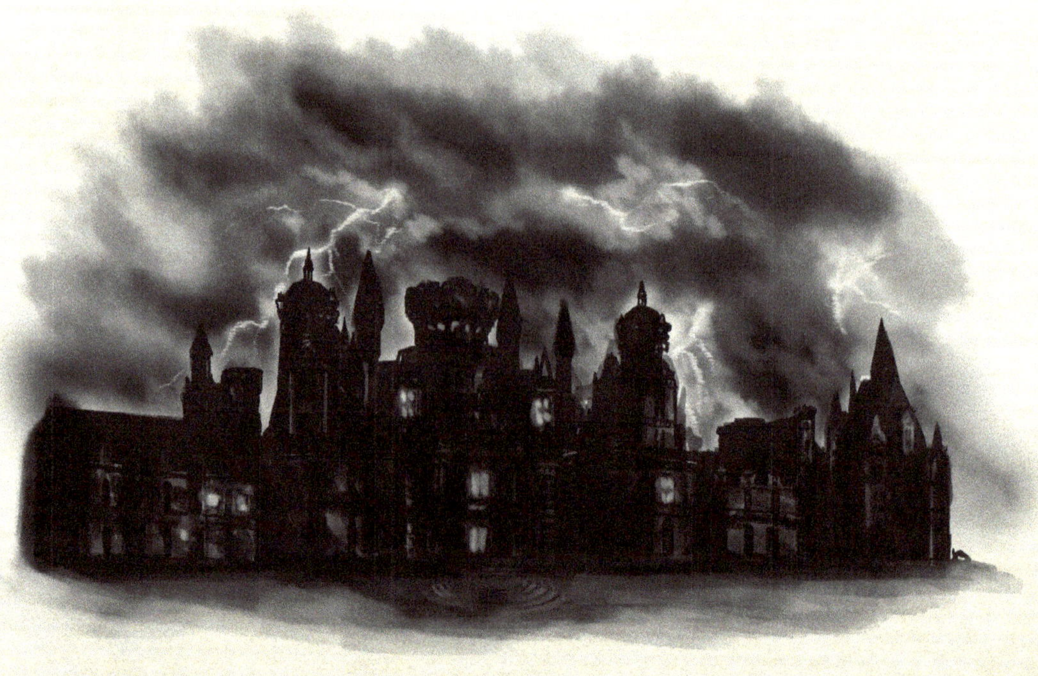

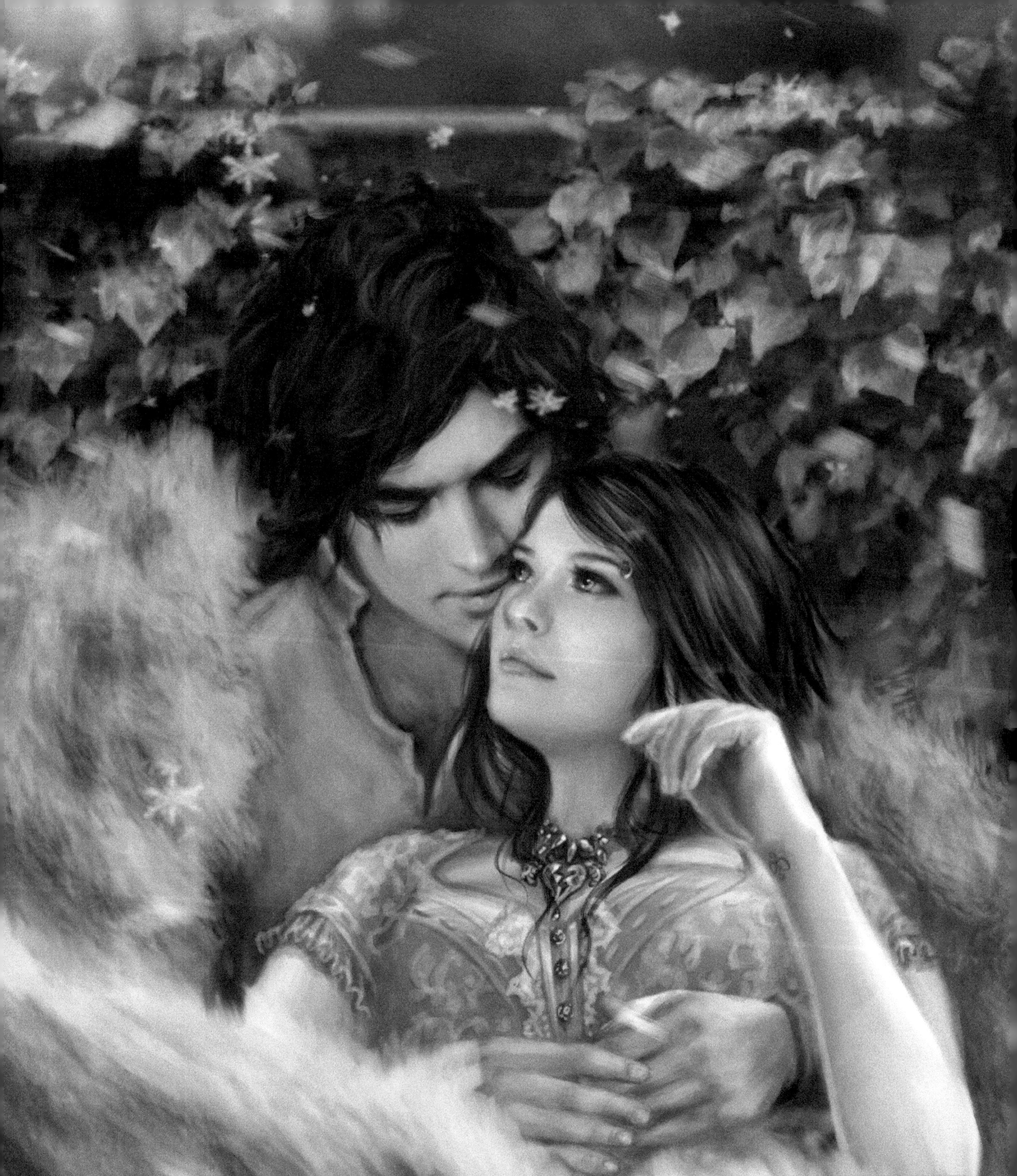

"I don't want to be scared anymore. For you, and for me, I don't want to be scared to live my life. And I want to live my life with you. Whatever the rules, whatever might happen, I don't ever want to be apart from you again."

"Worlds couldn't keep us apart," Memory replied. "Tried and failed already."

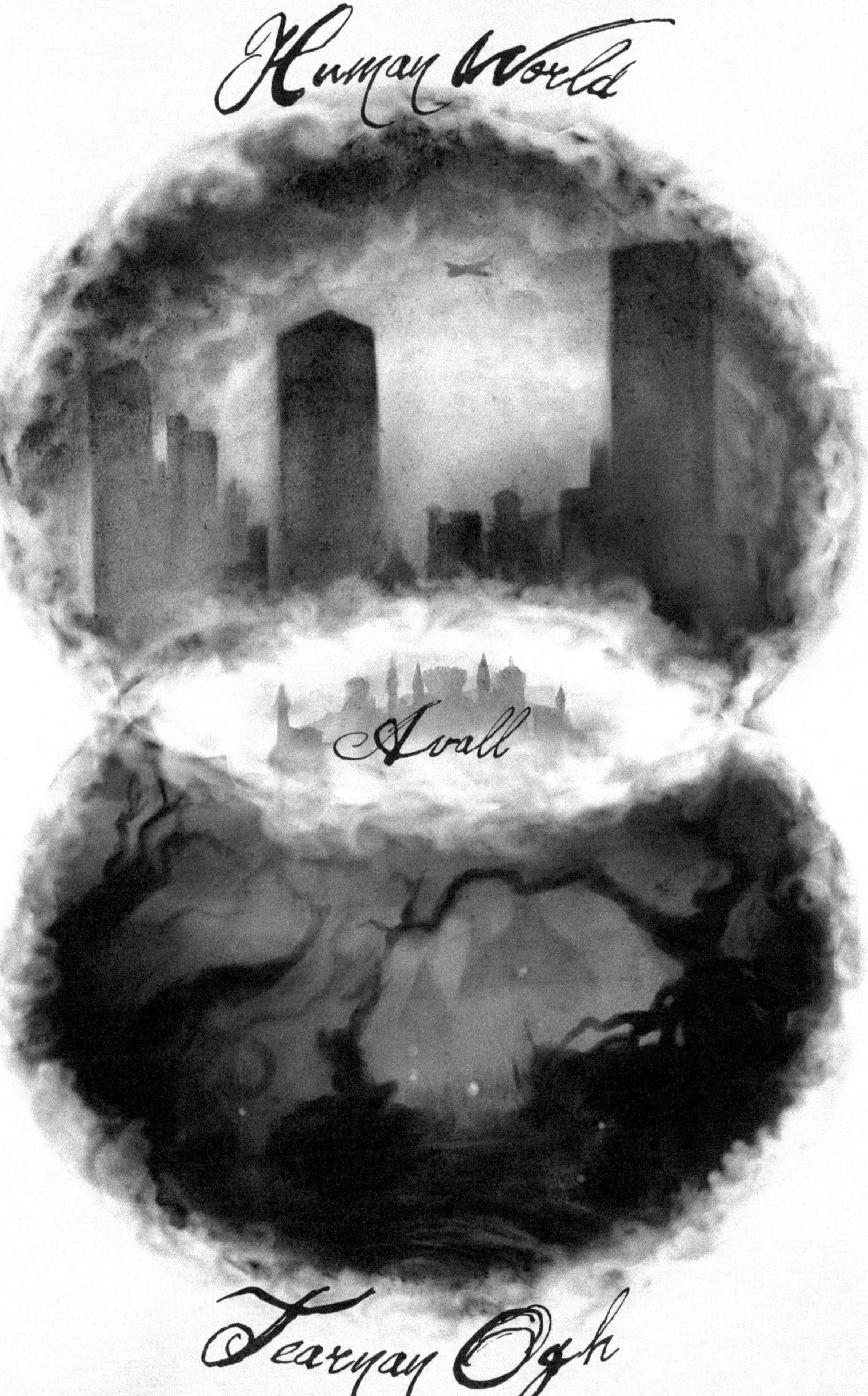
Human World
Avall
Tearnan Ogh

The Veil

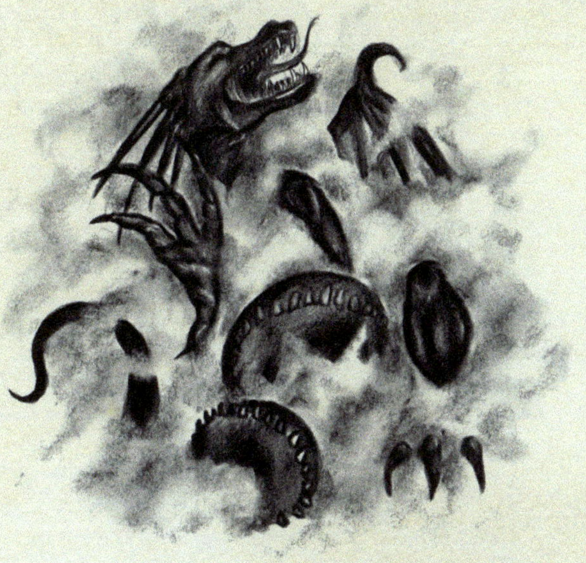

Hollowness and pure power surrounded them. She could almost see it moving, a force of nature and life within the gusts and ribbons of wind that flowed out like a golden tide.

Alward, in his research, describes the Veil as a semi-permeable membrane separating the worlds. The Veil is like the space between dimensions, with the earth on one side, and Tearnan Ogh on another.

There may be more dimensions that connect to the Veil as well.

At the forming of the Pact, Avall was drawn into the Veil, or the Veil wrapped around Avall where it existed in the rest of the world, hiding it and separating it from the world.

While Avall is a set of islands and the seas are regularly fished, all Avallians known not to sail too far from land, because there is only Veil beyond a certain point, and boats have been lost into it.

Memory describes being inside the Veil as a vast nothingness filled with roaring winds and wispy mists. The ebb and flow of life-magic can also be seem moving between the worlds through the Veil, and Memory describes it as a golden glow, rushing out of Avall like a tide, drawn to the iron in the rest of Earth.

The Veil can be used to travel quickly within Avall through the use of Veil Doors. The traveller is almost bending and stretching the veil to bring points of it closer, then slide along it to a different location in Avall. Traveling through the Veil completely between worlds is much more difficult.

At the end of the story, Memory has managed to restore balance to the worlds by creating a Veil Door that remains always open, syphoning life-magic from the rest of the world back into Avall.

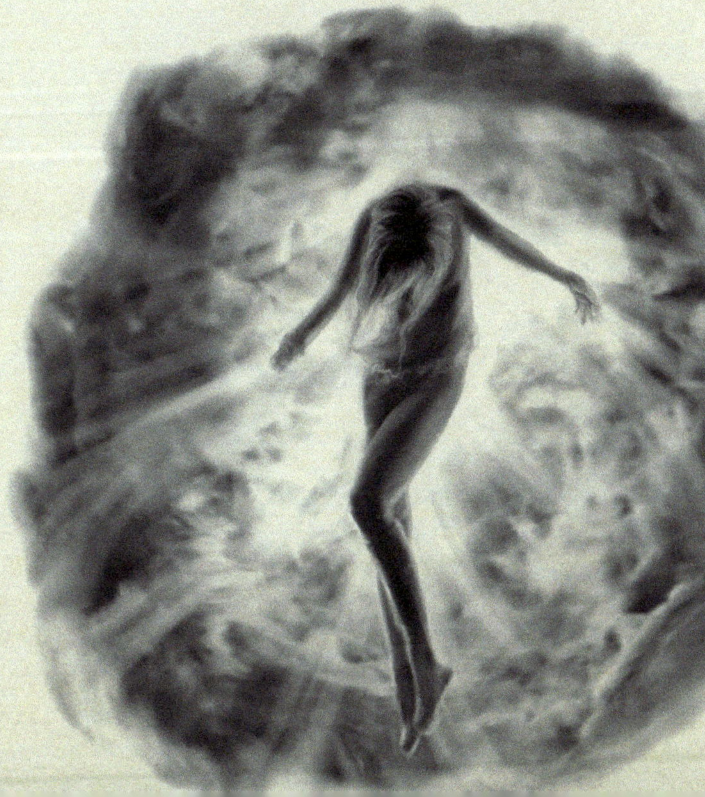

Tearnan Ogh

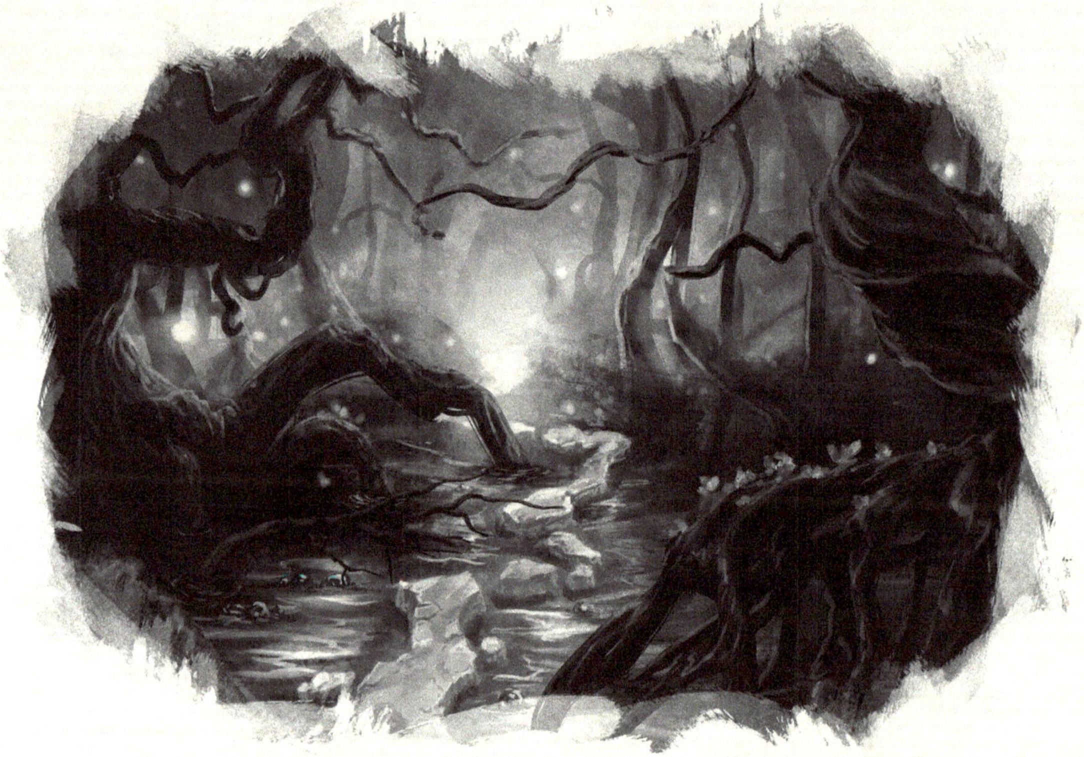

In her mind she'd imagined rainbows and sparkling streams where unicorns frolicked around pots of gold, or some other fairytale images. But the world she saw was bleak and lifeless. A shadowed husk of a world.

Although the fae have their own world, it is a dead place with no life-magic left. This is why they need to spend some time on Earth, in their sanctuary Avall, to be exposed to the life-magics they need to remain alive.

It is never revealed why the fae world has died, or what caused its death, however it is a land which no longer has any living plants or animals except the larger fae, who have kept themselves alive by drawing energy from Earth when they travel there.

There are remnants of life - fossilized forests, flash burned grass turned to ash in shape, and swamps that burble with the ghosts of fae creatures. And life

Author's Insight

The name Tearnan Ogh is derived from Tír na nÓg, the land of the fae from Irish mythology. Selina changed the spelling to a more phonetic variant.

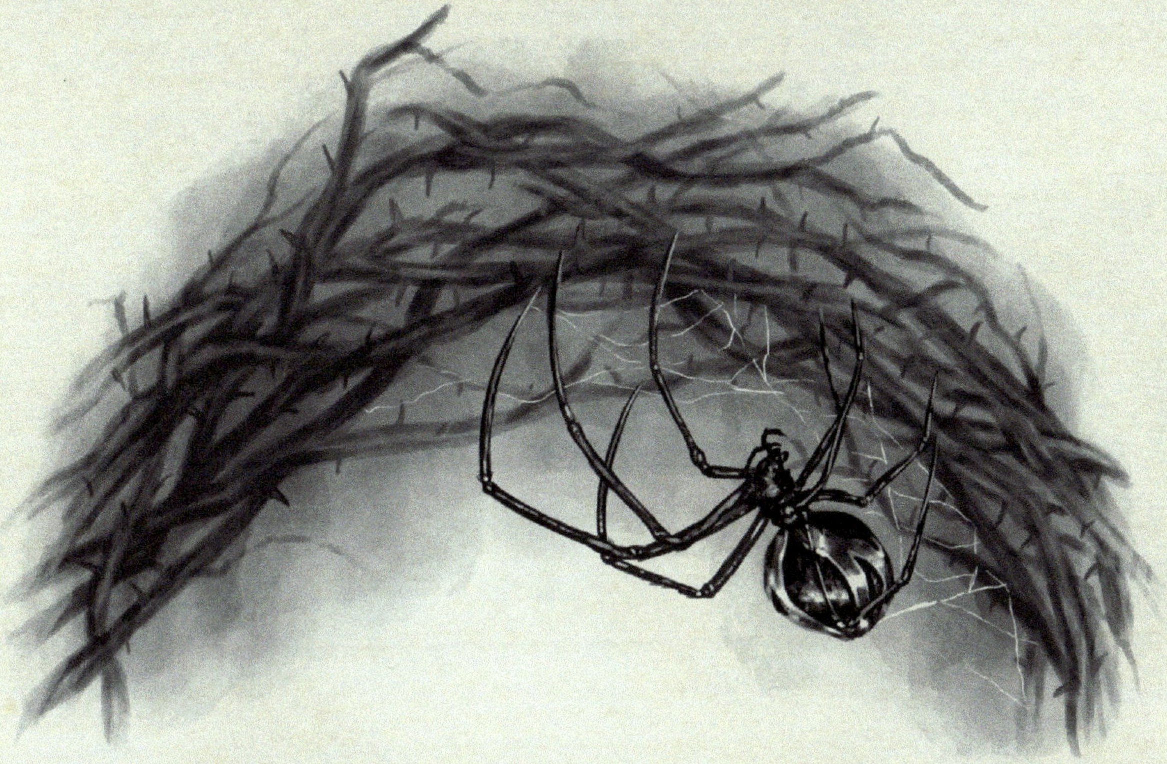

is also mirrored in the decorations and creations of the fae- glass flowers, trees made of silver and gold and enchanted with magically blooming crystal blossoms.

The world is divided into two distinct kingdoms, the summer court and the winter court. The summer court houses all the seelie fae races, and the winter court the unseelie.

Between the kingdoms, and with access points all across Tearnan Ogh, is the briar pathway. A magical passage which makes travel much faster across the world, the briars take their toll on any who travel through the thorny tunnel. With few fae left, and fewer needing or willing to travel, the briar path has too become a ghost of what it once was.

"Your Majesty, if you travel to Tearnan Ogh to recover Sir Will, you may not come back at all," Bedevere said. Memory held up a hand. "I'm getting Will, and we're coming back. That's happening.

Fairy Gold

It seemed the fashion for the fae to be seen with fairy gold weapons. Memory wondered if they were just status symbols or actually put to use.

One of the denizens of the fairy realms is the Rump of Steel-Skin spider. These metallic spiders live solely in the magical briar pathway tunnels and spin golden webs, which if collected, can be used to spin fairy gold. This of course is a reference to Rumplestiltskin who spins straw into gold.

Fairy gold is prized both by humans and by the fae. It is rare as it requires a lot of web to forge the gold from, and gathering the web is a dangerous task.

Only the fae can work fairy gold, forging it and forming it into weapons and ornaments. Being crystalline and brittle it is easily broken, and once broken, humans are unable to re-work it and it becomes useless to them.

The desperate have sometimes tried to pass worthless broken pieces of fairy gold off as normal gold.

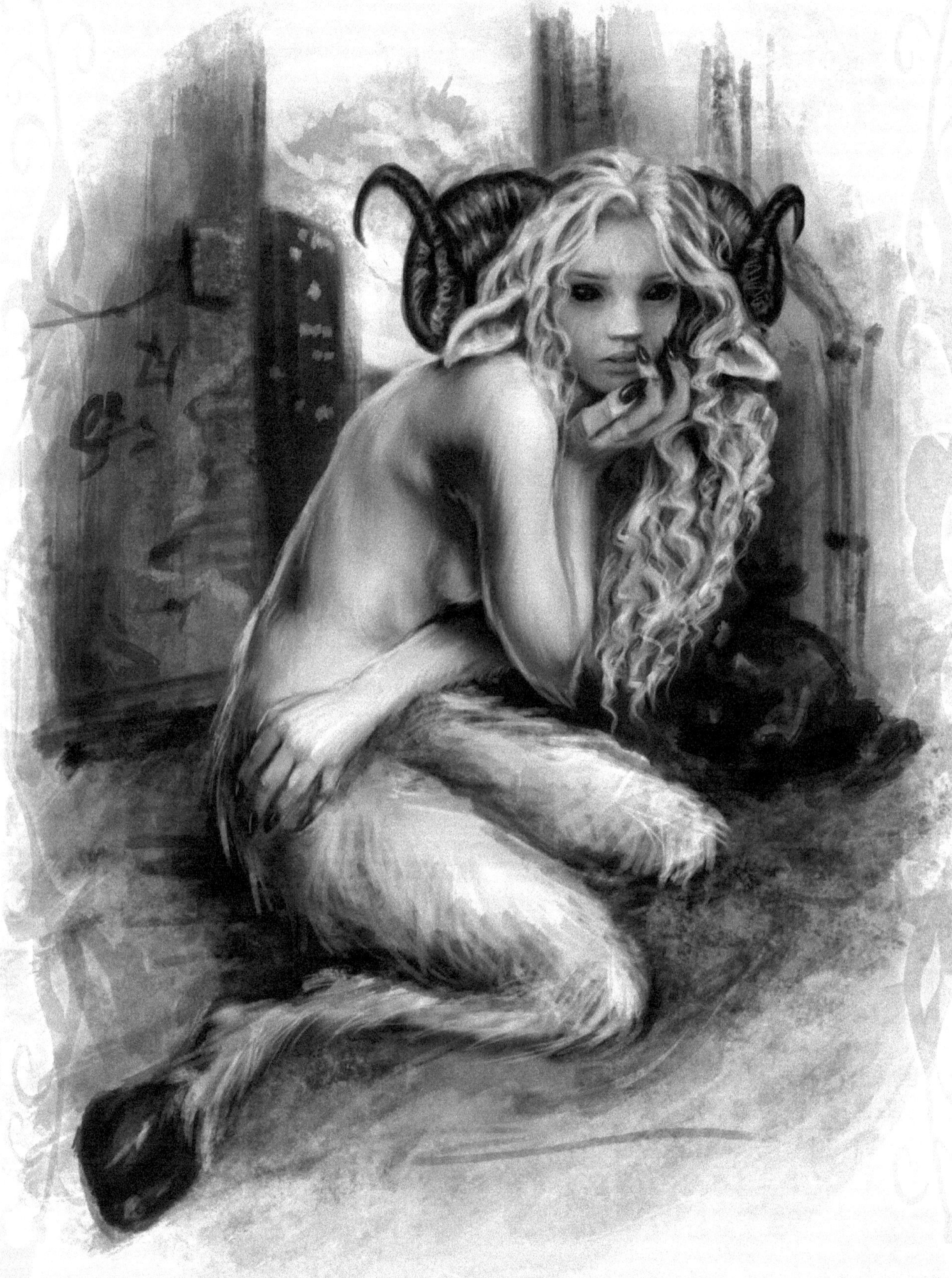

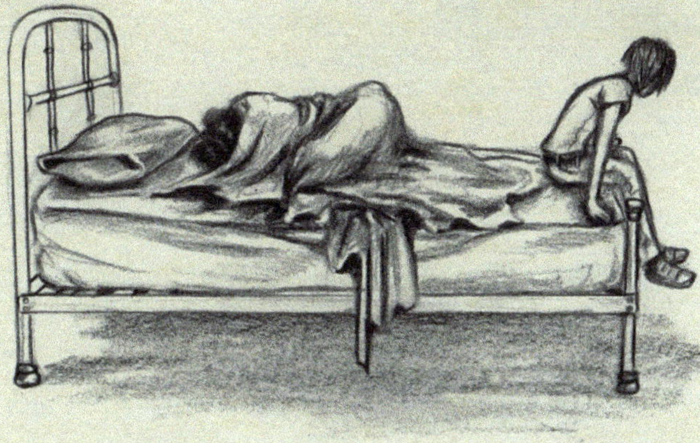

The Modern World

"I don't remember anything else before waking up here a few days ago. We were somewhere different? A different world? What does that even mean?"

The world which Avall was separated from is no different to the real world. It developed the same, has the same histories and mythology regarding Arthur, Avalon, and the fae, and is at a similar point in technology as the real world during the time frame of the story.

Any history of the lands of Avall were lost, or merged with the myths of Avalon, the land that "vanished into the mists". Fae no longer exist in the modern world, although the very few fae who brave the iron rich world are enough to keep their lore alive in the human psyche.

During the years after Avall was separated, some wizards explored ways to travel back to the rest of the world. Maybe they stumbled upon the truth that the other world did not become hell, or maybe they were simply curious. Some wizards did manage to travel to the rest of the world, but once there, were unable to travel back. It is through these wizards that the legends of King Arthur and Avall were continued in the rest of the world.

These wizards also retained their Spark of Connection, which they also would have passed on to their descendants. Magic would have built within them as it did within Memory, but was useless without the knowledge of it or behests. With the Spark of Connection being hereditary, there could be individuals in the world even in modern times with the ability to use magic.

Author's Insight

Although she purposefully left the exact location in the modern world where Memory grew up vague, Selina imagines it is probably somewhere in England.

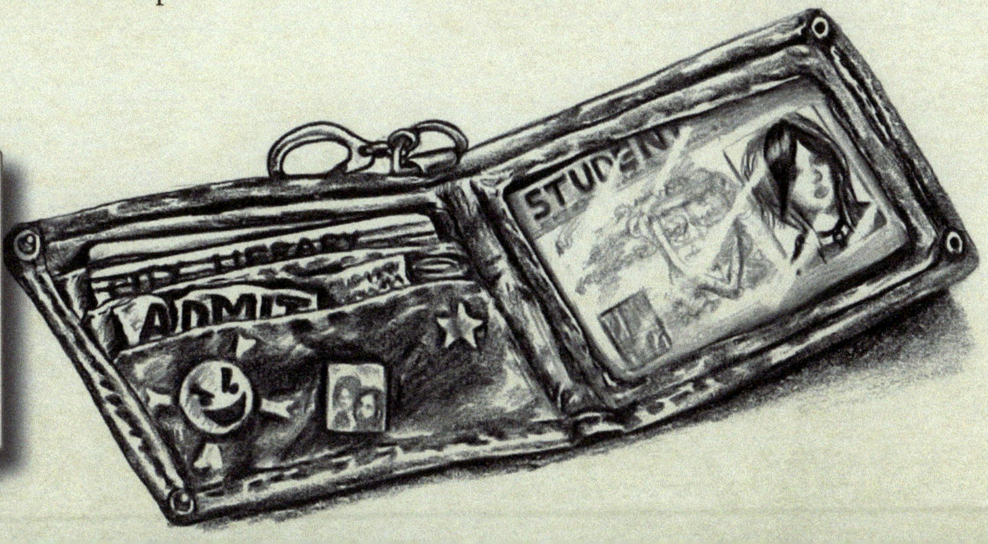

Caermaellan Palace

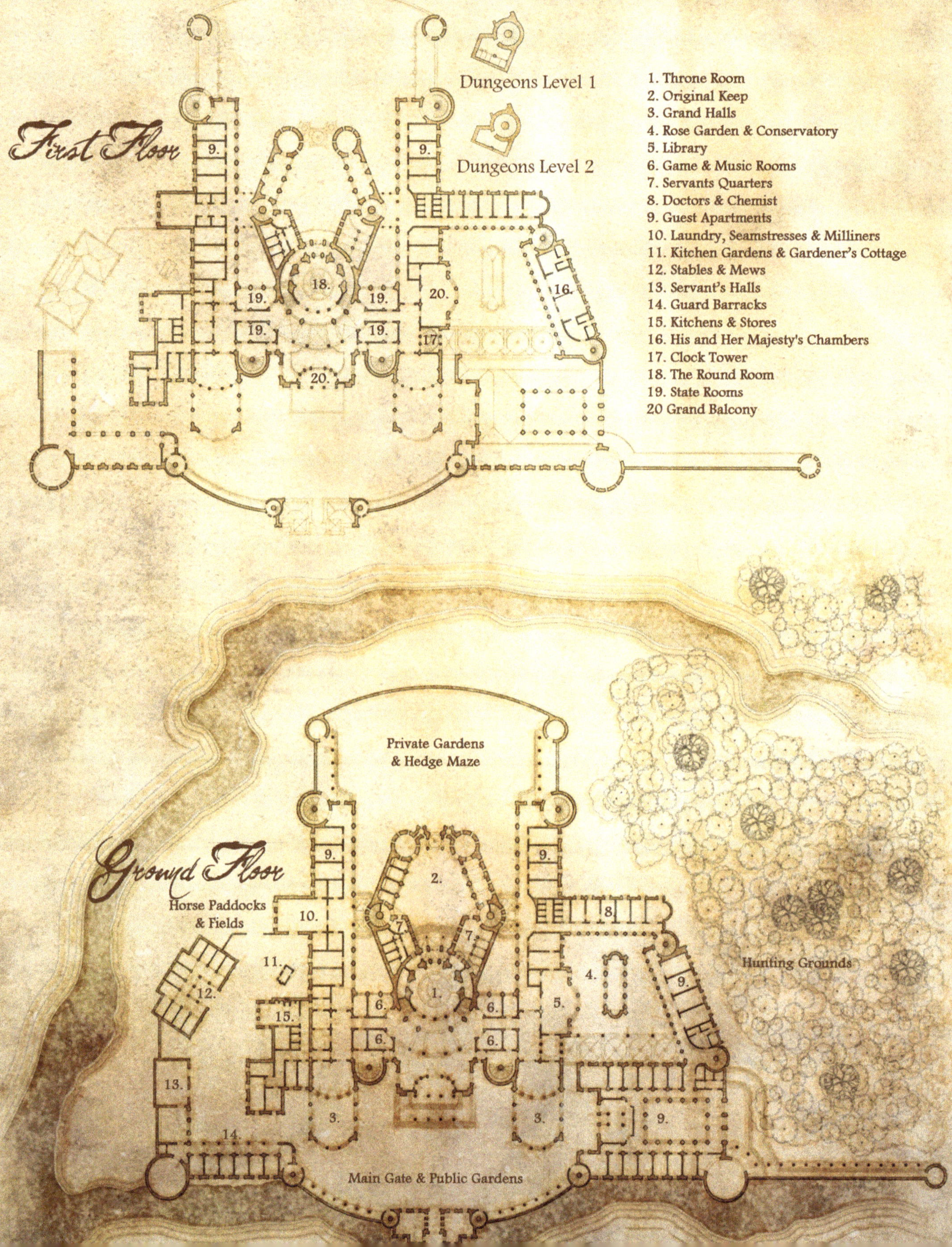

Caermaellan Palace

Living in the castle with her friends wasn't turning out to be the Happily Ever After that Memory thought it would be.

The home of Avall's ruler, Uther, could barely be called a castle. It was Arthur, who created the new capital, Caermaellan, and built the first great keep there once the lands became prosperous.

This original stone keep has lasted through the many centuries, and being such an important part of Avall history, was carefully preserved, including the grand Round Room and round table.

As time past, with changing needs, fashions, and technologies, the castle was expanded, but always while retaining the original stone keep at its heart.

Caermaellan palace became an extremely large estate which homes many noble families, Wizard's council members, serving staff, and guards.

Among the guards, are the brother's Peirs and Erec. Having been a leading force in the resistance against Thayl, Peirs quickly gained Memory's respect and friendship.

The palace of Caermaellan is like a small city, with a bustling workforce which keeps everything running within its walls with little regard for the politics of who is actually ruling over the land at the time. From the Maellans, to Thayl, to Eloryn, Hayes, or Memory, the staff have little interest beyond gossip as they busy themselves with the prestigious duties of maintaining Avall's most historically important building.

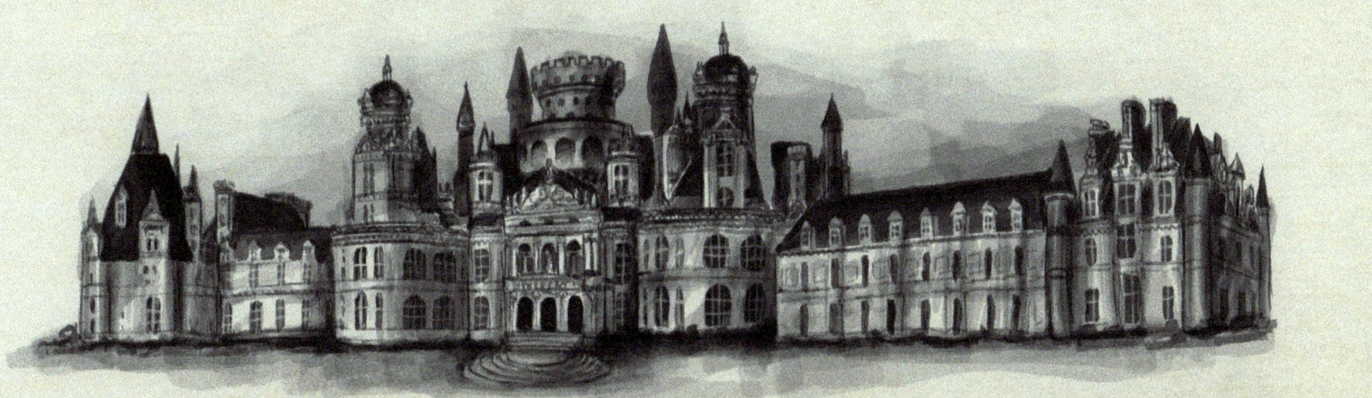

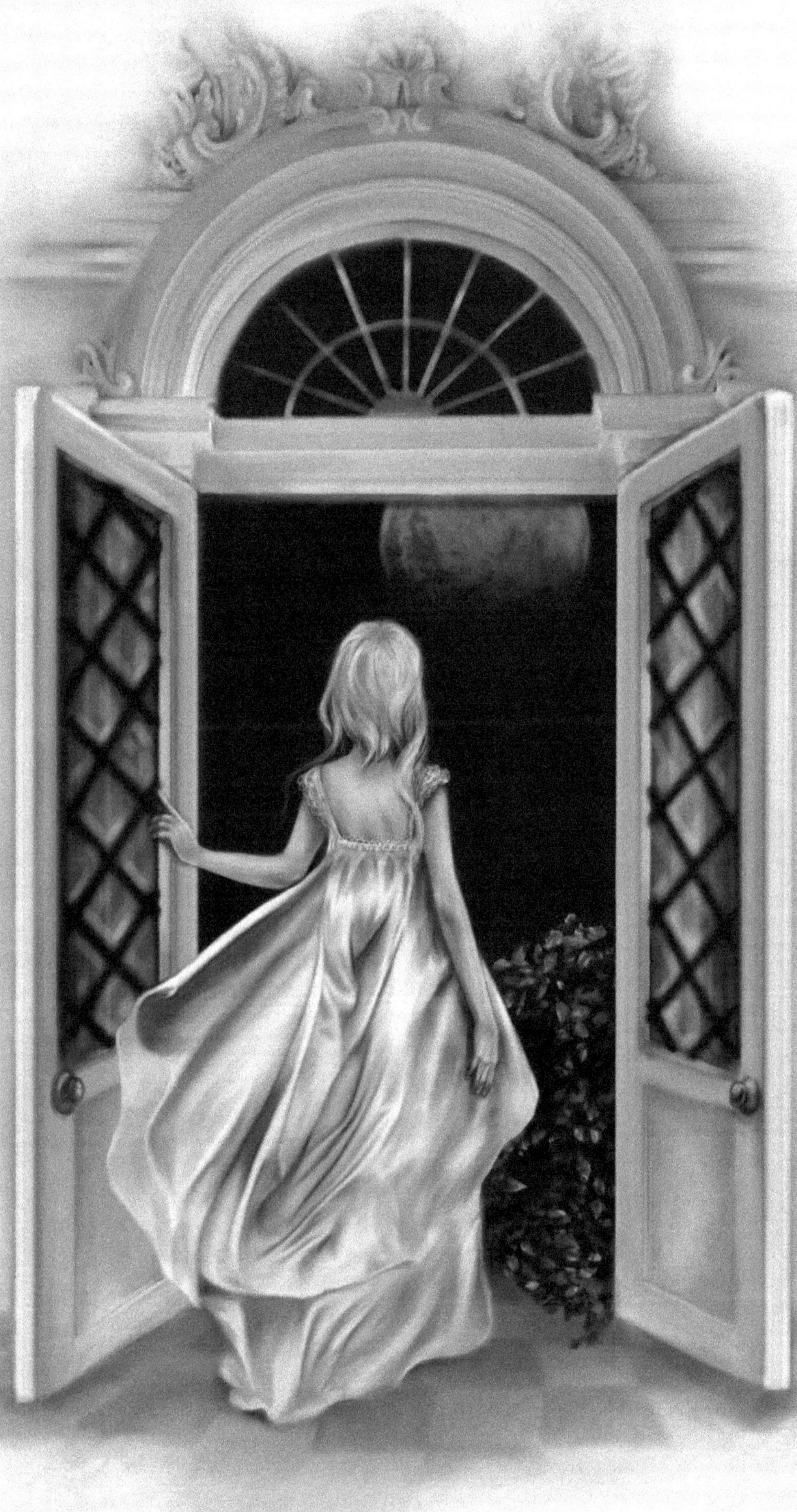

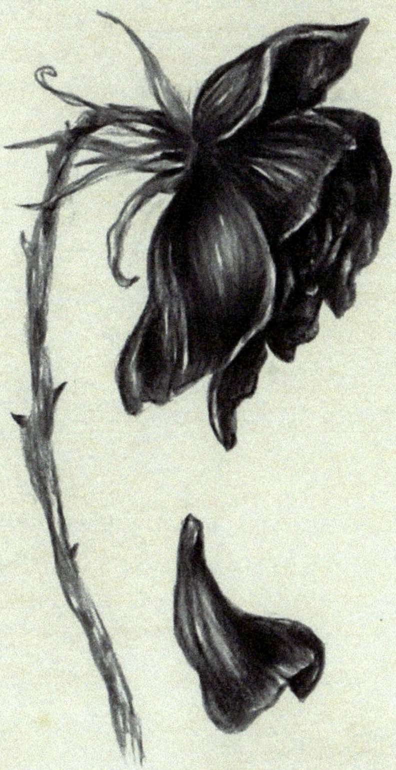

"This isn't me. Or maybe it is, but the point is I don't know yet. I'm a diary full of blank pages. I went from nothing, to forests and fear for my life, to crazy opulence."

Within one of the courtyards of the palace is a large rose garden which was established by Queen Loredanna.

The roses that grow there are behested to bloom in a rainbow of magical shades. It was a favored place of the short lived queen, and a place of many memories and sorrow for Thayl.

As he maintained her quarters after her death, he always kept a fresh cut bouquet of roses in a vase there.

The Ivy Room

Once Thayl came to power, the eastern wing of the castle that had held mostly Wizard Council's quarters and the chambers of the king and queen, were closed off. Apart from Loredanna's chambers, the wing fell to disrepair and neglect over the years.

Along an older section of castle wall, rose and ivy vines grew over those sixteen years to reach up and over the top (in a slight reference to the vines in Sleeping Beauty).

The vines also grew over an old guard room or bird house on top of the walls there, obscuring it from view. It was Will who rediscovered it, as he explored the grounds of the area he would make his new home. It seemed a perfect place for him and Memory to meet, private and away from prying eyes.

Dubbed the Ivy Room, the natural setting was comforting to Will and also became special to Memory. It was a great loss to her when her magic destroyed it when she was distraught believing Will had left her.

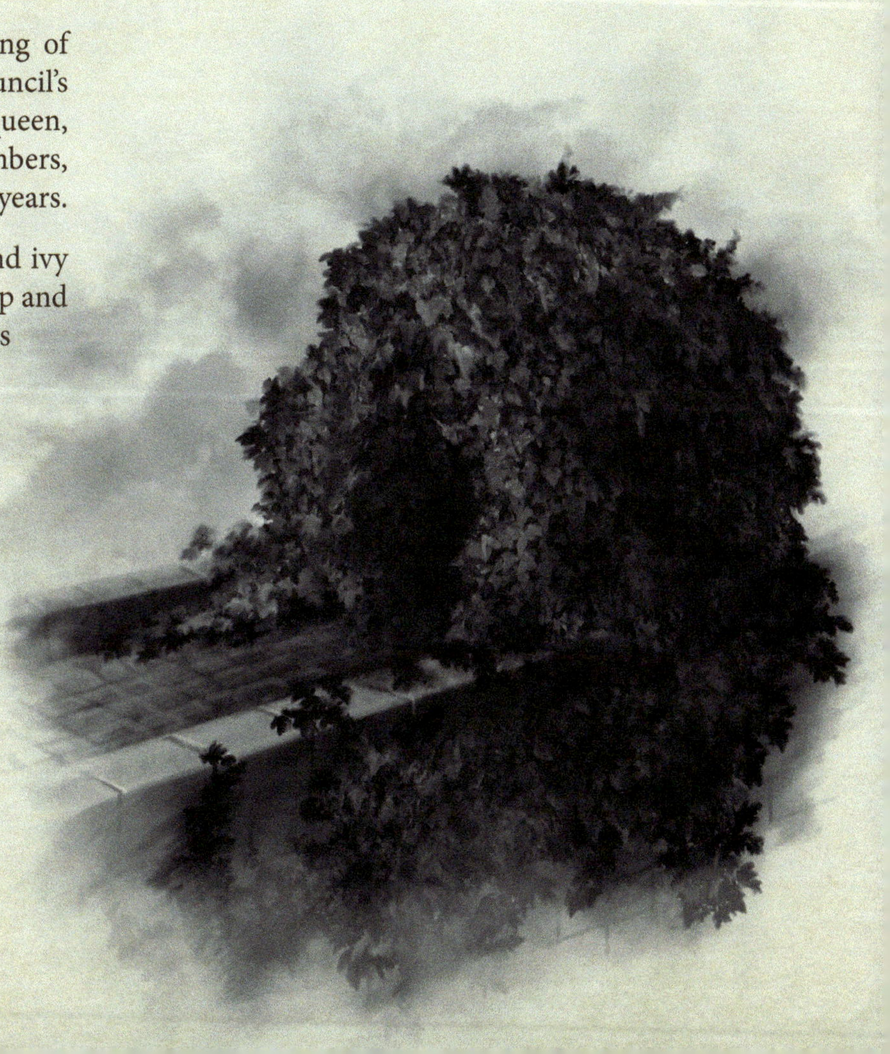

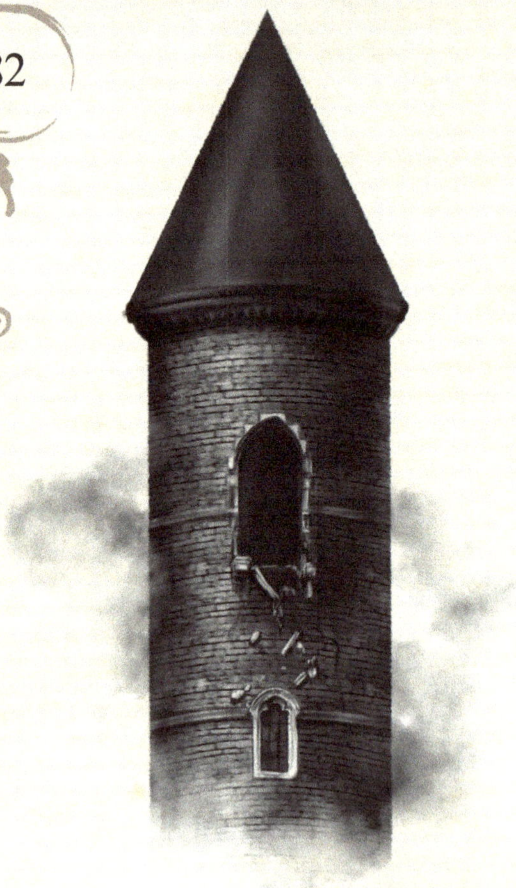

During the story, the palace of Caermaellan sustained a fair bit of damage. An entire tower was knocked down during the magical battle between Memory and Hope, and Hayes set off a bomb within the most sacred Round Room in order to continue his manipulations.

Destroying this room removed Hayes's strongest detractor, and allowed him further power to attack others who threatened his power. It is also symbolic of his desire for being in control, rather than sharing power.

While the tough stone structure of the original keep wasn't affected much by the explosion, the ancient round table was blasted to pieces. Eloryn spends a great deal of her time very carefully piecing it back together and mending it with her behests. It is a very important and symbolic action for her, healing and repairing such an old and powerful symbol of her family.

"King Arthur? Like King Arthur and the Knights of the Round Table?"

"I dunno. I just know Arthur Maellan was my ancestor who made the Pact. But you know the castle totally has a round table, I kid you not."

"Avall isn't Atlantis. It must be Avalon. From what I remember of the stories it fits, even the name. And Caermaellan, it's like Camelot."

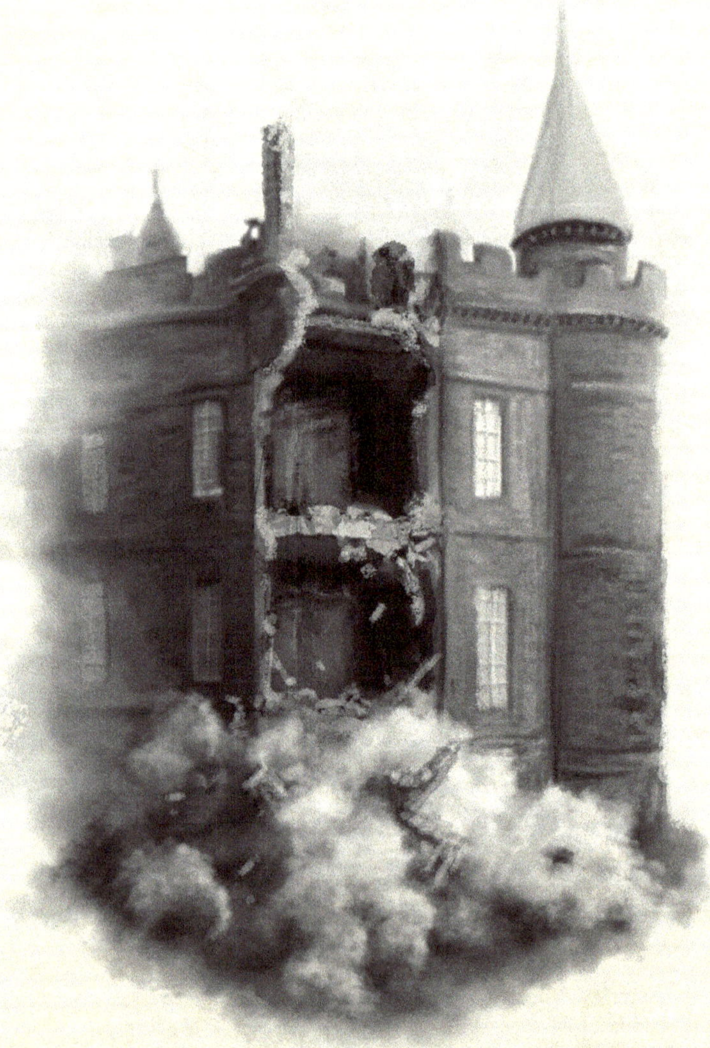

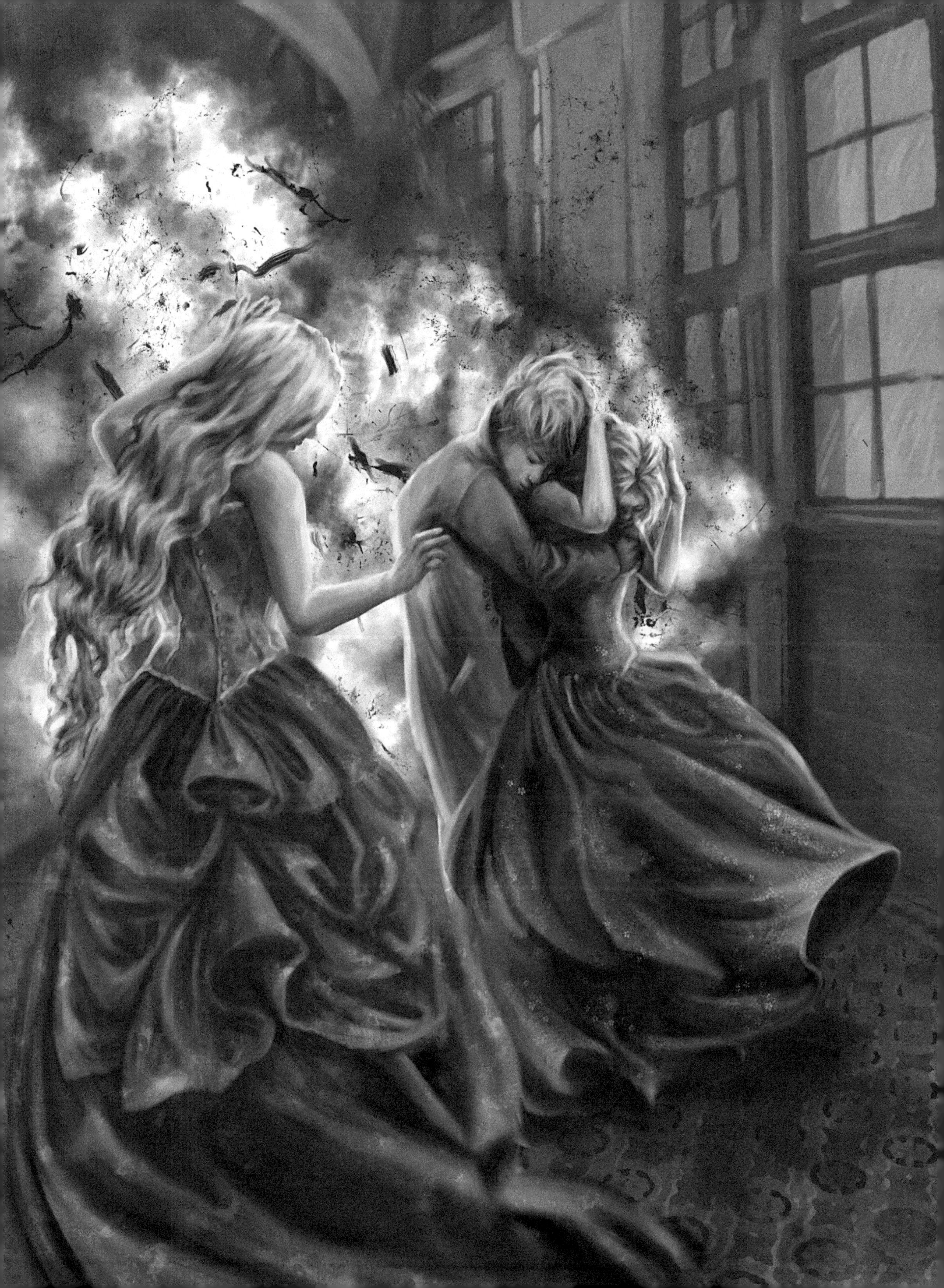

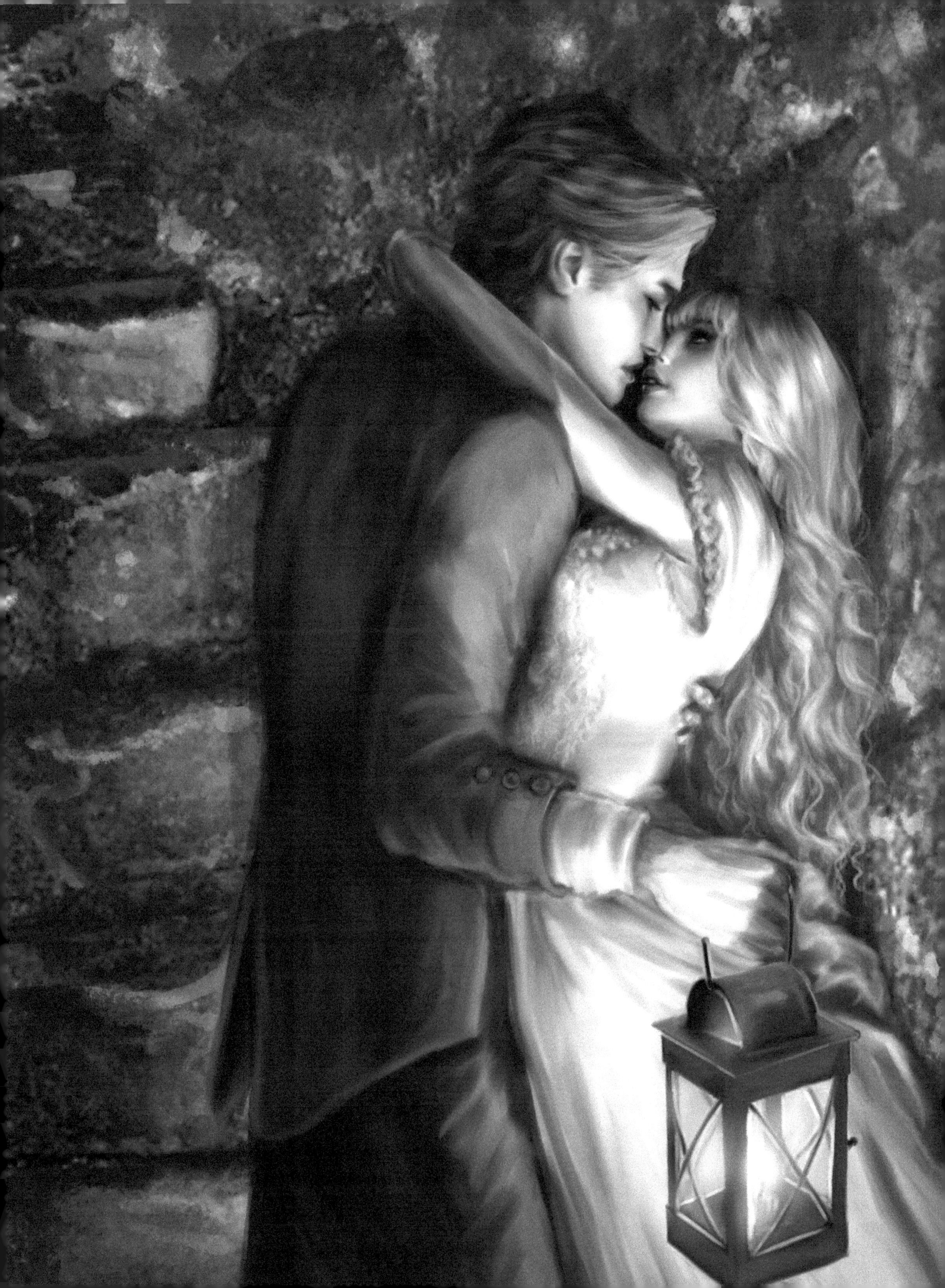

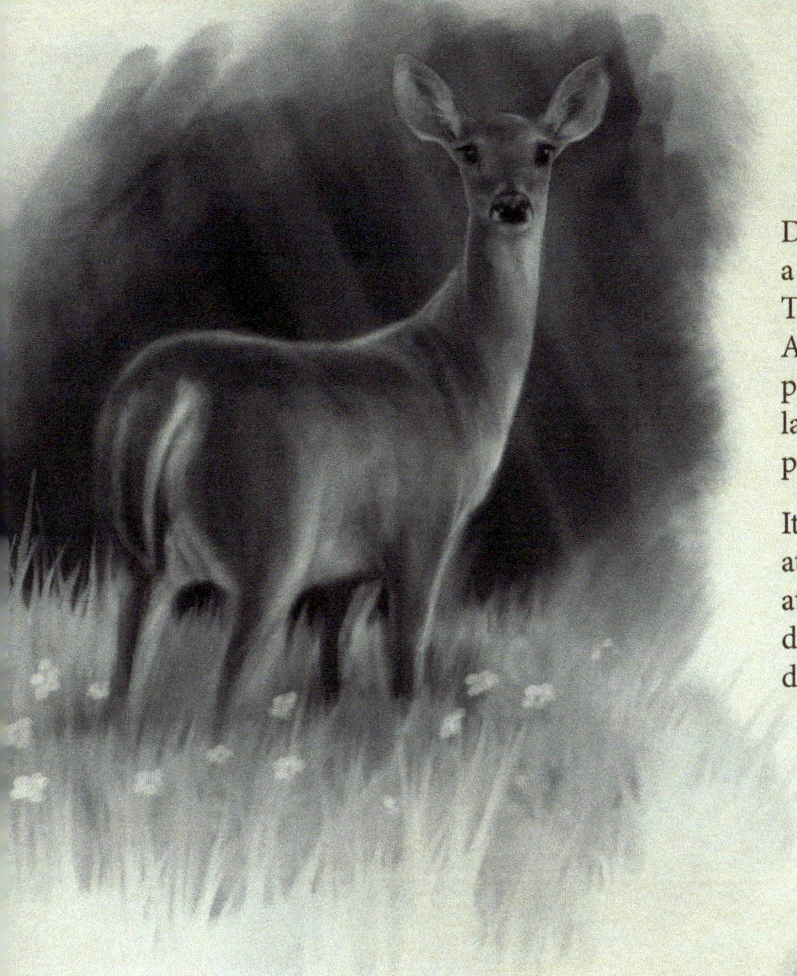

The Underground Lake

Deep under the grounds of Caermaellan palace, is a vast cave system with a large underground lake. The caves were discovered during the building of Arthur's keep, and he had his builders explore the passages, building steps and pathways down to the lake and out far from the castle, thinking of it as a potential escape route.

It was on the shores of this lake that Arthur, attempting to flee from his nephew Mordred's attacks, met his death. And it was here that Myrddin discovered him dead, and flung Caliburn into the deep black waters of the lake.

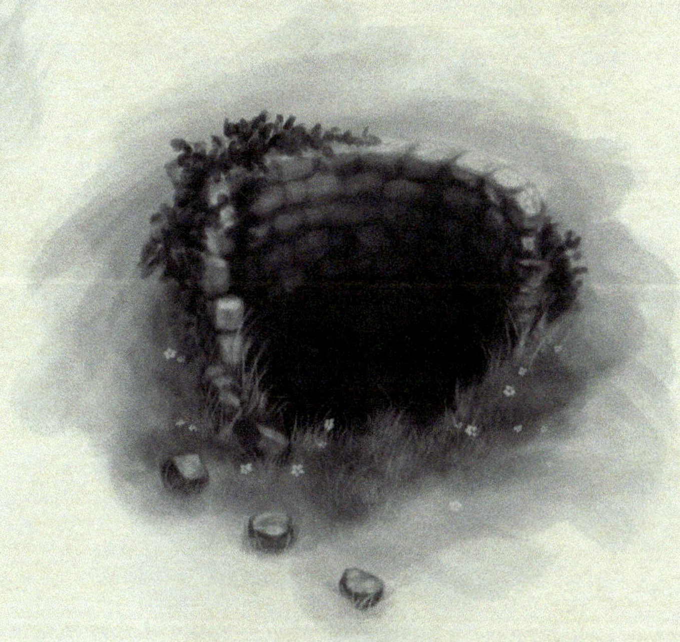

"Fine. I absolutely trust you are doing this to let me rest and not to take my sister off into a dark and isolated area."
Roen just shrugged. "It appears that my deception skills are getting sloppy through misuse."

After Arthur's time, most forgot about the lake and tunnels beneath the castle. Thayl rediscovered them, rebuilding a new secret entrance and using the area as a place to hide his growing iron collection.

The hunting grounds, which spread over a large area of wild forests on the east of the palace, quickly became Will's new home when he follows Memory there.

He learns of the old sunken well from Mina, who tells him the tunnel beneath is a place no fae ever travel. The well has sunken into some of the tunnels of the cavern system, and when explored, quickly led Memory and Will to the underground lake.

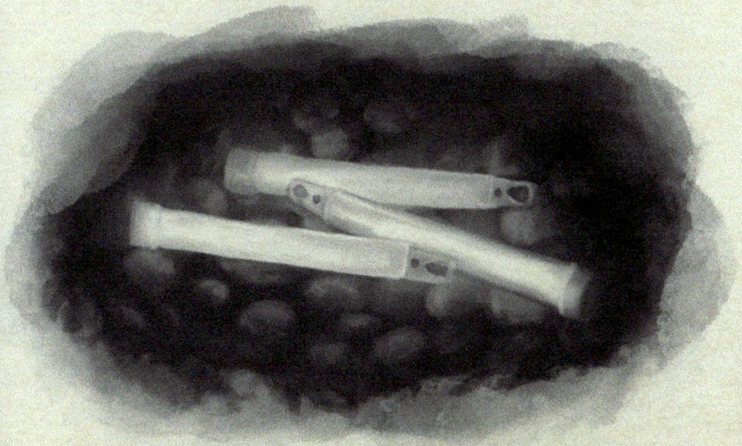

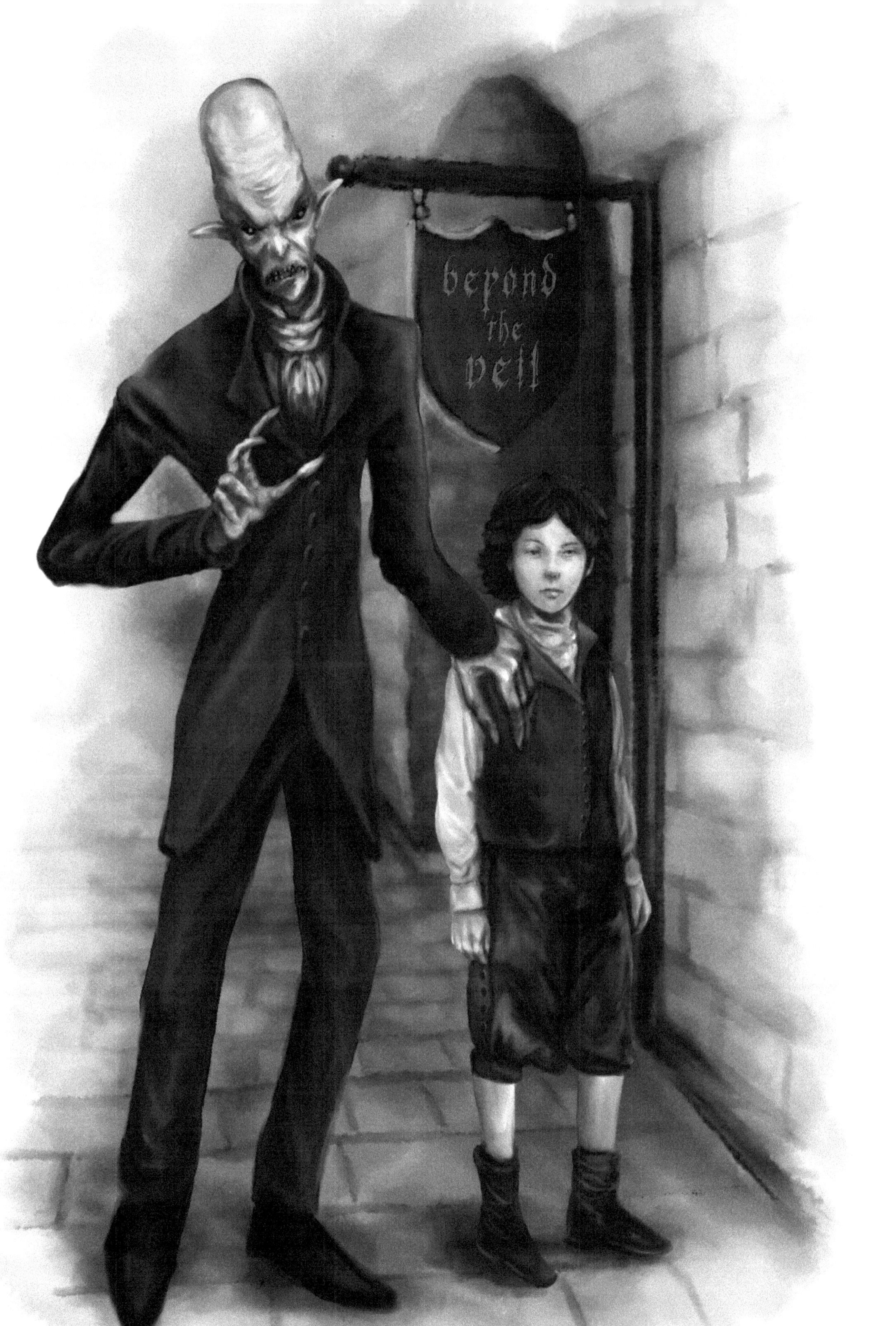
beyond
the
veil

Caermaellan City

Memory hopped down from the carriage, wanting to run off in every direction at once. The city was so enticing, full of misty secrets and winding pathways to explore.

Caermaellan is also the name of the capital city which surrounds Caermaellan palace. It is a coastal city and the largest in Avall, with a densely populated inner area and wide sprawling country estates surrounding.

The city landscape is dominated by stone architecture, cobbled streets and narrow, multi-story terrace housing. Decorative bronze is used instead of wrought iron in window guards and gateways. The people of the city travel mostly in carriages, on horseback, or on foot. The printing press had been developed in Avall based on imported schematics, and newspapers were just becoming popular and sold on the streets.

In the real world, during the Victorian era there was a great deal of interest in fairies, with many artists, authors, and craftsmen bringing fairy related works into popularity.

This fairy craze was a large inspiration to Selina in her own art and in writing Memory's Wake. In Avall, she imagined a land like fairy-crazed Victorian times, only one in which the fae were very much real and part of every day life.

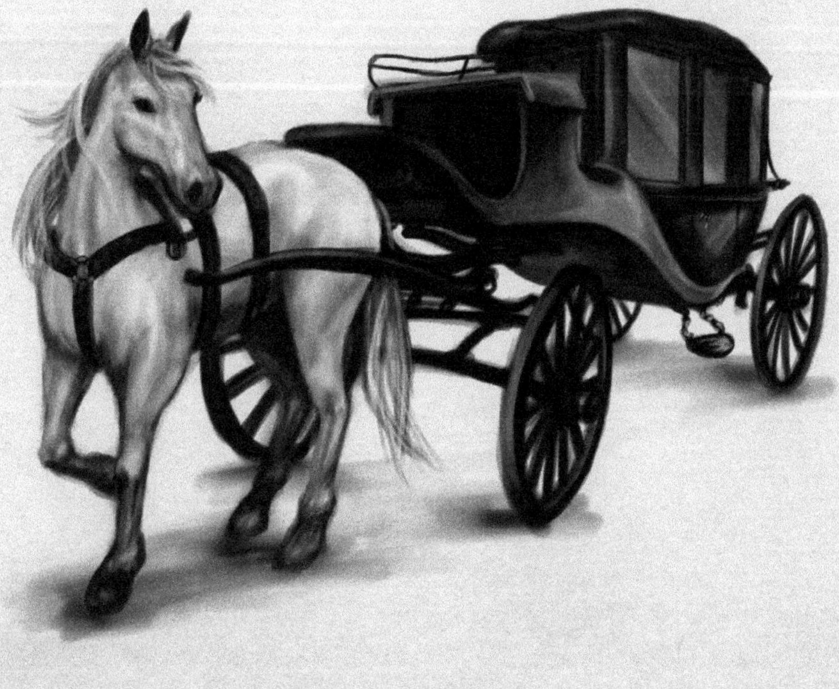

Memory's Orphanage

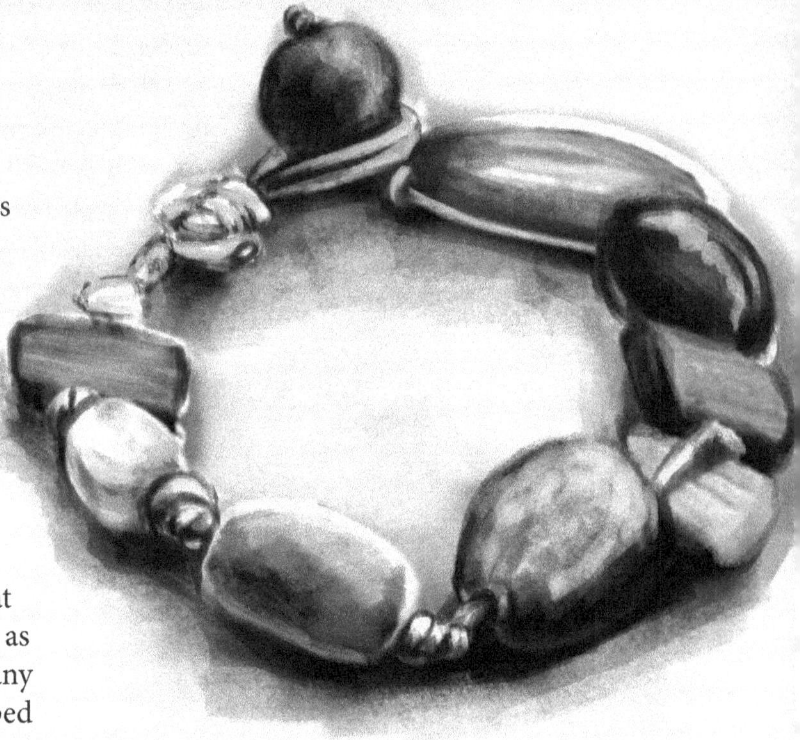

When Memory's needs and plans for the orphans in her care become more serious, she realizes she needs a base of operations to house the children and continue her work for them.

Through her royal connections, she is able to purchase a large although older building to become her orphanage. The running of that home and the help it provided was one of her proudest accomplishments.

It was through her work with the homeless that Memory met Maeve. Around the same age as Memory, Maeve had become a guardian of many of the younger orphans in the city, and helped Memory manage them and bring them into care at the orphanage.

Maeve became a close friend of Memory's, and understood her well, as in some ways their backgrounds were similar.

After Clara's death, Maeve took over the role as Memory's lead, and often only, serving staff member.

"I'm just going to have to buy it unseen. Apparently I can do stuff like that because I'm some rich princess."

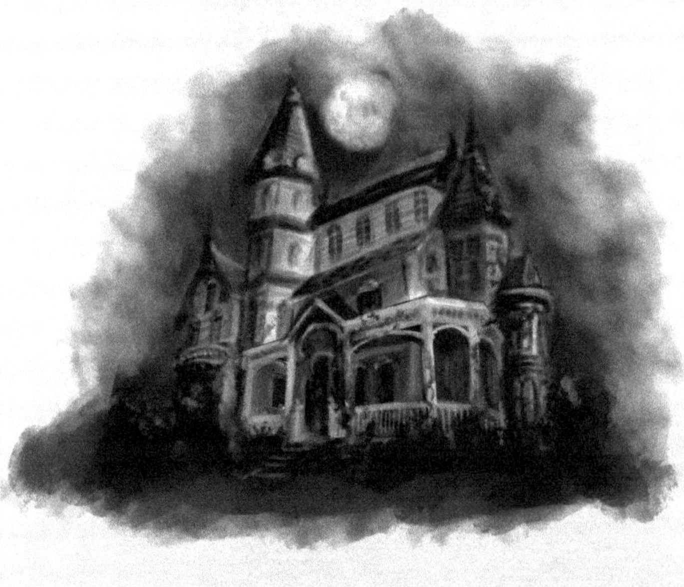

Across Avall, the fae have some areas that are designated as their official territory. Even within the city of Caermaellan, some abodes are considered fae territory. These were the first places searched when trying to find where the fae were taking the children they kidnapped.

Apart from official territory, some fae enjoy interaction with humans, and a number of inns and pubs through Caermaellan are known as fae bars, which the fae visit regularly. Even with the Pact, unseelie fae generally aren't welcomed, and the fae that visit are mostly seelie fae. Even still, the humans which visit these fae bars know to be on guard, and careful to follow the rules for when dealing with the fae.

Author's Insight

The image to the right is a version of Selina's "Lost Soul" artwork, which has been altered to have the character look like Memory. On completion of the first draft of Memory's Wake, Selina wanted a small number of copies printed for friends and family, but hadn't yet designed the official cover art. So this image was altered to create a stand in cover for these first copies of the book.

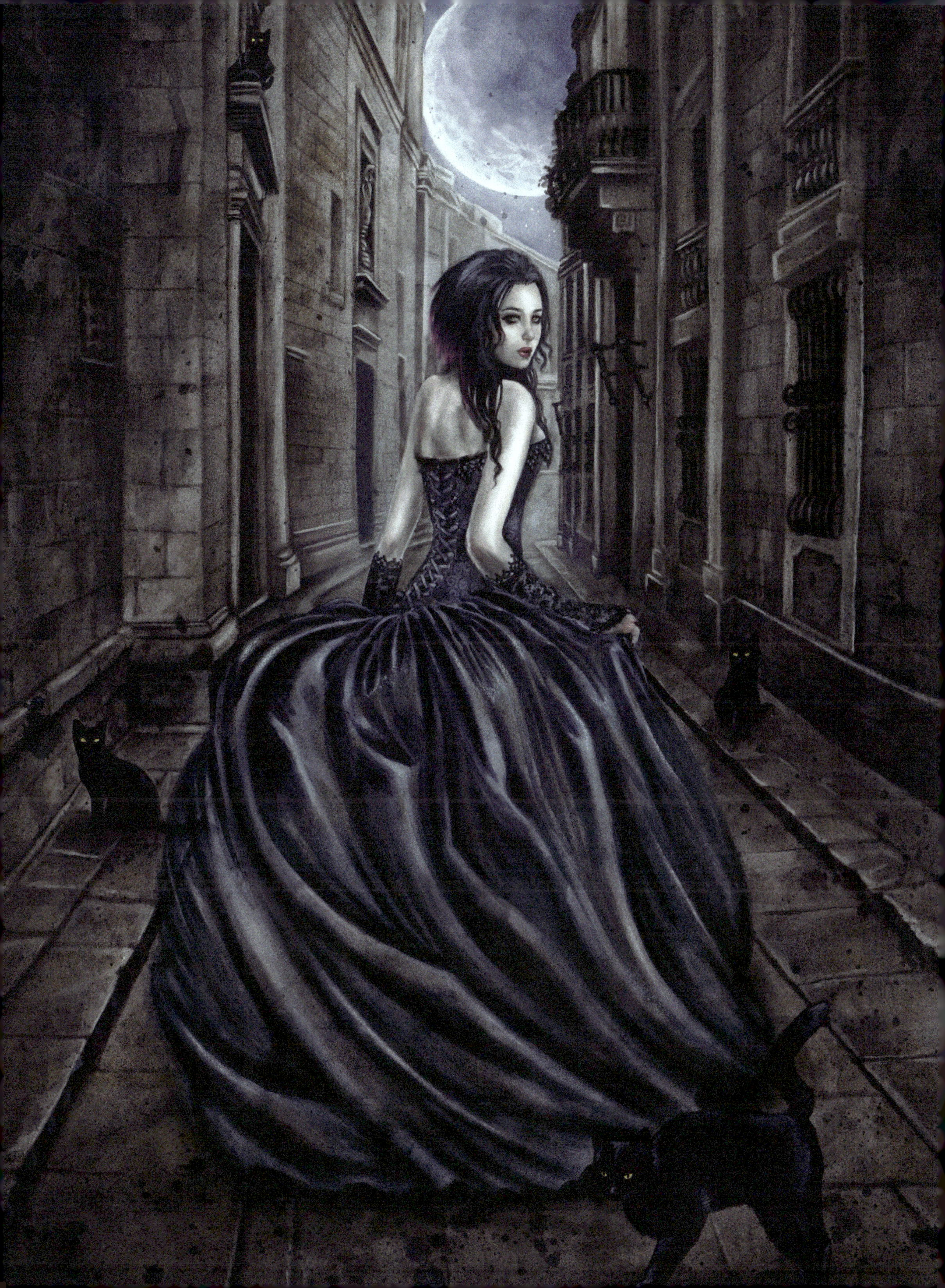

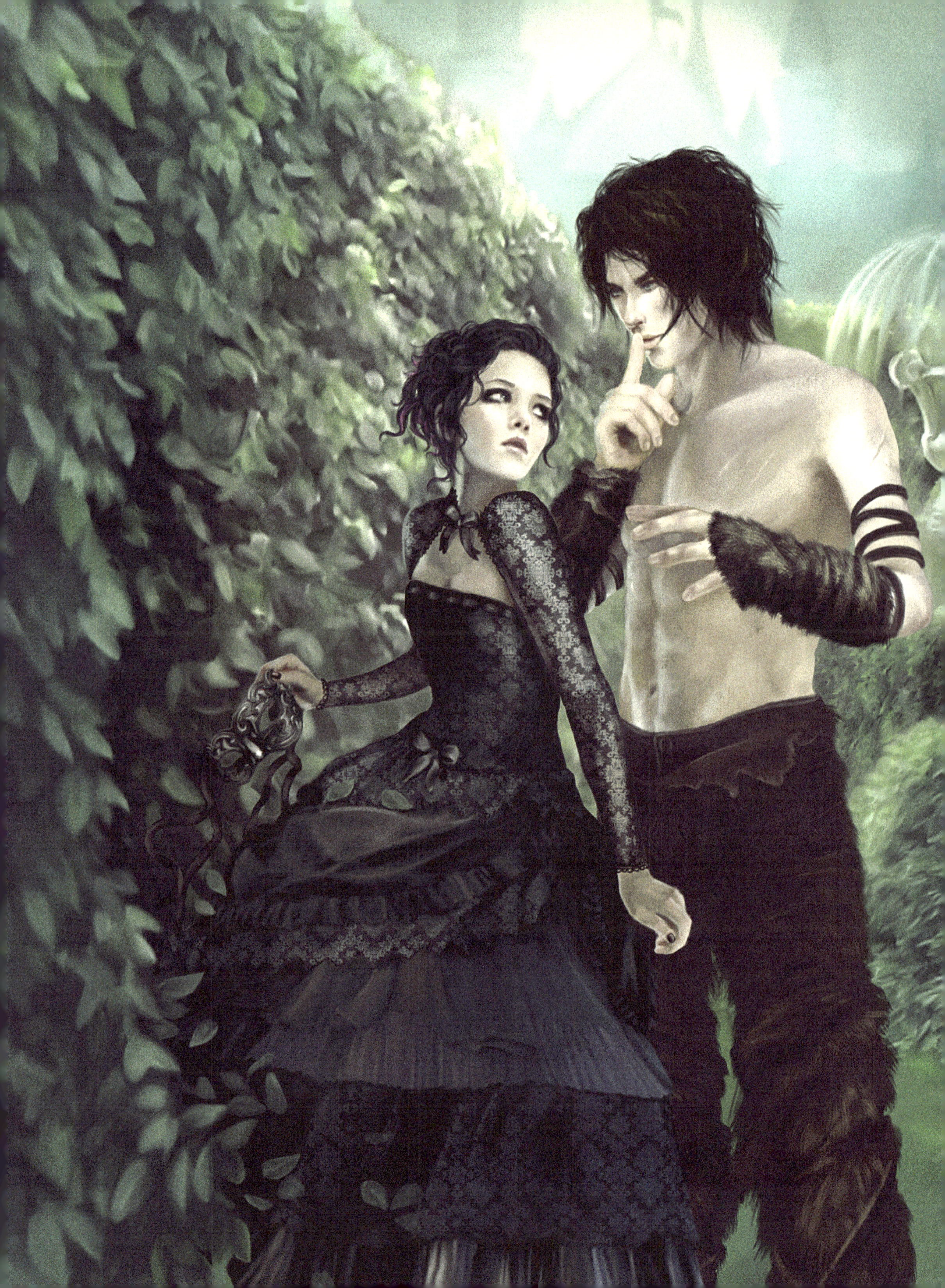

Palace de Montredeur

Looking back at the castle itself,
Memory blew out a low whistle.
The place had goddamned towers.

Palace de Montredeur is the home to Duke Lanval and Duchess Marian, who rule over the Danyn region, the capital of which is Maerranton.

The palace is the second largest in Avall with many luxuries such as advanced plumbing allowing for showers in many of the bathrooms. An entire river was diverted to run through the castle itself to provide water for it, inside and in the grounds which are full of fountains. The river mostly runs under the grounds, but is shown off as a feature in the entryway between the castle and the gardens.

It was here that Eloryn fell into the waters, and was pulled away by the current and washed down through the rest of the river.

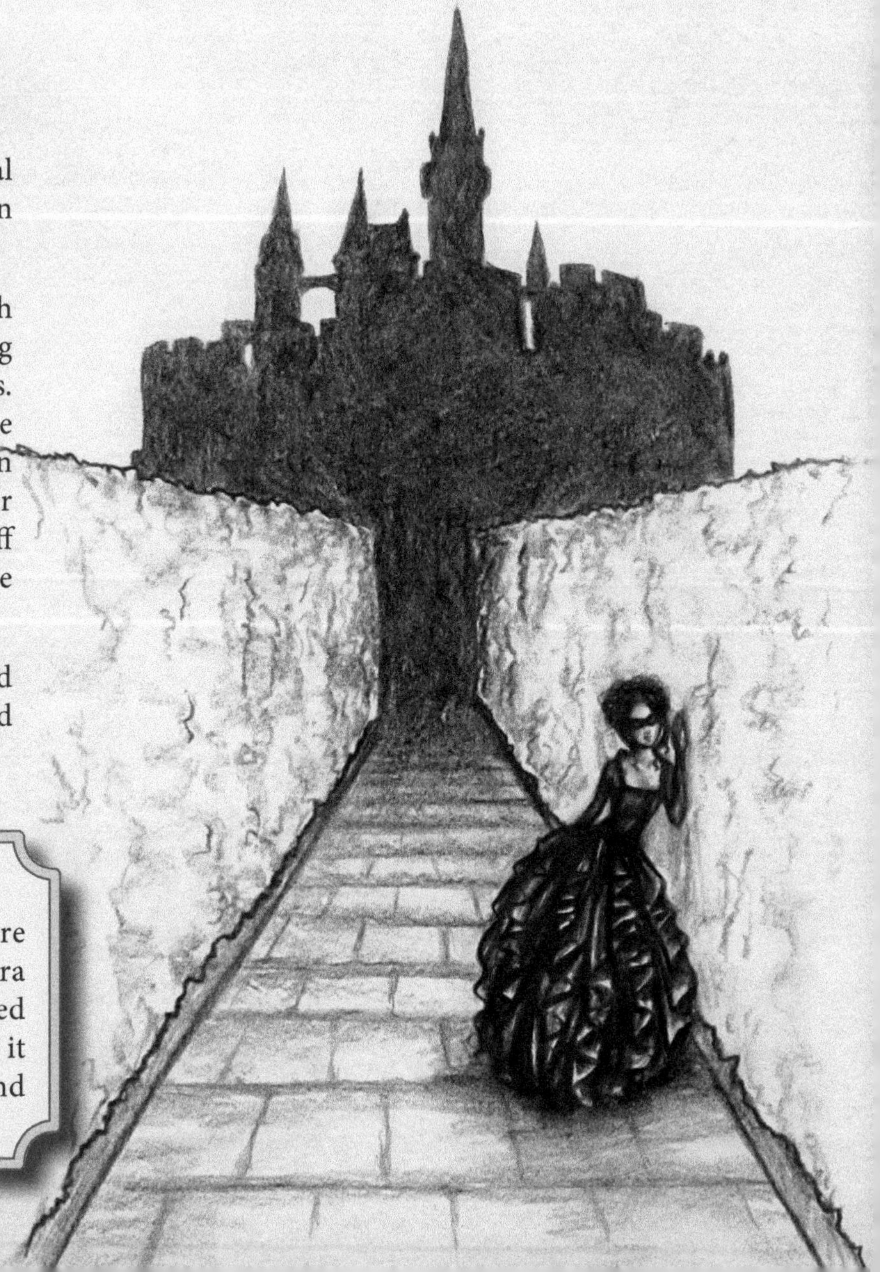

Author's Insight

The gardens of Palace de Montredeur were inspired by the gardens of the Alhambra which are full of water features. Selina visited the Alhambra with family as a child and it seemed like the most magical of places and remains a great inspiration to her.

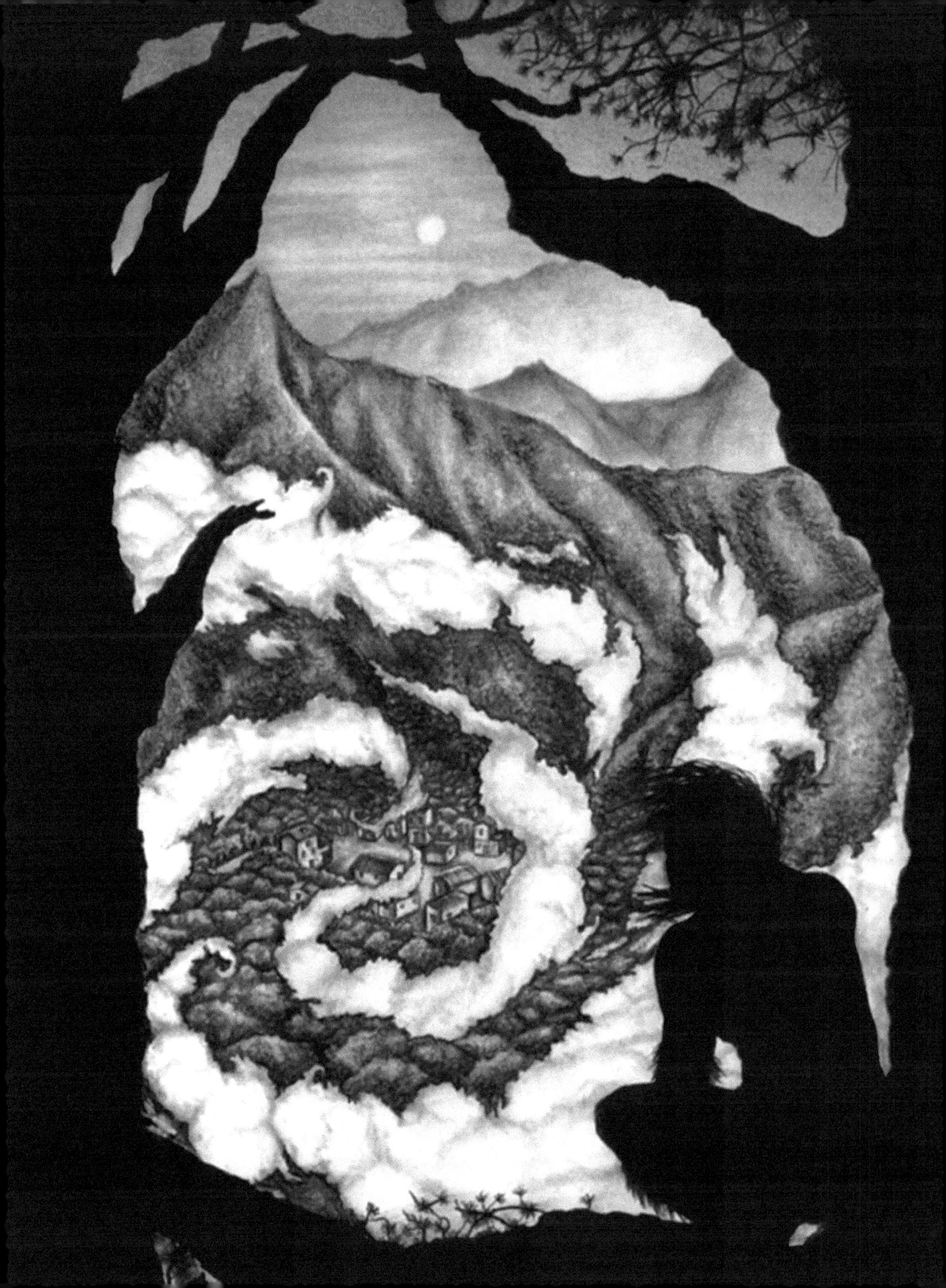

Maerranton, Aule, and Kenth

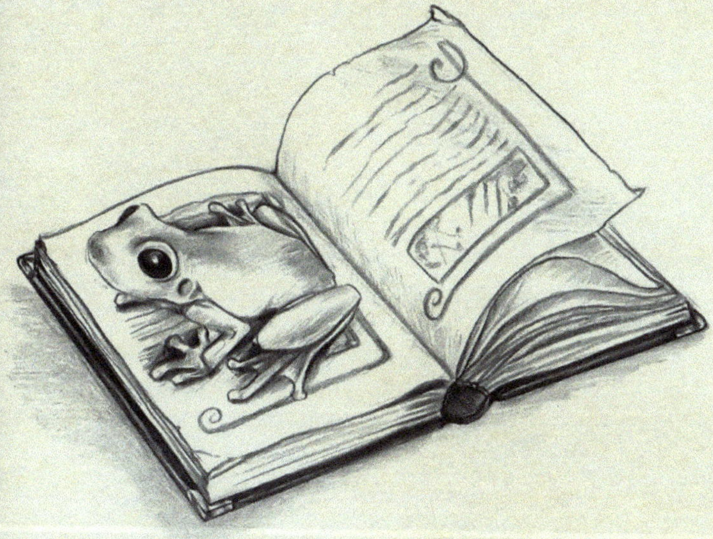

Author's Insight

In the early versions of Memory's Wake, the town near Eloryn's home was first called Caer. Caer is a Welsh term meaning "stronghold", "fortress", or "citadel". Once Selina had decided on the twin's family name, the capital became Caermaellan and the smaller town became Aule. It was a happy accident that Caermaellan had a similar sound to Camelot.

Three towns the characters travel through in the first book of Memory's Wake, are Aule, Maerranton, and Kenth.

Aule is the tiny mountain village closest to Eloryn and Alward's residence.

Maerranton is Roen's hometown, the largest the characters visit on their journey.

The underground tunnels, which were part of a water system similar to what is at the castle, had all been built a long time ago but neglected and run down, Roen uses them as escape tunnels, having explored them all thoroughly.

Kenth is the home of the wizard's council. The town was already suffering from the lack of fae in the land, then when the council moved there to hide, they used anti-fae wards which expelled all traces of fae from the area and the town became a "dead town", dead of the fae, where nothing would grow and all farmers and inhabitants left.

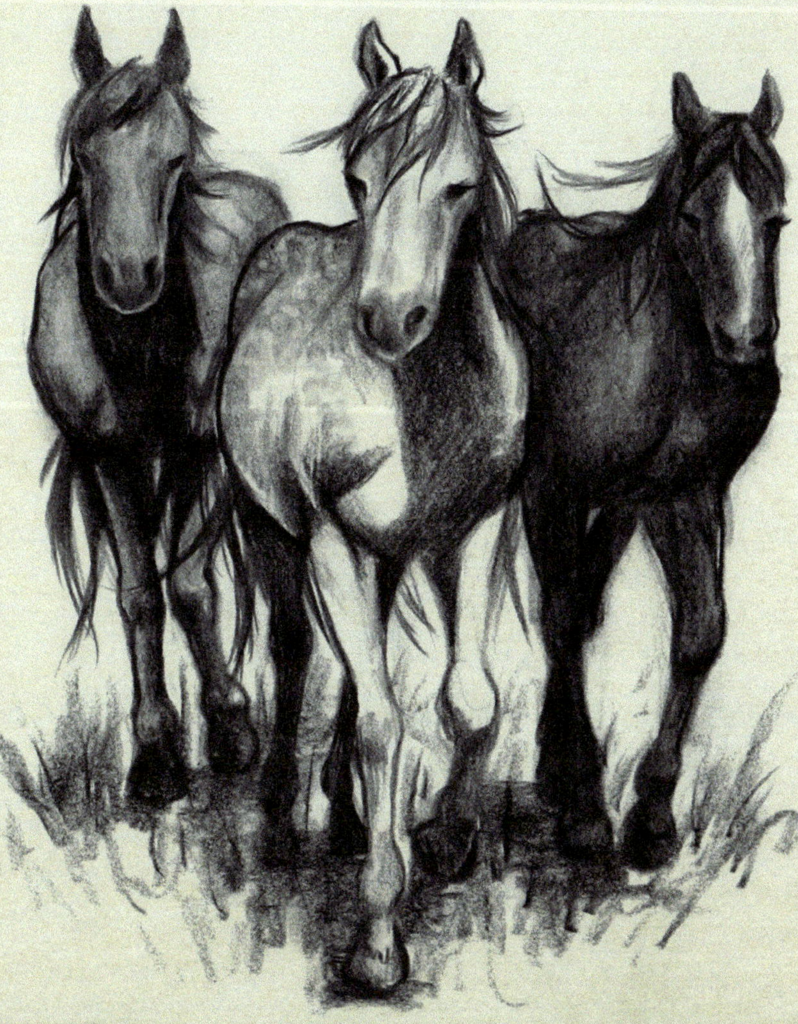

Speaking Mirrors

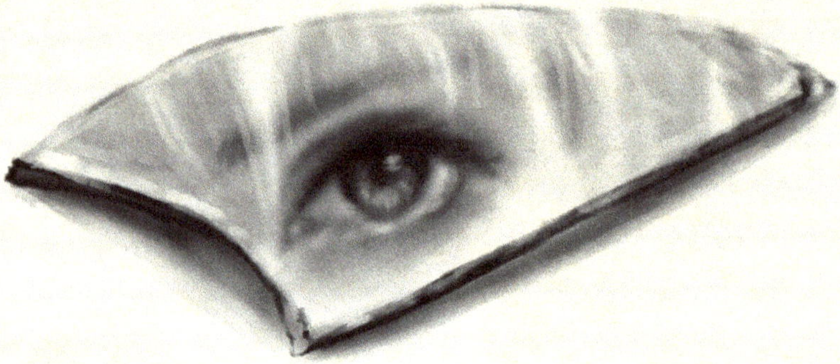

Speaking Mirrors are broken fragments of a once much larger enchanted mirror.

The story of their creation tells of one of the earliest Maellan Queens, strong in magic as all Maellan are, who was extremely vain and greedy. She enchanted a mirror to compliment how she looked and talk back to her when she asked questions, and she prized it as her favored advisor.

When the queen died, the mirror was found shattered. A wizard discovered that the parts of the mirror could still communicate with each other, in a fashion.

Shards of the valuable mirror are used as a communication system throughout the land of Avall.

Alward had two, one from the Wizard's Council and another taken from Loredanna's estate the night after she died. Eloryn used the one he kept at their Rhynn residence to speak with Lanval before they confronted Thayl.

The frame broke apart and the Speaking Mirror shattered into pieces.
Eloryn cried, "Are you insane? That is priceless! Irreplaceable!"
"So are you."

Fae Imports

"We fae, we travel, see many things. Or we did, before the human plague poisoned the world."

The fae, despite telling humans the rest of the world was hell, still sometimes travelled there and back. These trips were more frequent just after Avall's separation, and less frequent as the amount of iron increased in the world until travel all but ceased around the industrial revolution.

These fae would bring back with them things they thought the humans of Avall may value, interesting imports such as exotic foods, plants, books, technology, and fashion. They would trade these highly valuable imports, which the humans believed came at great risk to the fae who travelled into hell to retrieve them, for things the fae valued.

Payments could range from a year of a person's life, to their first kiss, a powerful memory from their past, even first-born children - things that have an intrinsic magical value, or the very least, are an amusement to the nearly immortal fae.

Maellan Royalty

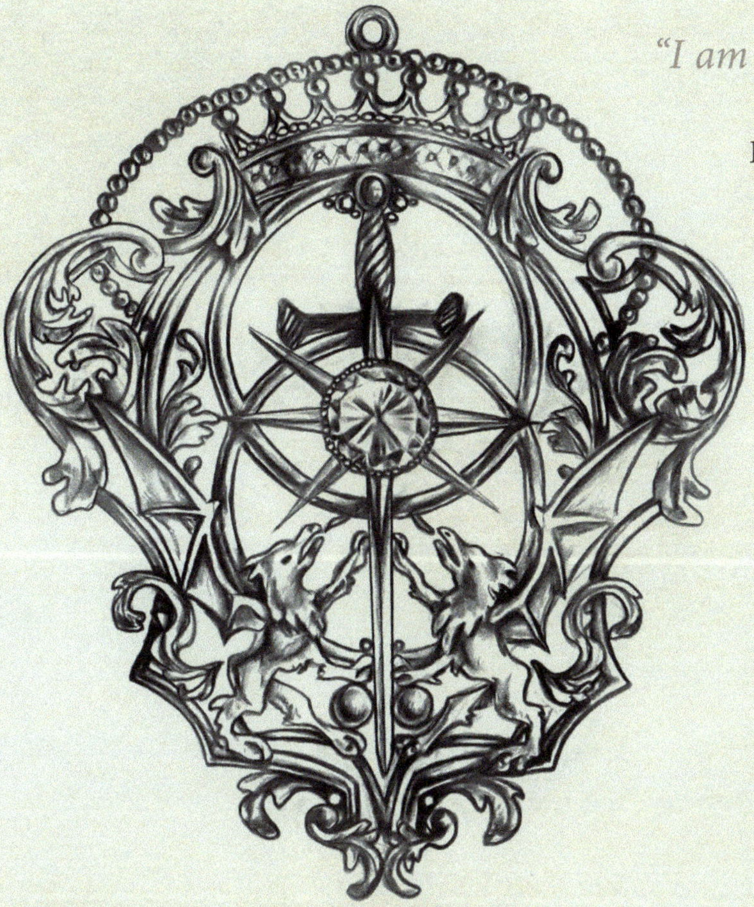

"I am Maellan. You bred me for this."

Before the Pact, the Aurelianus were the royal family, with Arthur Maellan being the first in the long line of Maellan royalty. Arthur is similar in many ways to the King Arthur of Arthurian mythology.

Over the next 1500 years, Maellans ruled almost continuously over Avall, despite many illnesses and accidents meaning the royal family often had short lifespans. Although never proven, these deaths were caused by Nyneve, acting on her grudge she held against Maellans based on Arthur and Myrddin's relationship.

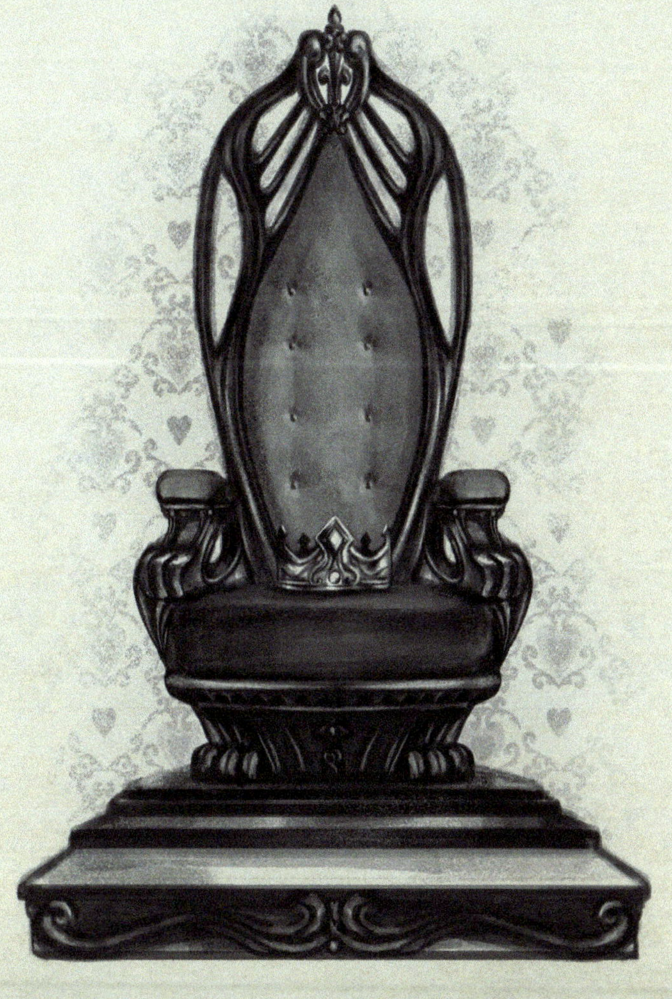

Arthur was a sensitive and empathic human, talented in communication, which is why he was already friends with the fae and quickly became talented in magic. The Wizard's Council continued to carefully breed the Maellan line to remain powerful in magic.

The crest of the Maellan family features Caliburn as its primary element, shining with a large ruby in the center.

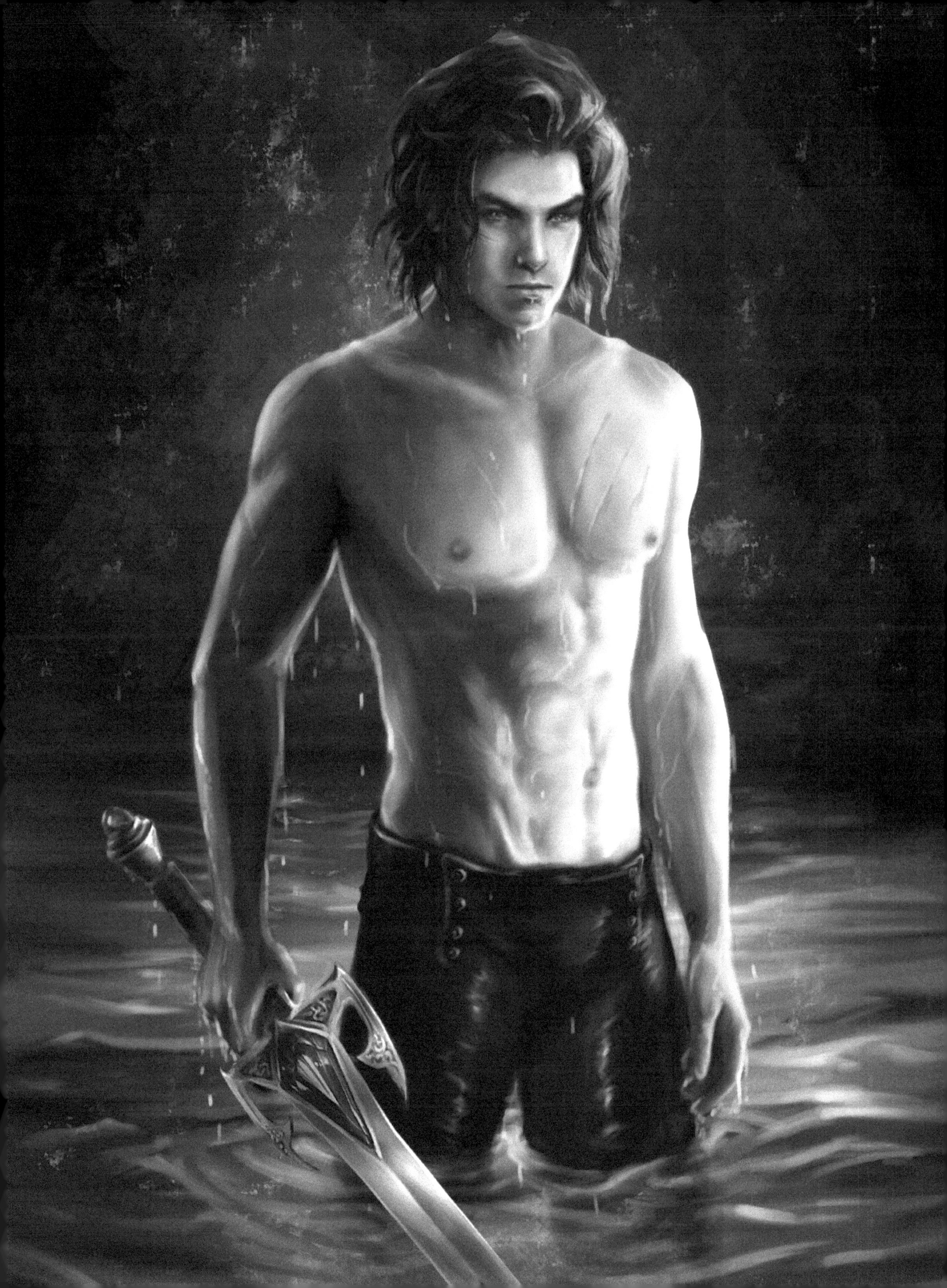

Caliburn

"In the stories I know, Arthur drew a sword from a stone, but it was way more literal."

Drawn from all the iron in the land by Myrddin and Arthur when the Pact was made, Caliburn is formed from an extremely magically dense iron.

Caliburn was not only a symbol of the human ruler's power, being the only iron allowed in Avall, it also channelled magic into the human wielder, making the bearer stronger. As very few humans in Avall had access to iron this ability was generally unused and unknown. However, Arthur's nephew, Mordred, realized the iron connection from seeing it in action for Arthur and tried to steal Caliburn to be more powerful himself. He fought Arthur, fatally wounding him just as Myrddin arrived. Myrddin tried to save Arthur but couldn't, and killed Mordred in return. In his last breaths, it was Mordred who Branded Myrddin.

Myrddin took Caliburn, which burned him but not as bad as full-blooded fae, and threw it into the underground lake under Caermaellan castle to stop it being misused again.

Caliburn is another name for Excalibur in Arthurian mythology.

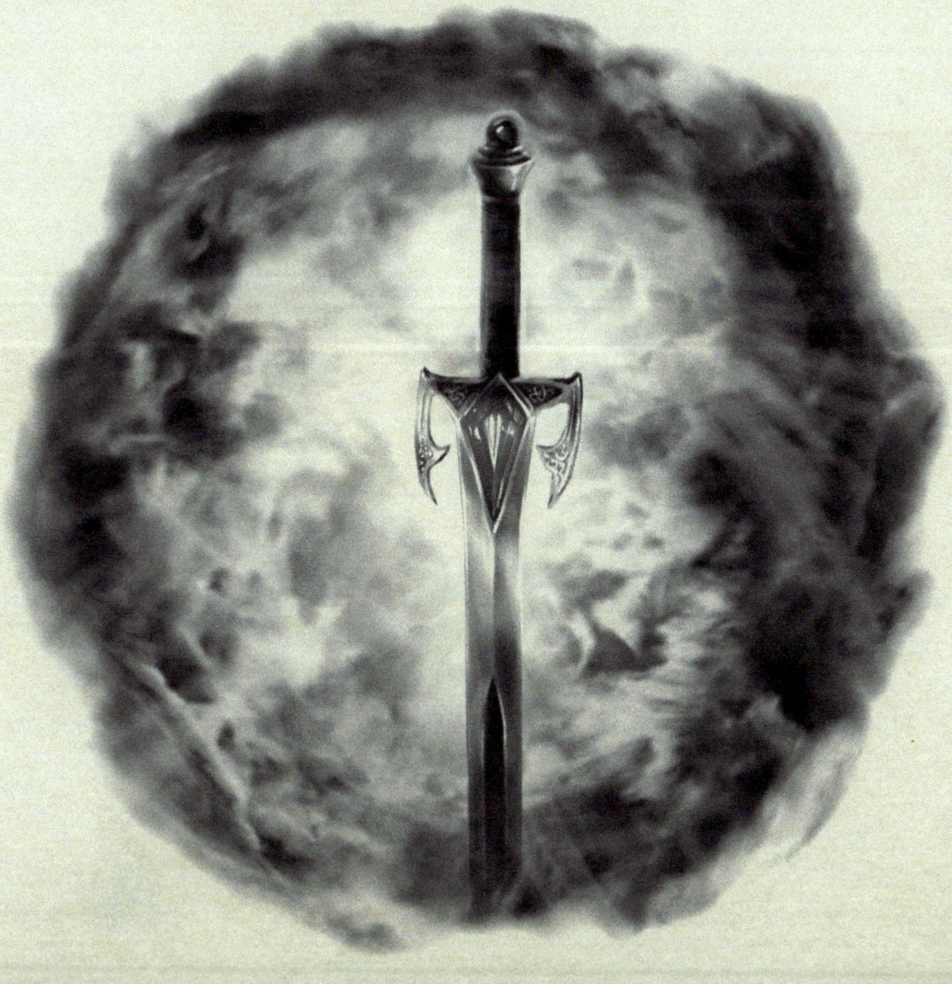

"I have a plan," she said again, studying Will's features, the earthy shade of his tangled hair and the way his dark brows made his blue eyes flash like lightning, trying to capture and lock them in her mind forever.

"And I know you won't like it. I know it might be goodbye. But I have the power to do this so I have to do it. I can save the humans, the fae, and Avall."

"It's time this vessel spilled."

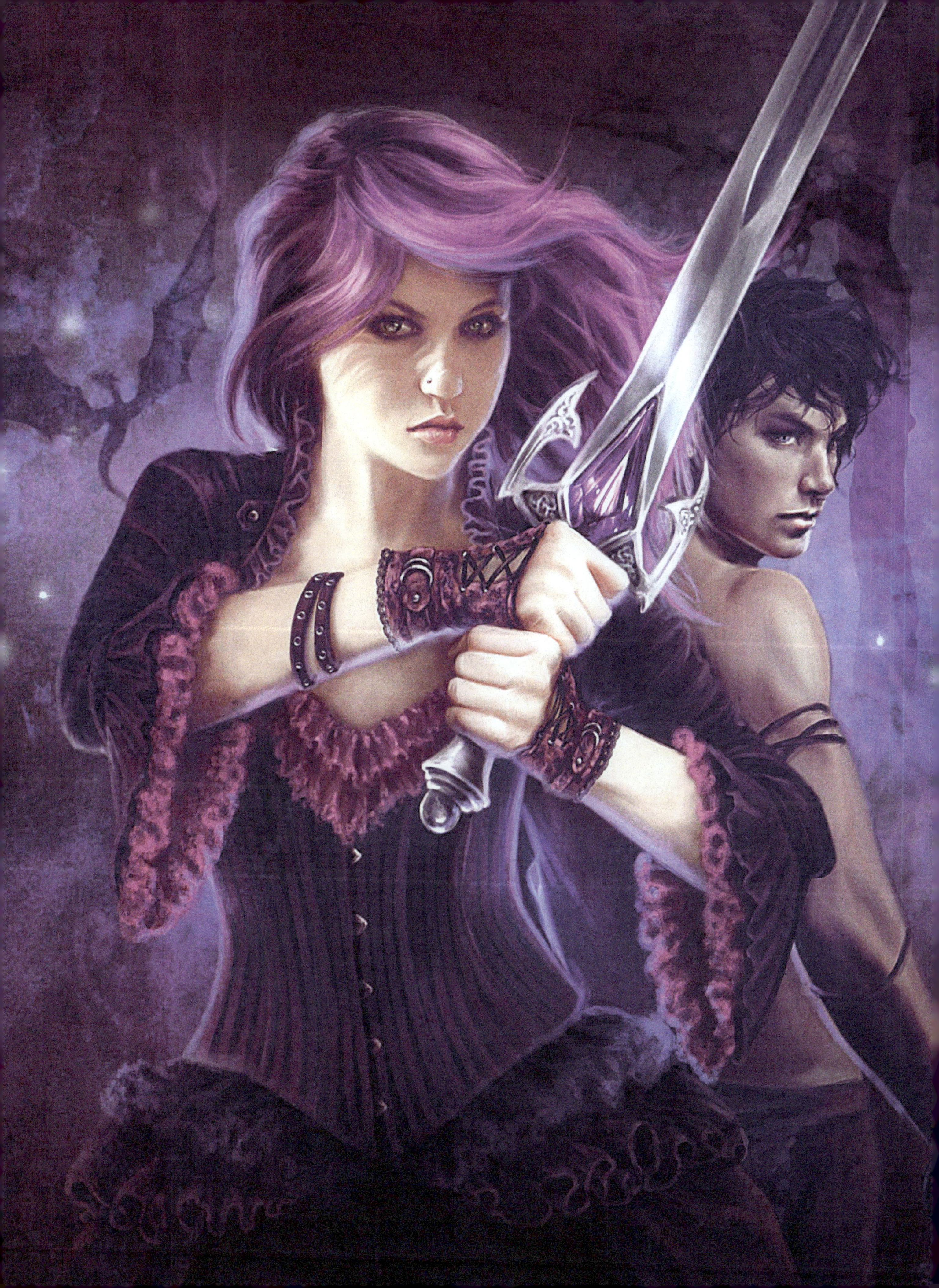

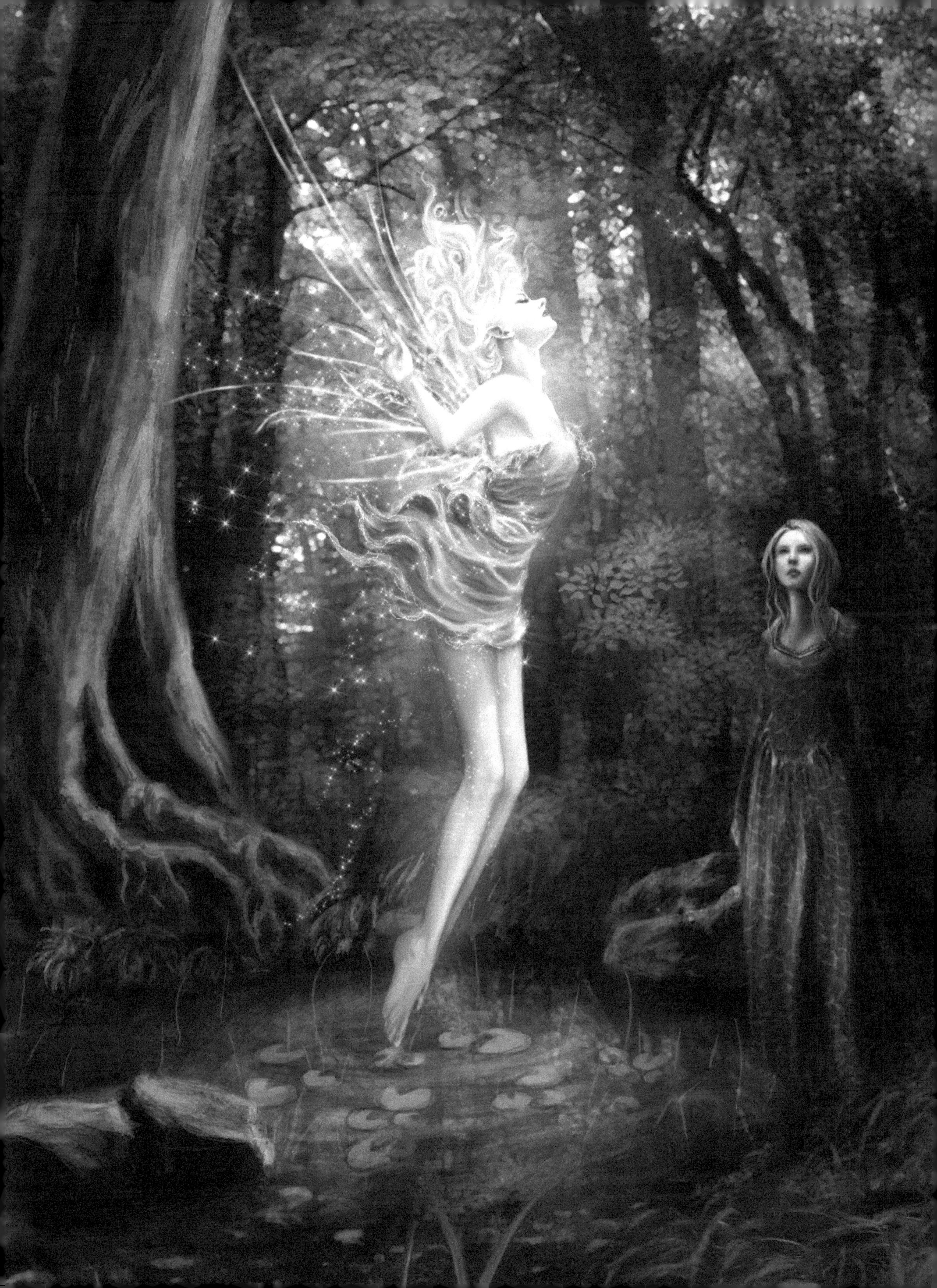

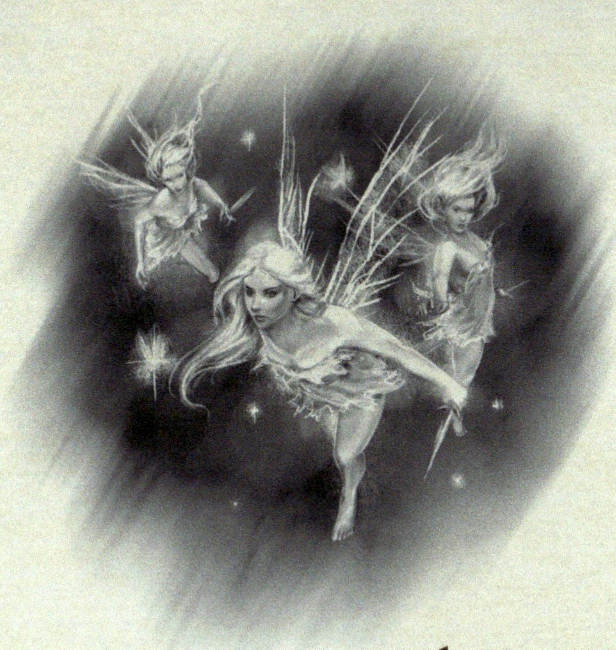

The Fae: Seelie

The court of the seelie fae generally includes creatures with humanoid forms and more human-like eyes and irises. Dominated by the classical types of winged fairies, creatures of the seelie court also include sprites, dryads, gnomes, unicorns, dragons, elves, naiads, dwarves and nymphs.

All fae creatures have the inherent ability to cast glamours (changing their appearance or the appearance of their surroundings), to travel through the veil at will, strength and keen senses, and extremely long lifespans- almost immortal in the right conditions.

Technically, all the fae in the story, both seelie and unseelie, are extra-dimensional beings. They come from an entirely different dimension to the human world, but choose to visit the human world frequently to absorb the life-magics they need to stay alive.

Within the seelie court, Aine and Lugh rule, but each subset of seelie race has their own prince or princess as well. Yvainne is the princess of the sprites, who is seen often with Mina and the other sprites who follow and watch over Memory's actions in the story.

Will spent his time almost exclusively with seelie fae creatures, particularly sprites, during his time growing up in Avall.

Although seelie fae are considered the light and good side of the fae realms, their personalities and behaviours can be just as tricksy as their unseelie brethren.

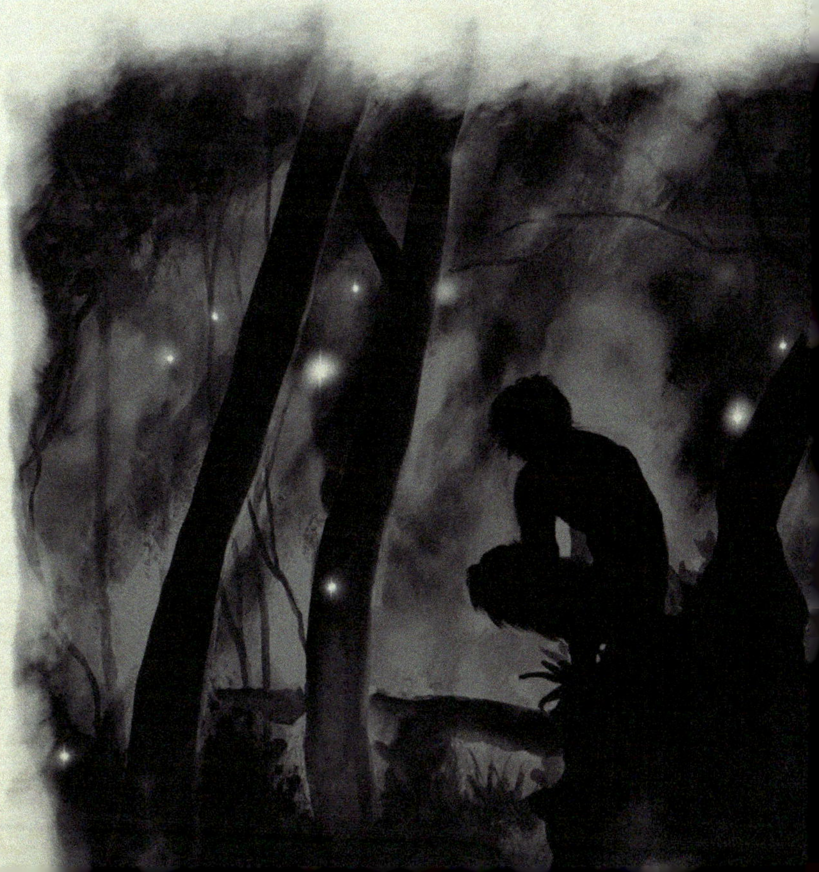

"My sweet pet," she sang, and twirled around him, dancing as he ate. She had delicate, tattered wings which trailed a stream of glittery light behind them.

Will ate and ate. Mina sang and smiled. He thought he'd received a miracle. He thought he was saved. He had no idea what had just happened. His life had become the property of the fairy before him.

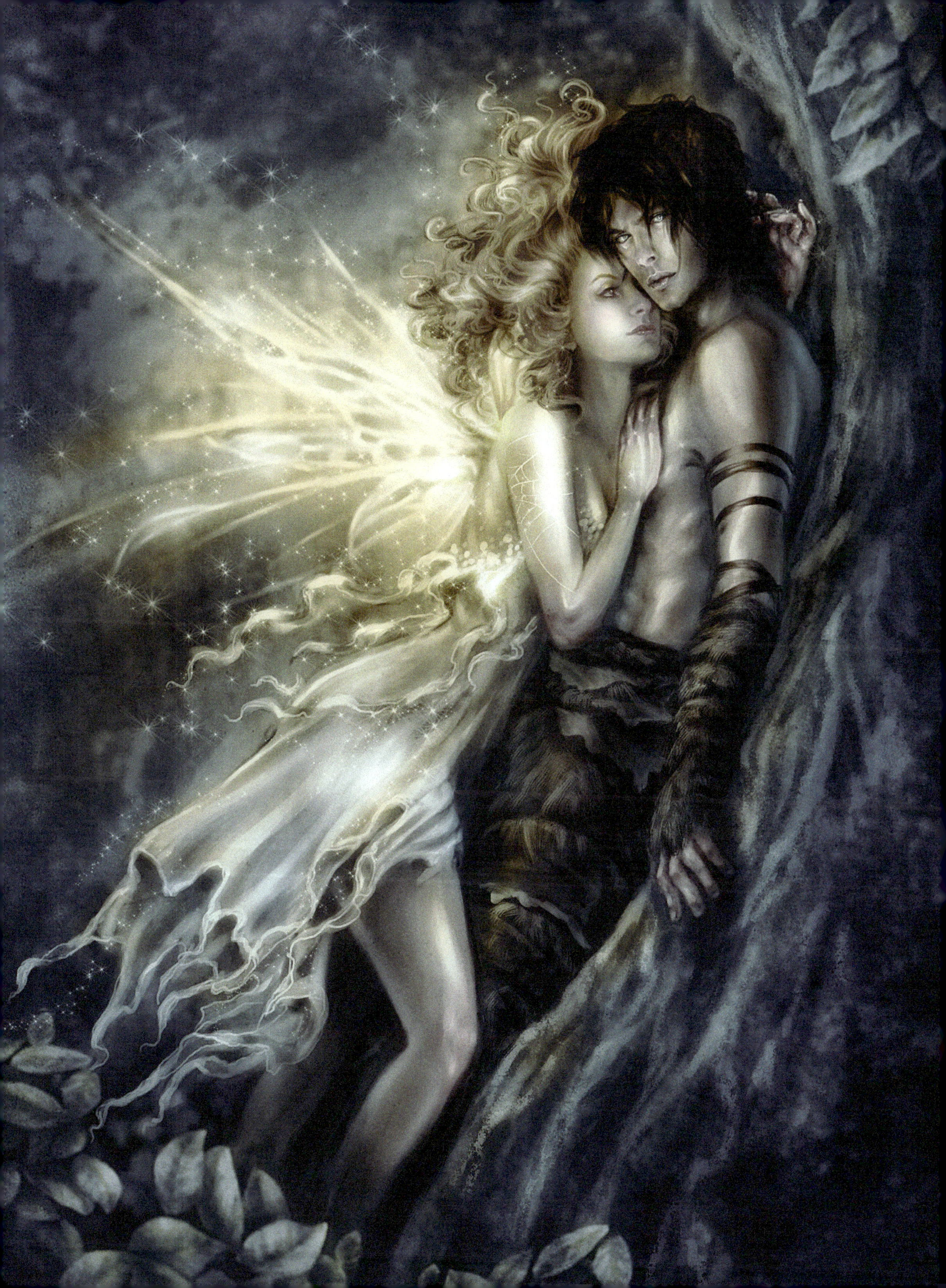

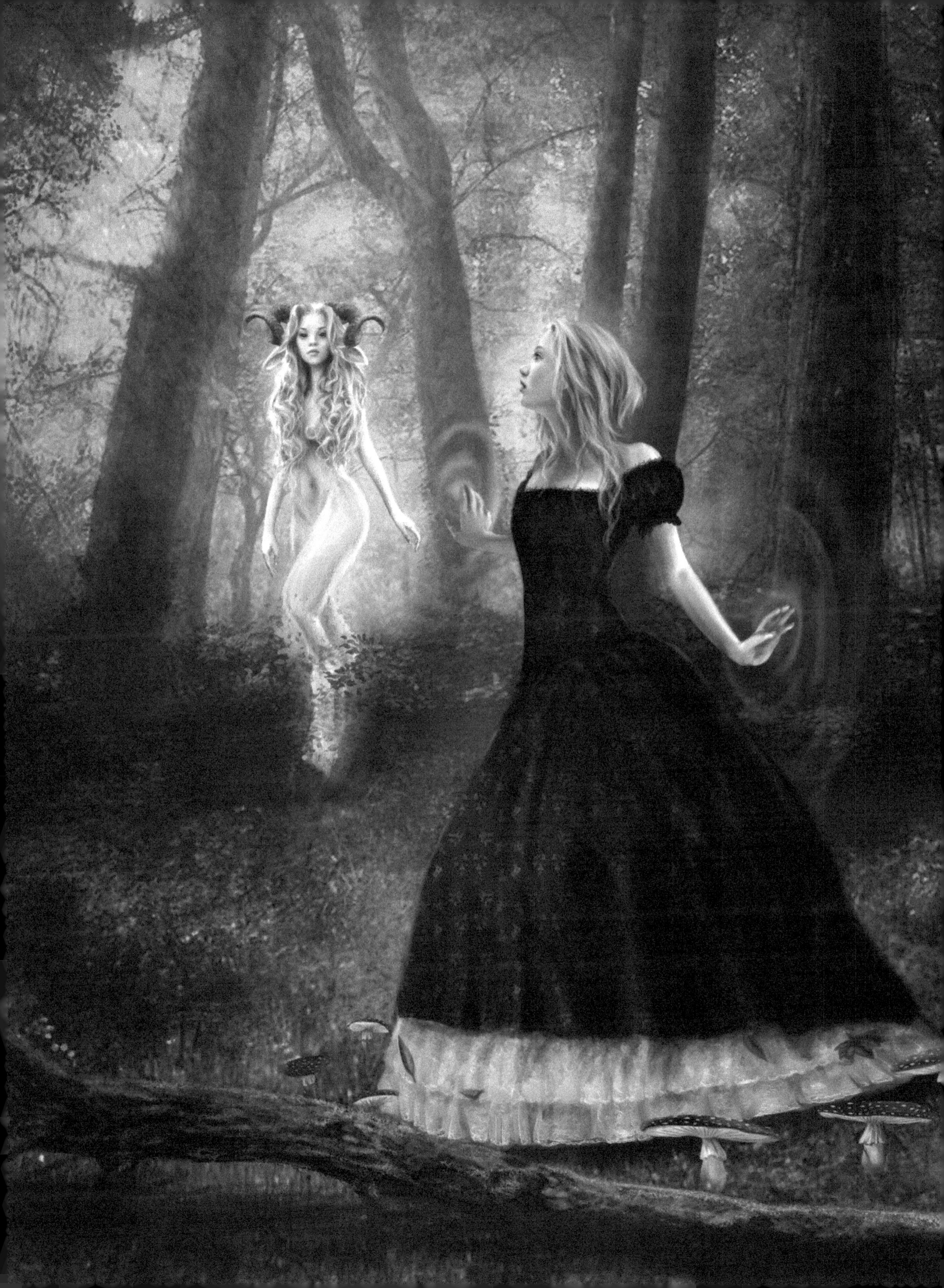

The Fae: Unseelie

"You prefer the human vermin over the unseelie fae, when we are your other halves, the dark to your light. We are your balance."

The races of the unseelie court are similar to the seelie fae in many ways, such as their abilities to glamour, travel through the veil, and immortality. Visually though, the unseelie races are less humanoid or more monstrous in appearance, and always have fully black eyes. The unseelie fae say their eyes are evidence that they were "born of the night".

Races found in the unseelie court include sluagh, griffons, gaunts, weepers, dark hounds, goblins, bogarts, hags, banshees, ogres, giants, succubae, imps, harpies, sirens, mermaids, selkies, trolls, kelpies, phooka, gargoyles, and fauns.

In behavior, the unseelie aren't generally more evil or dangerous than the seelie fae, however a number of elements have combined to mean they are often more aggressive or harmful to humans. Unseelie fae have lived with the disadvantage of their monstrous appearances, and have been hunted by humans throughout history often for nothing more than their appearance.

When something is treated as a monster, it can often quickly become that.

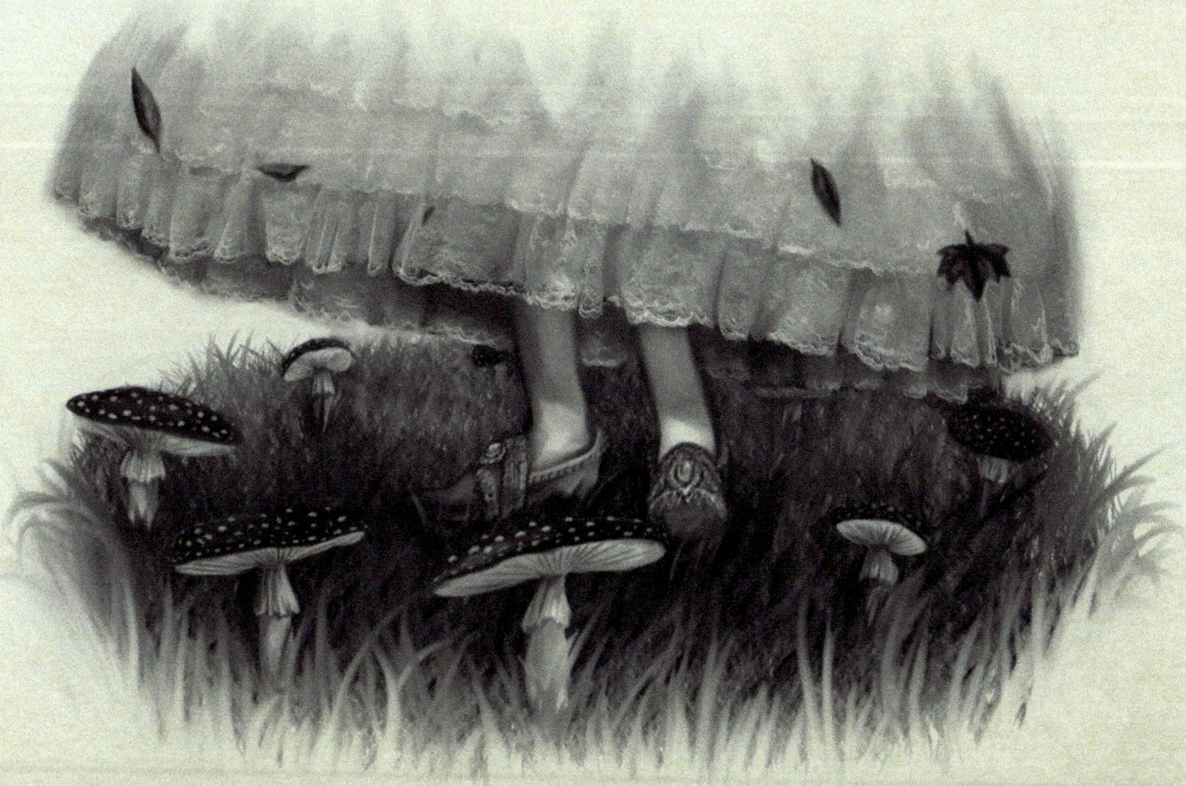

Rules When Dealing With The Fae

Never accept food from a fae.

Don't agree to do anything for them, allow them to do you a favour, or go into debt with them.

They may sometimes appear human so always be on guard.

If in doubt about whether someone is really a human, offer to share some bread or some salted food, which they will not eat.

Keep an eye out for fairy rings and don't step within them.

Stay out of fae territory.

Do not travel to the fairy world.

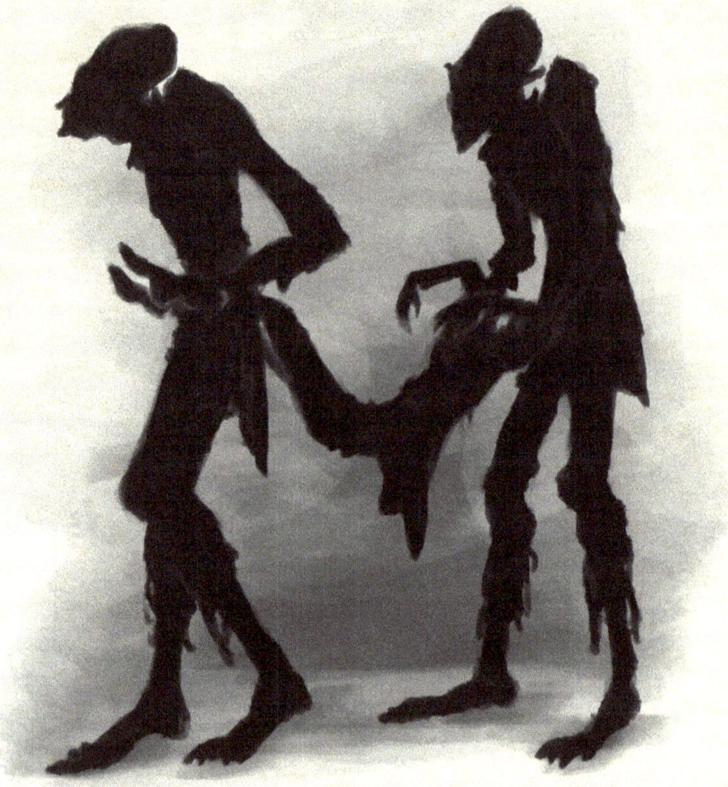

"Would you call a snake or spider evil? They are creatures of nature, same as the unseelie, same as all fae, same as humans. We are as we are and all have our place in the balance."

The unseelie ruler Finvarra also had a great dislike of humans, believing them inferior creatures to the fae, and his dislike grew to a twisted hatred as he grew madder with age. He also soon came to believe that the humans of Avall were using up in frivolous behests the precious life-magics he and his kind needed to live. Over time, he attracted to him the worst of all unseelie fae, his court filled with the darkest and most vicious of all races.

Nyneve's scheming also allowed these most evil individuals to act out. As her father's dementia grew stronger, she subtly took control of the unseelie court. She built her own network of dark fae who were loyal to her and her cause, like members of the unseelie griffon-knights and her small army of gaunts.

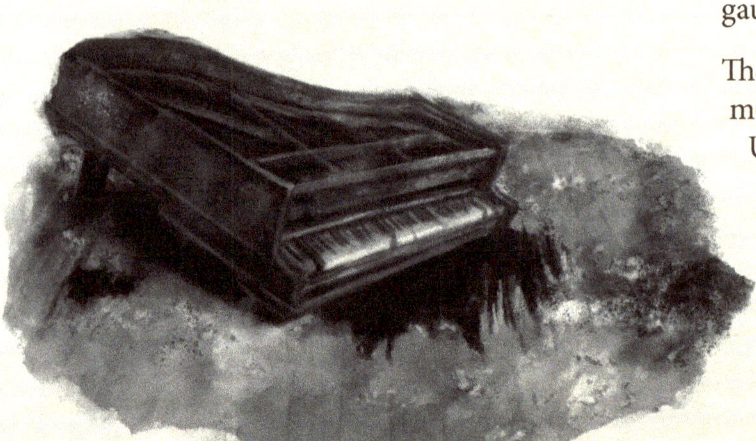

The unseelie fae races also include many of the more solitary creatures, like kelpies and fauns. Unlike the seelie sprites who are communal and group together, fauns like Shonae live alone, a single faun taking up a large area of forest for themselves where they can live alone and undisturbed by the other creatures of their race or court. Despite being grouped into courts, many of the fae only ever live in the wilds and have little to do with the rulers or politics of their kind.

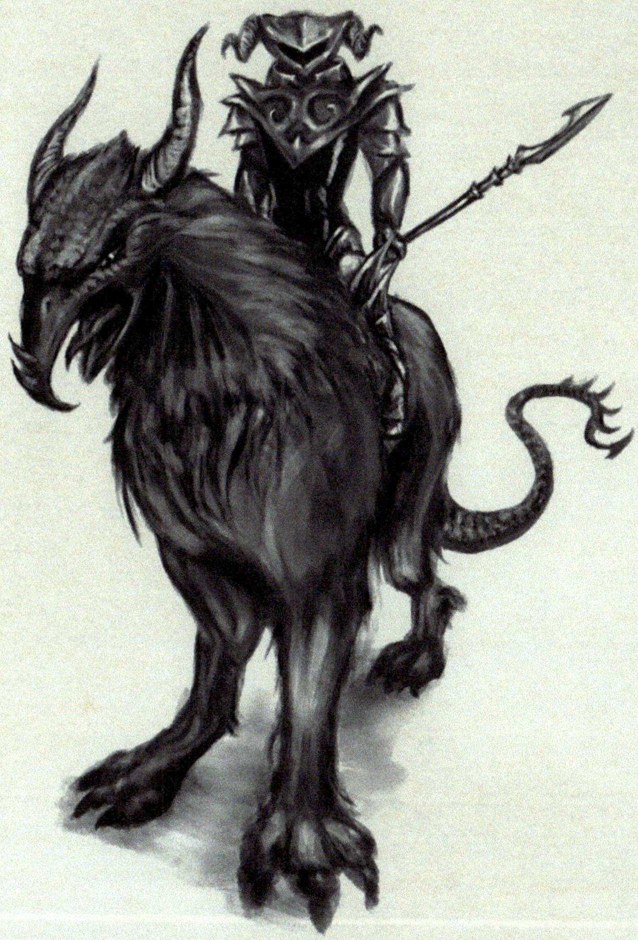

Branding

"Branding is a horrible death. An unfair thing. I saw it happen to someone I loved, once, long ago."

When the Pact was formed, it was Arthur's opinion that Avall couldn't be filled with the seelie and unseelie fae without there being some kind of protection between the races. He proposed Branding, a way in which any creature committing a crime against a creature of another race could be magically punished.

The unseelie agreed to the idea, because in truth they were just as threatened by humans as humans were of them, with the long history of humans hunting them like monsters.

If a creature harms someone of a different race, the victim can speak the words of the Brand, and the magic of the Pact will act if the guilt is true, and place a Brand mark on the attacker. The Brand kills on its own within 24 hours, but death often comes sooner as having the mark of the Brand means the creature is fair game for any attack or punishment from any race.

Many from all sides have criticized the Brand as cruel an ineffective, a punishment and deterrent rather than any true means of peace between the races.

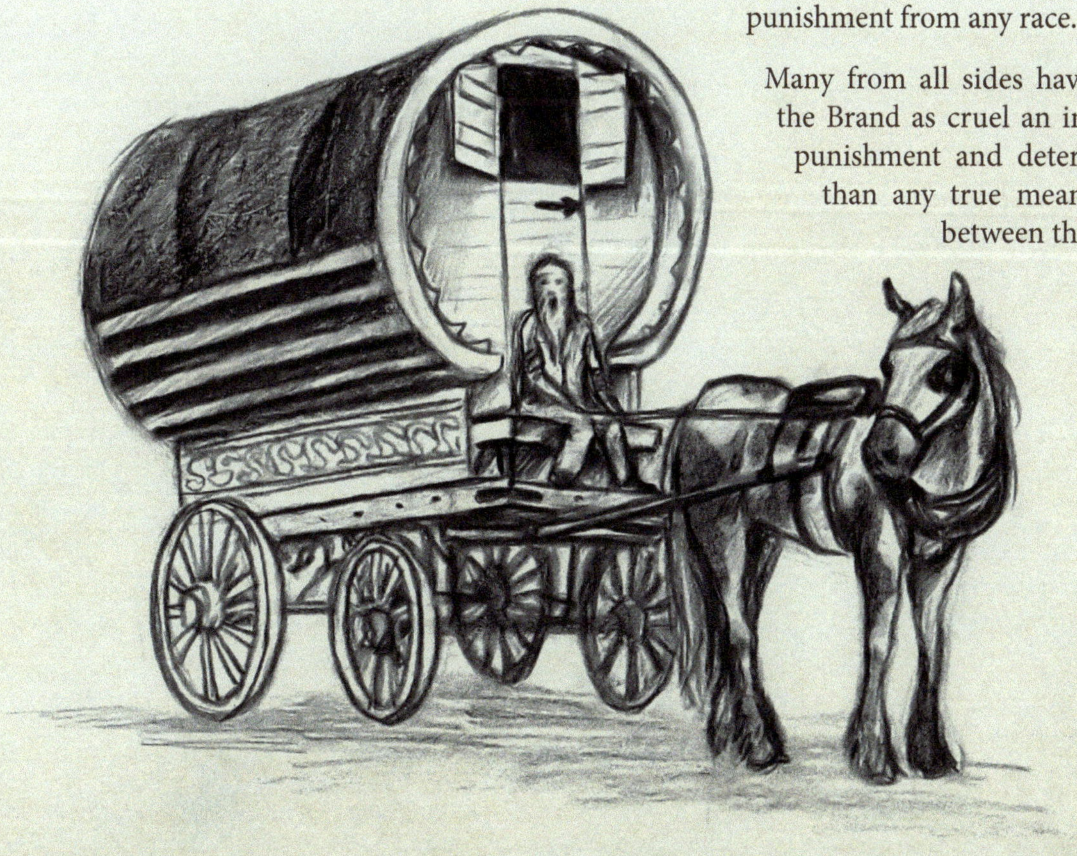

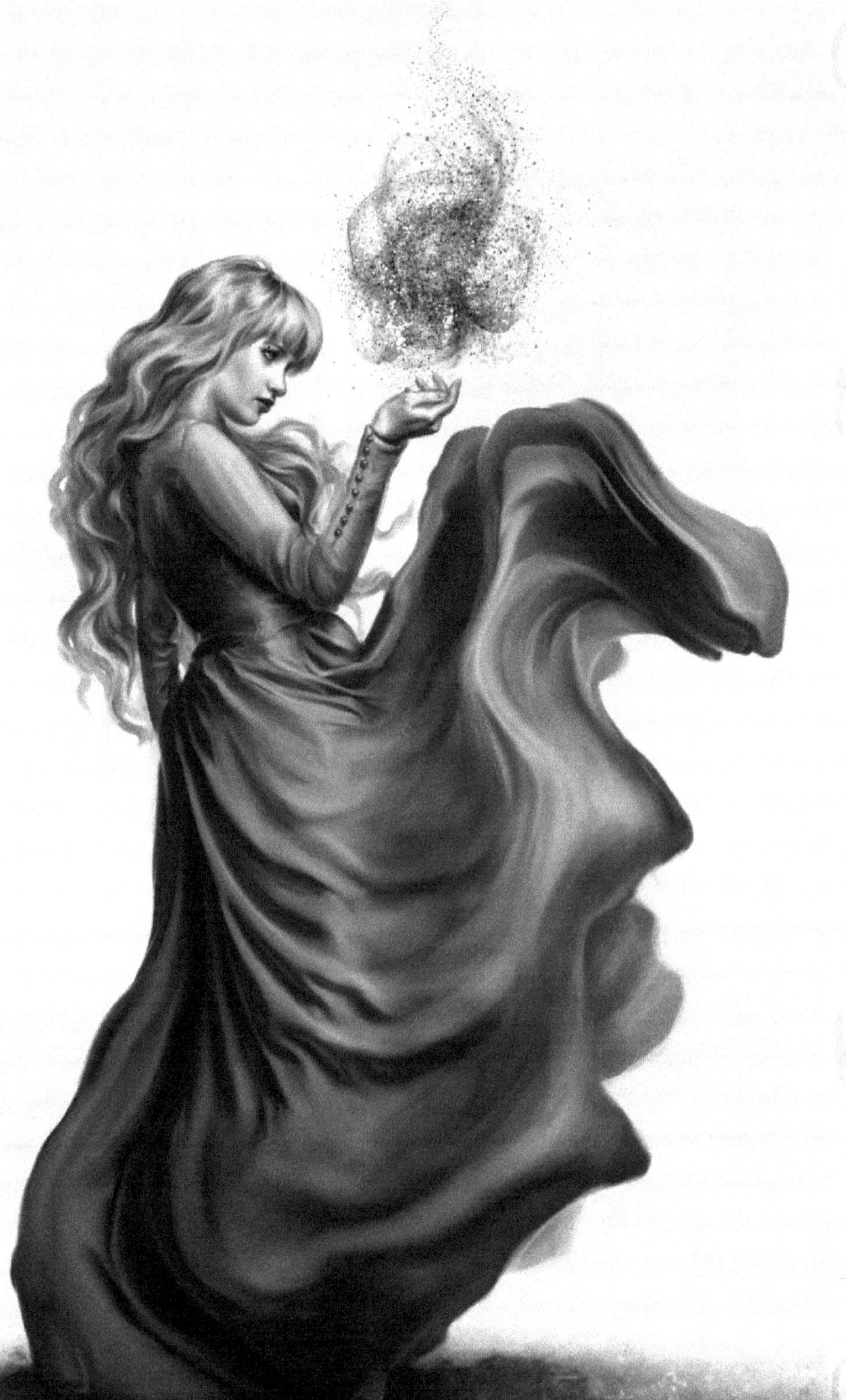

Magic

"So, it's just pretty please, but in fancy magic words?"

The human magic of Avall is centered around behests, a form of request and contract spoken in the magical language created by Arthur and Myrddin.

All humans of Avall received a Spark of Connection as part of the Pact agreement. The Spark of Connection is passed down from generation to generation, and is like a small light of life-magics within a person, which allows them to connect to the larger forces of magic in the world around them. Once connected, it's the words of the behest that shapes the magic to their desires.

Being a form of spoken contract, behests need to be well structured and proven through testing in order to work. It is part of the duties of the council of wizards to plan, test, and share the wording of new behests with the populous- when such behests are deemed useful to the common people. The majority of complicated behests are restricted purely to wizards and those trained by wizards in roles of healers, communication providers, and metal workers. These are all roles that rely heavily on magic in Avall. Doctors rely on healing behests, messages can be sent across the land faster with behests than normal letters, and without iron, metal workers are trained to use behests to help strengthen the softer or weaker

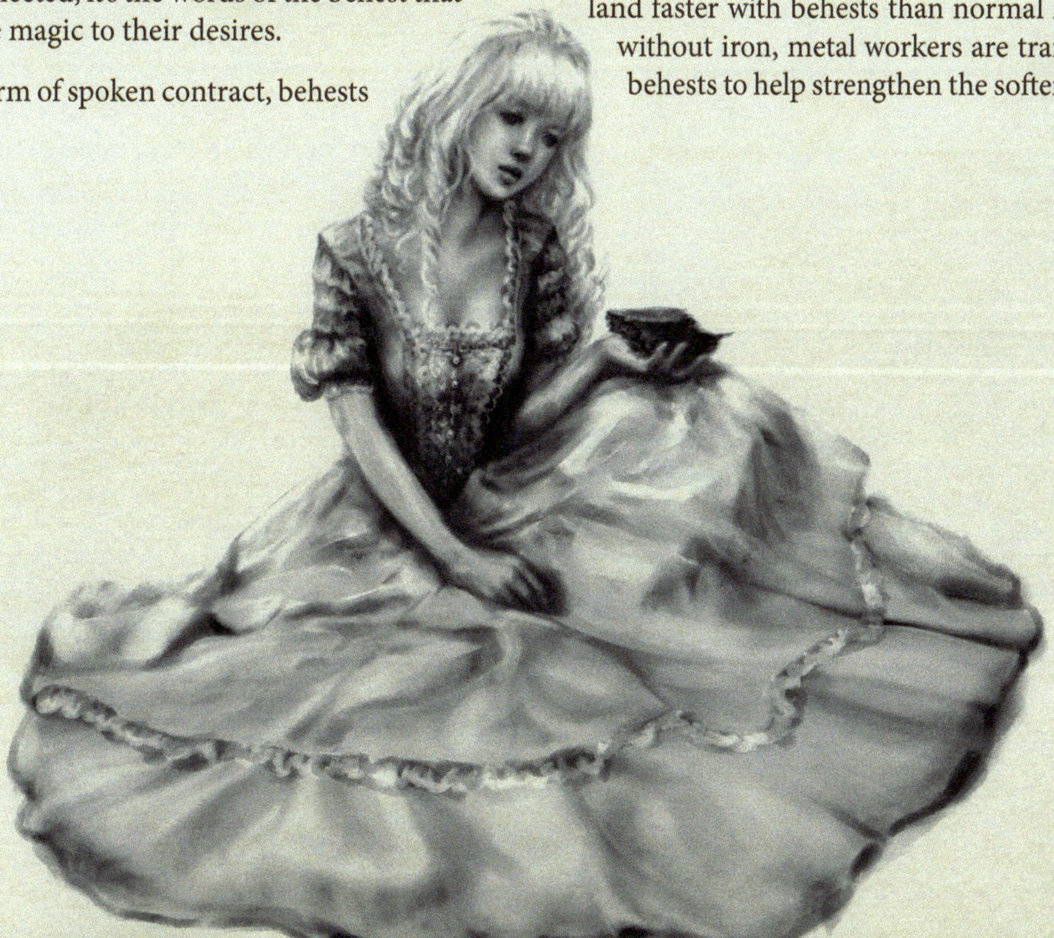

"Yeah, like I can control when and for what reasons my magic splurts out. You've got so much control and power. You can ask anything of anything and just, bam, done. My magic is more bam, HAHAHA DID SOMETHING YOU WEREN'T EXPECTING LOLZ."

metals allowed in the land to be more comparable in strength to iron.

The magical language for behests was based loosely on Irish Gaelic. While the general population know a number of behests, only wizards know the complete magical language. Eloryn was also taught the complete magical language by Alward, and with her magical lineage, she is able to use it to speak on-the-fly behests that haven't been scripted or proven like those the wizards use. While wizards do memorize some of the more complicated spells, they rely more often on reading them.

Another core rule in the magic of Avall, is that "like calls to like". Items of similar properties are drawn together. When Eloryn traveled through the veil in the faulty veil door spell, her DNA being a match to Memory's meant that Memory, who had been trapped in the veil, was drawn to her and drawn out of the veil with her.

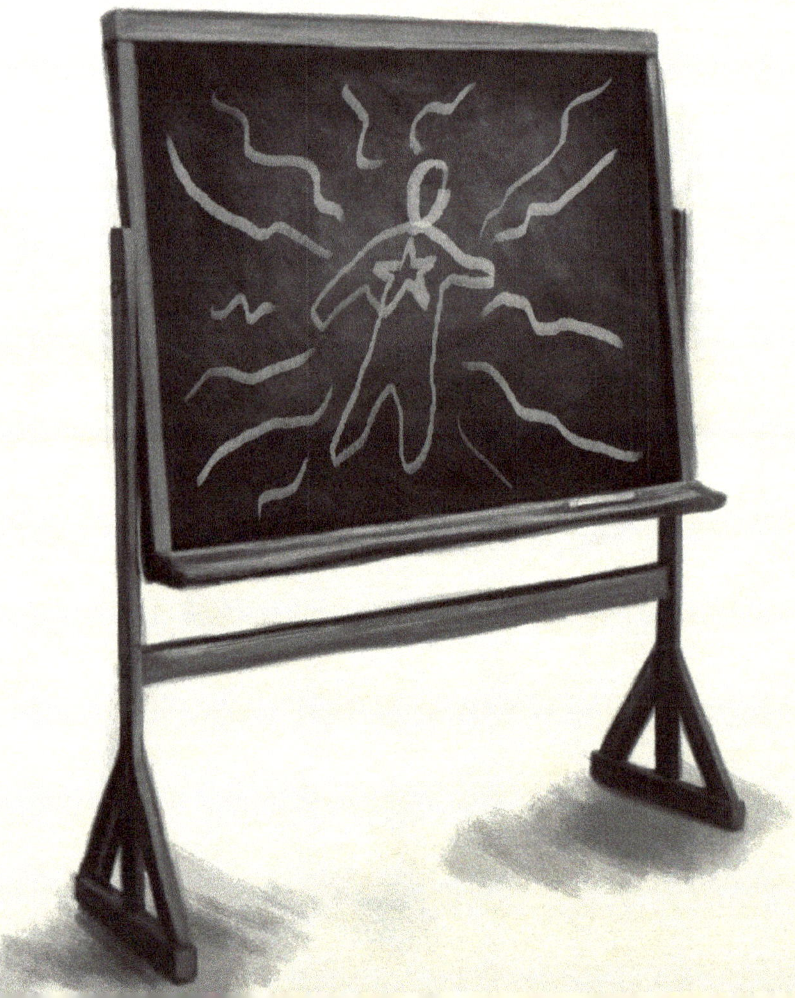

When Eloryn planned to cut off Thayl's hand, she theorized that due to like calling to like, the magic and memories that had been stolen from Memory would return to her if she was nearby at the time.

Like calling to like could also explain Memory's ability to heal Eloryn with magic when she wasn't able to heal others, and also how magic continued to be drawn into Thayl so he never ran out- the large store he had within him became a magnet for magic around him.

Some of this is also similar to how iron affects magic within Avall. The life-magics of the earth are meant to be a continuous and balanced flow through all creatures, plants, and the earth itself. But when man forge iron ore into cold iron, or steel, that conduit for magic becomes affiliated to man, drawing in any surrounding magic then channelling it into nearby humans. When the rest of the earth became full of iron, all the natural magics of Avall were being drawn from there to the iron.

When a human has the Spark of Connection as Memory did, the iron not only channels magic through them, but also stores it within them adding to that little piece of magic already there, due to like calling to like. After sixteen years of absorbing magic in this way, Memory could be said to have had an entire world's worth of magic within her.

"What does it feel like? Having the connection to magic?"
"Like a bonfire burning me away from the inside."

Behest Pronunciation Guide

Light- Summons a Wisp

Àlaich las - A-lay lash

Heal - Minor injuries and pain relief

Cairadh maith feòil - Care-ash may fee-ol

Fire- Small sparks to start a fire

Sraide teann - Srayj tee-an

Hone- Sharpens dulled blades

Bleith daingich - Bly dayn-eech

Branding - Brands a being who has broken the Pact

Bronmarbh Aileadh - Bron-mairv Allay-ee

Summon Object

Beirsinn fair nalldomh - Bare-shen fair nalldom

Banish - Ends another behest

Cuirdhùnadh fanhl - Cur-ee-un-ach fa-nal

Faster - Allows for faster movement

Deann-ruith - Deen rue

Death Spell

Guidhe beag lugha ob ciorram greim-bàis spad eucail spad eug

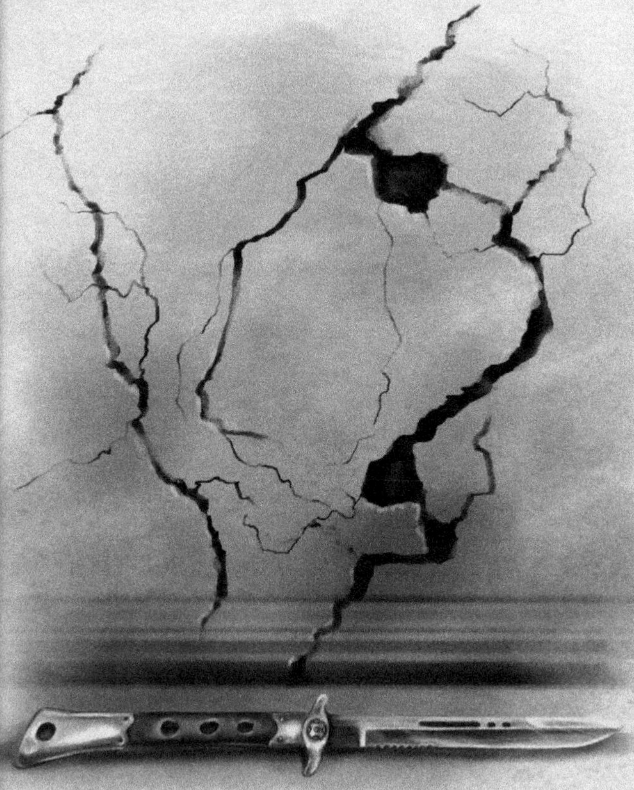

"Magic? Is that why my skin's tingling like this? But magic's not real."

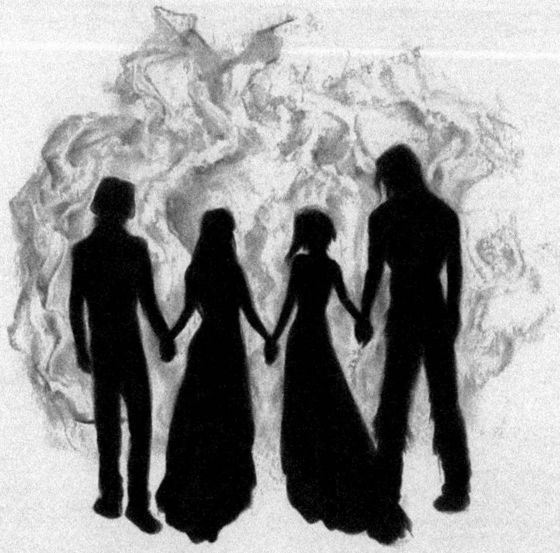

She still felt fragile, brittle like fairy gold, from the return of her old memories. But she also felt stronger from the return of her newer ones.

She no longer burned inside with all the excess magic she had felt her whole life. All that was left was just the normal, small Spark of Connection.

No missing soul, no missing past, no longing for a family she didn't know.

She had everything she always wanted.

She finally felt whole and complete.

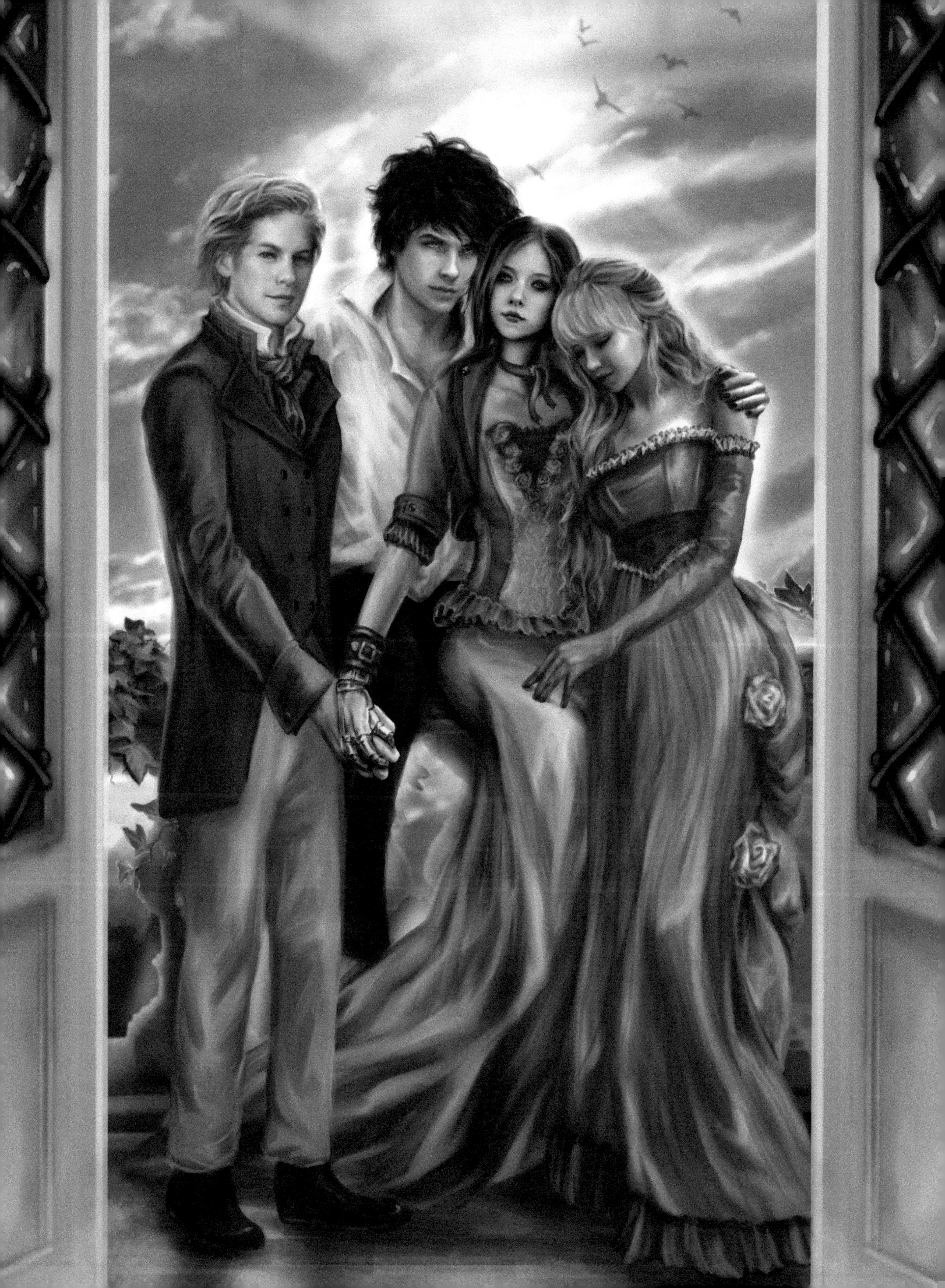

Early Concepts for Memory's Wake

The earliest ideas for Memory's Wake began in 2001 and before. Even then, it had the name Memory's Wake, but it was a very different concept.

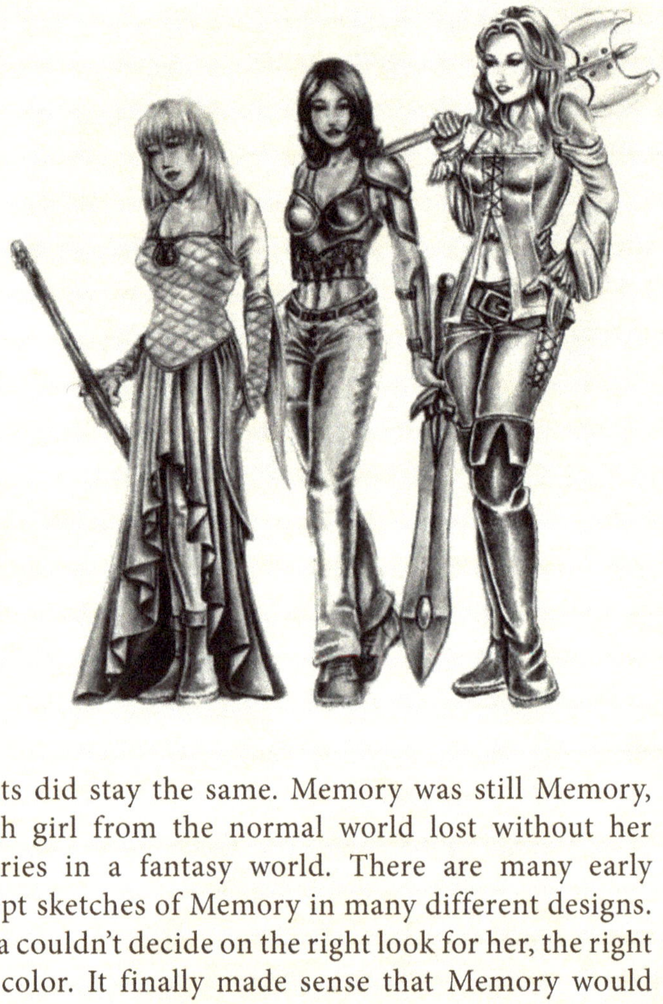

It began as a plan for an ongoing comic book, as Selina was very interested in becoming a comic illustrator at the time. The world was not the Victorian style, fairy filled, lost Avalon it is in the series, but a rather generic fantasy world.

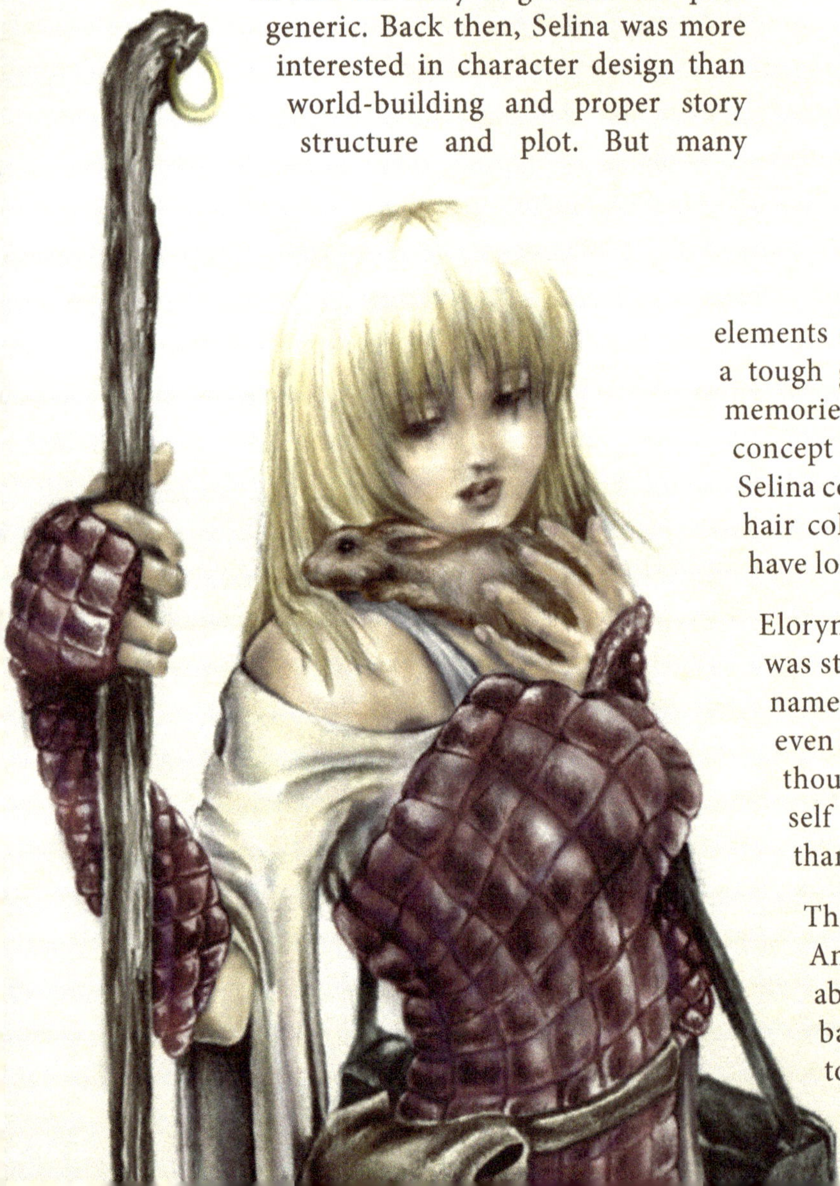

In fact the story in general was quite generic. Back then, Selina was more interested in character design than world-building and proper story structure and plot. But many elements did stay the same. Memory was still Memory, a tough girl from the normal world lost without her memories in a fantasy world. There are many early concept sketches of Memory in many different designs. Selina couldn't decide on the right look for her, the right hair color. It finally made sense that Memory would have lots of hair colors.

Eloryn was the character who changed the least. She was still a princess, raised in hiding by a wizard. Her name was originally Caellin, and the story focused even more on her in that version than Memory. Then, though still shy, she came into the story with more self confidence and more in tune with her magic than in the final version. She also had a pet bunny.

There was a third female lead, Syndra, an Amazonian ex-barmaid with wicked combat abilities (it appealed to Selina's humor that a barmaid in a fantasy world would have to be tough to survive). Although she was completely written out of the final story, parts of her personality lived on in Clara, and in the red-headed barmaid from Elder's Bridge Inn.

Roen changed very little, ever the rogue with the heart of gold. His noble back story was a new addition to the final version.

Will wore less- a classic leather loincloth rather than the old pants and fur wrappings of the new character design. He was also originally half Asian in race, but was still the devoted friend of Memory's who would follow in the shadows and be her guardian angel.

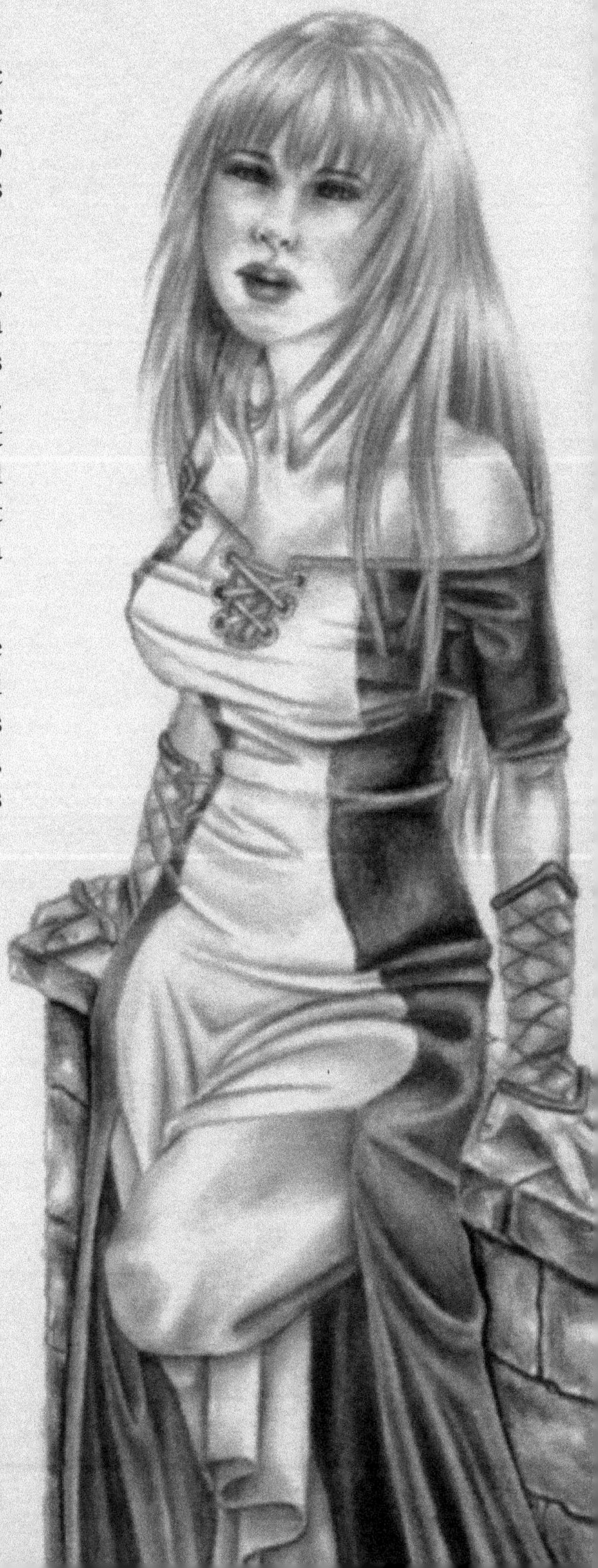

At some point, Selina's plans to illustrate the story as a comic were abandoned. A few years after that time, unable to let the characters and story go, Selina turned the comic book script into a short novella version, to feel as though she'd given the characters some closure, but it wasn't enough.

In around 2007, Selina shared the story with her husband-to-be, and he encouraged her to work on it again. He handed Selina a copy of "Story: Style, Structure, Substance, and the Principles of Screenwriting" by Robert McKee and it changed her world. Selina learned so much about writing and story-telling from that book. It opened her eyes and she became hungry for more, and she learned about writing from every source she could find. It became clear the novella version was drastically flawed, and not a suitable resting place for her beloved characters.

Selina took to the story with an axe and spent the next couple of years plotting, world building, redesigning the characters, and learning. The new version of Memory's Wake was to be a full length novel, with two following books plotted as well to create a trilogy.

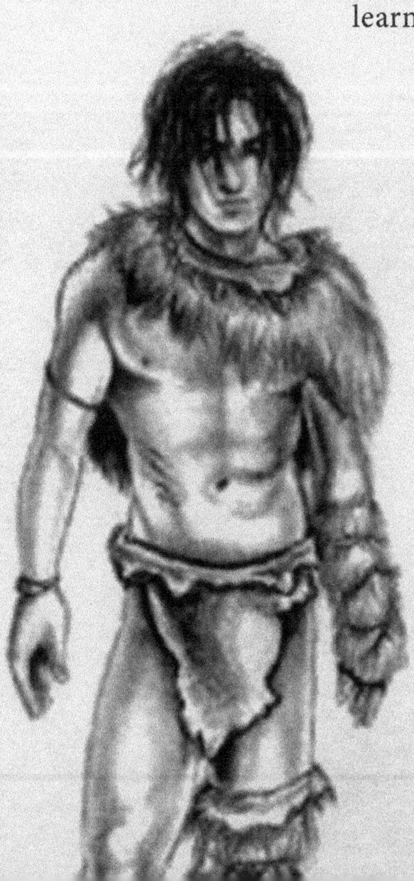

Once the first novel was written, Selina wasn't sure if she would illustrate it at all. She wanted to, it seemed natural too, but she hadn't heard of any young adult illustrated novels before.

But in the end, how could she not illustrate it?

Will wore less, and was half Asian.
Eloryn had a pet bunny.

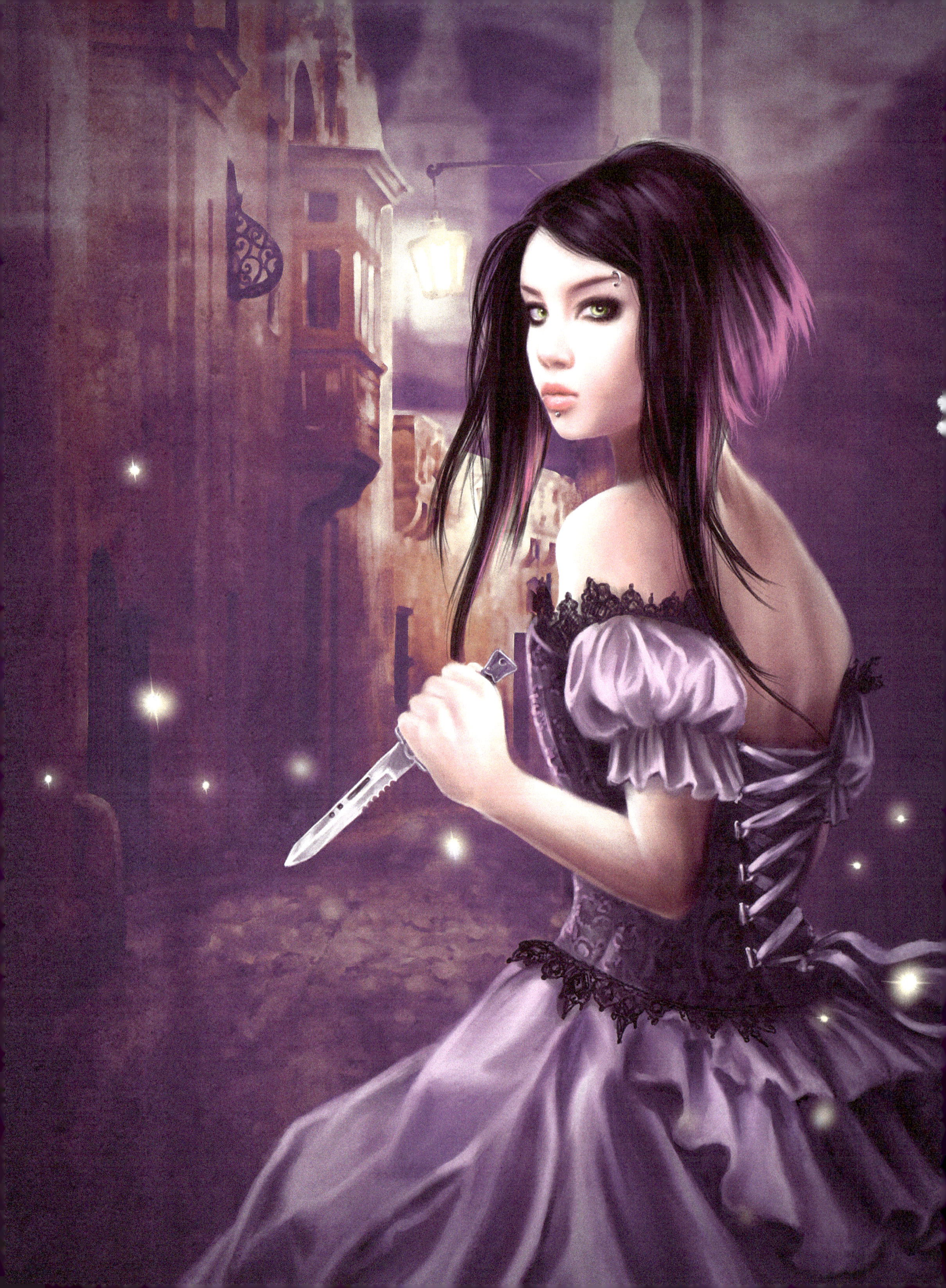

About the Author and Artist

During her life Selina has found ancient Roman treasure, survived cancer, had knights joust at her wedding, been mugged for doughnuts, made a living as an artist, eaten every bizarre and wonderful food put in front of her, and created new worlds in her novels. Born in 1981 to Australian and Maltese parents, Selina lives near Sydney with her family.

Completing the Memory's Wake trilogy is one of my greatest accomplishments. Sometimes I look back on it all and think, wow, where did that all come from!?

As I look forward to stories I want to tell in the future, I can't help but worry and hope that they will be able to top what I created in this tale.

Thank you deeply for sharing Avall and Memory and my other characters with me. I hope you love them as much as I do.

~ Selina

It's an undeniable truth that Selina Fenech has been lost to the realms of fantasy since she first laid hands on books. Faced with overwhelming heartache that our own world wasn't so full of magic and adventure, Selina did the only thing she could. She began creating her own worlds of magic by painting and writing.

Then one day, the other children told her that books weren't cool. Selina turned away from books and writing and submerged herself in her visual art. She became a successful fantasy illustrator, supporting herself with sales of her art that now has a worldwide following.

But the desire to tell stories remained, and once again, Selina embraced them and her writing to create some new worlds.

Because books are cool. Don't let anyone ever tell you otherwise.

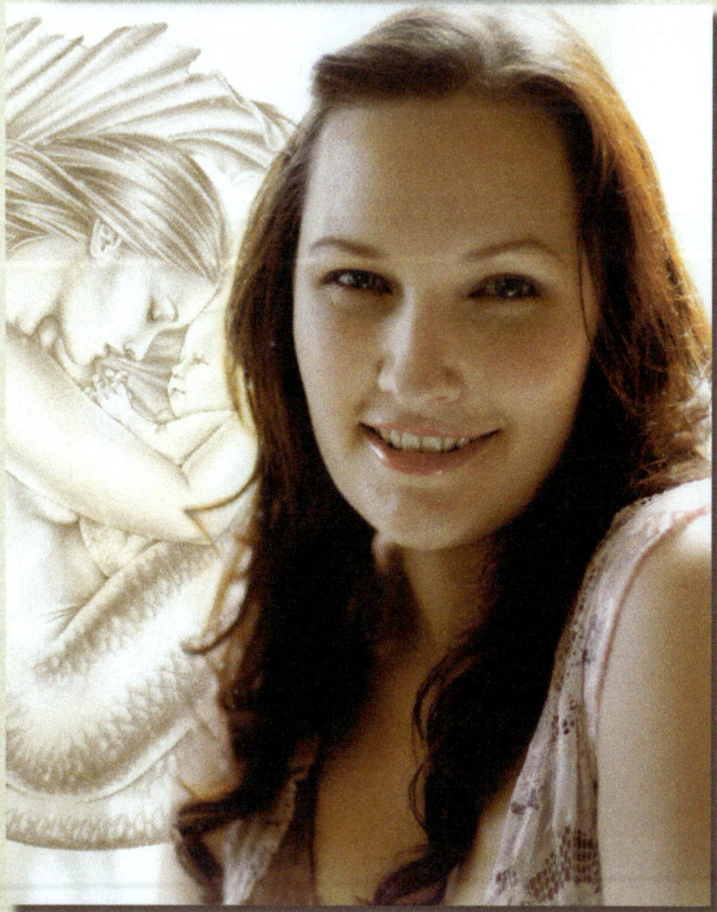

www.ingramcontent.com/pod-product-compliance
Ingram Content Group UK Ltd.
Pitfield, Milton Keynes, MK11 3LW, UK
UKHW060120010826
14089UKWH00005B/85

9 780